THE HABERMAS–GADAMER DEBATE AND THE NATURE OF THE SOCIAL

For
P. J. L. How (1906–83)
and
D. M. How (1912–)

The Habermas–Gadamer Debate and the Nature of the Social

Back to Bedrock

ALAN HOW

Avebury
Aldershot · Brookfield USA · Hong Kong · Singapore · Sydney

© A. How 1995

All rights reserved. No part of this publication may be reproduced, stored in a retrieval system, or transmitted in any form or by any means, electronic, mechanical, photocopying, recording or otherwise without the prior permission of the publisher.

Published by
Avebury
Ashgate Publishing Ltd
Gower House
Croft Road
Aldershot
Hants. GU11 3HR
England

Ashgate Publishing Company
Old Post Road
Brookfield
Vermont 05036
USA

British Library Cataloguing in Publication Data

How, Alan
  Habermas–Gadamer Debate and the Nature
  of the Social: Back to Bedrock. -
  (Philosophy Series)
    I. Title II. Series
  121.68

ISBN 1 85628 179 5

Library of Congress Catalog Card Number: 94-73467

Printed in Great Britain by Ipswich Book Co. Ltd., Ipswich, Suffolk.

Contents

Preface VII
Acknowledgements XI

Section One
The Context Of The Debate

1. The origins of the debate: hermeneutics and Critical Theory 1
2. The disputed territory: the first part of Truth and Method 23
3. The second part of Truth and Method:
   understanding and the human sciences (a) 36
4. The second part of Truth and Method:
   understanding and the human sciences (b) 59
5. The third part of Truth and Method:
   on language and reality 86

Section Two
The Debate

6. Introductory issues:
    Popper, Adorno, and the concept of totality 101
7. Round one: Habermas' first critique (a)
    on the virtues of hermeneutics 116
8. Round one: Habermas' first critique (b)
    on the vices of hermeneutics 139
9. Round two: Gadamer's first reply (a)
    on the real scope of hermeneutics 155
10. Round two: Gadamer's first reply (b)
    language is more than it seems 164
11. Round three: Habermas' second critique
    method reaches the parts that hermeneutics can't 180
12. Round four: Gadamer's second reply
    on the dangers of ideal speech, and the importance of modesty 200

Section Three
Afterthoughts

13. A discussion and evaluation of the debate 213
14. Concluding remarks and some possibilities 225
Bibliography 229
Index   245

Preface

The original purpose in writing this book was to provide my social theory students with an accessible guide to the debate between Jurgen Habermas and Hans-Georg Gadamer, a debate I still regard as probably the most important one of the last 25 years for anyone working in the humanities or social sciences. There have been some good commentaries on it, and the primary texts have gradually become available in translation, but the commentaries always seemed to assume too great a level of prior knowledge, and the primary texts are dense and convoluted essays in their own right. The task as I saw it was to situate the issues that lay between them in the wider framework of their ideas, thence to unravel the closely woven arguments that are *actually* found in their essays. Too often commentaries bypass the actual claims authors make in favour stylised versions that simplify, and generally tidy up matters that should be thought more obstinate and deserving of more attention.

However beyond the rather neutral desire to clarify the details of the debate lies my belief that their work is of great intellectual significance. It has always struck me that what both of them show, and is often missing from the theoretical work of some authors in the area, is a certain 'fidelity to the object'. By this I mean that there is an authentic sense of *the social* in their work, an appreciation of the real nature of the matter with which they are concerned. Despite the abstractness of their writing it is imbued with a sense of what human existence is like, it has an awareness of the finite nature of our lives, of the 'linguistic' quality of our understanding, and of the way values and rationality are always interwoven in everyday life. For this reason I have subtitled the book *Back To Bedrock*. By this I want to suggest that the issues generated by the debate speak to the most fundamental questions affecting not only my own discipline of sociology, but other social sciences and the humanities generally. Though neither author is a foundationalist in the philosophical sense, their debate was a kind of excavation, it dug down and revealed the foundations of the social world, and does, I think, provide the best context in which analysis and discussion of theoretical matters affecting these disciplines can take place.

The work of Jurgen Habermas is well known in the English speaking world, he is perhaps the foremost developer of the tradition of thought known as Critical Theory. His ideas though have ranged far and wide from those of Horkheimer, Adorno, and Marcuse, with whom the tradition was first associated, indeed such is the current reach of his work it is now difficult to discern exactly what its central tenets are. One way 'into it' is via his debate with Gadamer for it seems to me that its effect continues to the present day. Habermas' claim that the underlying telos or aim of language involves the reaching of common understanding and agreement, is one that has its source in Gadamer's hermeneutic account of language. This universalising potential of language can be seen to feed into the heart of Habermas' subsequent projects, such as 'communicative action' and 'discourse ethics' where the universal potential of rational argumentation *through language* is used to underpin his case. Indeed, insofar as he identifies his overall project as overcoming the pessimism of Adorno and Horkheimer, which sprang from their fear that there was no ground for reason, then Gadamer's hermeneutics has provided a significant part of the solution.

However, whether Gadamer's account of language *should* be thought to serve Habermas' 'universalising' ambitions is much less clear, and is one of the themes of this book. The importance of hermeneutics to Habermas is often remarked on, but rarely given much attention. Sociological commentary on Habermas' work has tended, more or less, to assume him the victor and hermeneutics but a station along the way of Critical Theory's development. Perhaps this is understandable given the speed with which Habermas moves from one field of endeavour to another, the Habermas follower must have great powers of endurance to keep up with the master. Nevertheless, my case overall is that Gadamer's work stands up well to Habermas' critique, and that Habermas' criticisms are effective only insofar as they are based on his own subtle redescription of Gadamer's case, one that suits his own very different project. This is not to say that such redescriptions are automatically invalid, as Gadamer himself acknowledges, when we come to understand something we always understand it differently. Nevertheless, there is a point at which we can decide between two interpretations, and I believe there remains in Gadamer's work a quality and substance that resists reduction by Critical Theory, and for which I think the English word - wisdom - stands as well as any. My hope is that this book might contribute something to increasing an awareness of the fruitfulness of his ideas and thereby to the widening of his influence.

The book

Early on in the writing of the book it became apparent to me that in order to do justice to *this* debate I would have to exclude a number of issues and debates that were pertinent to it, but not part of it. The contemporary outlooks known as postmodernism and realism have a considerable bearing on the issues raised in the Habermas-Gadamer debate, but here are either pressed to the margins or left out altogether.

Roy Bhaskar's realist philosophy of science is of particular importance as it, like Gadamer and Habermas' work, challenges the intellectual imperialism of positivist conceptions of social explanation. However, while it rejects the idea of a unified science based on positivist principles, it affirms the possibility of an essential of unity of method between the social and natural sciences based on realist principles; principles that acknowledge differences exist between the equally real subject matter of both.

To some extent in their debate both Gadamer and Habermas too readily assume the validity of positivism's own description of natural science, even though they rail against the way the validity of this description has been allowed to pervade the human sciences. It could be argued, for example that the post-empiricist philosophy of science, from Kuhn onwards, has effectively undermined and dispersed the more grandiose claims of positivism, arguing that science is an essentially *social* activity, and not an unmediated source of truth. If this is a weakness in Gadamer's and Habermas' case it is largely explainable in terms of the publication date of the key text, *Truth and Method,* which first appeared in 1960. Gadamer has remarked that he feared the twenty years it took him to gather the ideas for *Truth and Method* would prove to be too long. He doubted that a book on hermeneutics could make any impression in a philosophical world (still) dominated by logical positivism and buttressed by the ever increasing success of natural science.

Moreover, neither Gadamer nor Habermas are *simply* reaffirming the old distinctions between the natural and the human sciences. Habermas is concerned with the interface between the two as it affects social analysis, while Gadamer, amongst other things, is concerned to show that a hermeneutic dimension exists even in the natural sciences. In this sense there is, I believe, a certain common ground between them and Bhaskar, though it is beyond the scope of this book to deal with it.

The book is divided into three sections. Section one deals with the intellectual background to the debate, and includes a fairly extensive commentary on *Truth and Method*. I have included this because discussions of the debate often prematurely side with Habermas in limiting their accounts of the comprehensiveness of Gadamer's position. *Truth and Method*, which is Gadamer's masterwork, is at the heart of the debate though it often seems to function as a silent partner, i.e. as *only* that which Habermas critiqued. Habermas may have initiated the debate and Gadamer duly responded, but *Truth and Method* is the key to all that followed.

Section two deals with the details of the debate and draws heavily on the actual texts written by Habermas and Gadamer which made up the debate. A central theme here is that when Habermas draws out elements from hermeneutics to incorporate into his own theory he redescribes them in such a way as to make them amenable to his project, while those elements he will reject are made more vulnerable to criticism.

In section three I evaluate the debate, finding Gadamer's work well able to resist Habermas' criticisms, and in its turn capable of challenging Habermas' ambitions for a new Critical Theory. Where Habermas claims that hermeneutics needs to be more like Critical Theory to avoid being politically and ideologically naive, I claim the opposite is the case, and that ideology-critique needs to recognise itself as a variety of hermeneutics. The final chapter deals briefly with some implications the hermeneutic case may have for practising historians and sociologists.

Acknowledgements

Most books take time to gestate in the author's mind and this one is no exception. As a result there are many people who in conversation have contributed wittingly or unwittingly to it. Of particular importance in this regard are Richard Hopkins and Bob Carter. The conversations Richard and I had as undergraduates many years ago were amongst the most rewarding and formative for me, and thanks must go to him for setting me on a path from which I have never looked back with any regret. More recently Bob Carter joined the staff of Worcester College of Higher Education and to him also special thanks must go. His patient and thoughtful comments on this text and other matters have been invaluable. His proof reading was always more than just proof reading.

More than once the support staff at Worcester College rescued me from the ensnarements of different word processing packages. Thanks for this must go to Ruth Powell, Kate Peel, Ann Bennett, Cath Morris and Sue Evans. Last but not least thanks must go to Lynne for her endless patience with this unreconstructed academic.

1 The origins of the debate: Hermeneutics and Critical Theory

Introduction

I first came across the Gadamer-Habermas debate as a social science undergraduate in the mid 1970's, when I read Janet Woolf's book *Hermeneutics and The Sociology of Art* (1975). I was already fairly familiar with the work of the older members of the Frankfurt School and had found it both stirring and insightful. Once the density of their style had been unravelled a little by helpful tutors, that mixture of intellection and commitment which characterises their work, provided me with an unending source of illumination. There were times though, when the brilliance of their critical strictures was at odds with my own response to things. I admired their relentless exposure of uncritical, positivistic social science, and their ability to cut through the spurious sense of vitality and liberation that marked many the products of the culture industry. But sometimes I felt uneasy about that same remorseless critical tone, which for all its dialectical subtlety invariably seemed to end on a downbeat. Their tireless pursuit of negation grated a little if I applied it to those artworks that I found moving, be they low or high culture products. The encompassing nature of their critical method, I found, could have the effect of reining in the sense of delight and celebration which accompanies the experience of art. When I read Woolf's account of Gadamer, and then Gadamer's own account of the experience of art, which he uses as a kind of model for all human understanding, the validity of my own concrete experience came more sharply into focus. Moreover, Gadamer's views bore some resemblance to those of the Frankfurt School, for he also emphasised the experience of art as something that was beyond the control of scientific method, and thereby spoke of human freedom. Like them he opposed the idea of art as the mere decoration of reality, insisting instead that it could bring the truth of reality into being. Like them he argued that art had some power to transcend the circumstances of its production, and yet must carry with it the marks of its historical tradition of origin. What surprised me was that there was a body of thought, quite unknown to me at the time, which contained so much that I found apt, and yet whose tenor was quite different from that of any of the Frankfurt School authors.

Background

The debate between Hans-Georg Gadamer and Jurgen Habermas was one of the most unexpected and productive of scholarly debates. It was unexpected because the traditions of thought from which each came, had never previously shown much interest in or sympathy for the other, indeed the one, had sometimes engaged in vitriolic opposition to the other(1). Gadamer's intellectual origins were to be found in the tradition of hermeneutics and existential phenomenology, with a particular debt to Heidegger, while Habermas's forebears were the Frankfurt School Critical Theorists, notably Adorno and Marcuse. As neo-Marxists, the Frankfurt School theorists had always regarded existentialism and the tributaries of thought that made it up, with great suspicion. Their political senses were roused to hostility by a tradition that was not only apolitical, but which, as they saw it, paraded spurious spiritual solutions to the real problems that beset Western Europe in the 1920's and 1930's. In a world increasingly dominated by scientific rationality, existentialism's appeal lay in the misguided allure of an 'authentic experience' which would cut through the mundanities of an increasingly controlled, rationalised everyday life. It provided inner solace to people for whom the world had become innately meaningless and dangerously out of control. It was the existentialist's *jargon of authenticity*, especially that found in Heidegger's in *Being and Time* (1927), that Frankfurt School authors like Adorno, objected to so much. It expressed, with a peculiar resonance for Germans, an amalgam of heroism and pathos, of action for action's sake, that needed only minor adjustments to be the intellectual echo of the *volkisch* spirit celebrated by the Nazis. And though, according to Marcuse (1977), it came as a complete surprise when, in 1933, Heidegger declared his allegiance to Hitler, (as no-one had recognised any political implications in his work prior to that), with hindsight the relationship was clear. Many of the key concepts used by Heidegger in *Being and Time*, (anxiety, boredom, being-toward-death, dread, thrownness etc), reflected the joyless existence of life in an oppressive society, for which the 'resolution' was "authentic existence". This notion of authenticity, argued Marcuse, involved individuals in turning inwards, away from the real world, and from there developing an iron resolve "to determine every phase, every situation, every moment of one's existence". However, any actual decisions that might be made were neutral, in the sense that their empirical content and consequences were irrelevant in being bracketed off from consideration. *Any* substantive decision could be authentic, so long as it was self-assertive and not self-deceptive. Karl Lowith (1988:115-117), a student and friend of Heideggers', recalls the last meeting he had with his mentor in 1936, and confirmed that, at least at that time, Heidegger himself saw no discrepancy between his philosophy and his partisanship for National Socialism (2).

In spite of their repeated rejections of Heidegger's work, none of the Frankfurt School authors were simply dismissive of his philosophical achievement, and in a broad sense he shared with them an opposition to the scientization of reality, the steady undermining of those forms of thought which fall outside the remit of scientific method, and their replacement by forms that are amenable to scientific analysis. Questions relating to moral judgement, or the experience of art, for example, could not provide the observational data required for scientific knowledge, and as a result had been pressed to the margins of knowledge, being regarded as merely subjective phenomena. While Frankfurt School authors never accepted the idea of an 'authentic experience' as an alternative to this process, they did recognise how deleterious the process was to human potential. Indeed recently Stauth and Turner (1992), have drawn fairly explicit lines across the borders of the traditions, arguing that a common sense of the repressiveness of the modern, rational world can be traced from Adorno and Horkheimer's *Dialectic of Enlightenment* via Max Weber's *Protestant Ethic And The Spirit Of Capitalism*, to Nietzsche's *The Birth Of Tragedy*.

Marcuse himself had briefly been a student of Heideggers', and had originally wanted to bring his work to bear on Marx's 'historical materialism'. Indeed, it was the *concreteness* of Heidegger's concepts that actually attracted Marcuse in 1928, the feeling that the more affective dimensions of lived experience could be brought to light. This feeling he claimed, was the result of a double reaction. On the one hand he rejected the dryness of the neo-Kantian, and the positivist schools that dominated German universities after the first world war. On the other hand he reacted against the "no mans land" into which left-wing thought had been driven after the defeat of the German Communist

Party in 1921, a defeat that included the murder of Karl Liebnecht and Rosa Luxembourg

> The failure of the German revolution - which my friends and I actually experienced in 1921, if not earlier with Karl and Rosa's murder - was decisive. There didn't seem to be anything with which we could identify. Then Heidegger came along. Sein und Zeit appeared in 1927...What happens after a revolution fails ? A decisive question for us...and then suddenly Sein und Zeit appeared as a really concrete philosophy. (Marcuse 1980:125)

Initially there were few reservations in Marcuse's mind over Heidegger's work. For what he saw in it was the hugely valuable attempt to move philosophy beyond abstract principles, toward a concern with the real nature of human existence, something which he also saw underlying Marx's emphasis on social praxis. It is interesting to note that in his 1928 essay 'Contributions to a Phenomenology of Historical Materialism', Marcuse puts quotations from Marx, rather than Heidegger, in inverted commas, suggesting that it is Marx who is further from his position, and in need of rejuvenation from the other source. It was 'historical materialism' that mistakenly saw history as a process going on independent of human beings, and failed to appreciate that it was the historicity of human existence that made history possible. The idea of revolutionary change, that Marxism made central to its understanding of history, depended on the possibility of there being a 'before' and an 'after', a 'better' and a 'worse', which in turn had been shown by Heidegger to depend on the temporal and affective nature of human existence. Without incorporating this, the Marxist account of history would describe a mechanical and undifferentiated process. Marcuse quite unselfconsciously superimposed Heideggerian concepts onto Marxist ones, arguing that the inevitability of revolutionary action depends not on economic circumstances, but on a "radical act" internal to the agent's own existence. He does qualify this by pointing out that it is the proletariat, who by virtue of their position in the production process, are likely to be the ones for whom the need for authentic- radical action will arise. This marrying up of the Marxist idea of a revolutionary act, an existentialist idea of an authentic act, and calling the result, a "radical act", has evoked doubts in some otherwise sympathetic authors such as Alfred Schmidt [1968 (1988)]. It seemed to lead even in his later work, to an un-Marxist *actionism*, where any group is sought out that might pull off the radical act.

However Marcuse's acceptance of Heidegger's ideas even at this stage, were fairly restrained, and he never drew explicitly on them again. Even in his 1928 essay it was plain that the concreteness he found in Heidegger's phenomenology of existence, on its own was insufficient, and would in its turn have to be related dialectically to history. Certainly on his own account (1977), he came to recognise, after Heidegger declared his allegiance to Hitler, the false concreteness of the concepts he had found in his work. These led not toward a better understanding of history, but in their abstractness and neutrality, away from it.

Ironically, some forty years later, Jurgen Habermas in his own renewal of Critical Theory, looked across for support toward Gadamer's hermeneutics, a body of thought much influenced by Heidegger. Like Marcuse before him, he felt that the reconstruction of historical materialism required greater purchase on lived experience, if it was to break with misleading views that saw human action as just the effect of material causes outside it. Like Marcuse, Habermas was seeking firmer ground on which to base his general theory of society. Gadamer's ideas in *Truth and Method*, like Heidegger's in *Being and Time*, seemed to provide a framework that was general and systematic, and yet avoided the naiveties of more objectivistic outlooks. Though Habermas would never use the language of ontology as Gadamer did, his appropriation of Gadamer's ideas does suggest that he wanted to ground his work internally, as it were, in the human condition, rather than the more familiar assumptions of science.

How best can we account for this borrowing of ideas from a tradition that seemed so politically at odds with Frankfurt School Marxism ? At one level it may be accounted for by the different circumstances that characterised the 1930's and the 1960's. Both existentialism and nazism had a popular force in the 1930's, but their intellectual and political importance had faded by the 1960's and the relationship between them was no longer an issue. What had gone on apace was the incorporation of the social sciences into the broad programme of a unified science. Yet by the mid-1960's Habermas, unlike his predecessors, was able to draw on a range of authors whose work had broken through the pervasive grip of natural science assumptions. He saw Gadamer's ideas as the most subtle and comprehensive in a range that included Schutz, Cicourel, Garfinkel, (the later) Wittgenstein and Peter Winch.

But beyond this there were wider intellectual circumstances that conditioned the move. At the risk of oversimplifying, one might say that with the apparent decline in the revolutionary potential of the Western working class, those on the left who wished to sustain a credible intellectual Marxism, were set a foundational problem. If the transcendental role of 'realising history', that had been assigned to the working class by influential Marxists, such as Georg Lukacs (1922), could no longer be believed, and if history did not obviously have a directional purpose built into it, i.e. it was not leading to the designated Marxian conclusion, then Frankfurt School writings were bound to be treading on uneven ground. This resulted, naturally enough, in the need to explain why the working class were not fulfilling their appointed task; but also in a need to find conceptual tools *outside* Marxism, that would provide an adequate explanation. On the other hand they always had an aversion to 'first philosophies' or "traditional theories" as Max Horkheimer called them, theories based on fixed principles which were thought to be valid in all historical circumstances, science being the most obviously successful modern example. To adopt these, for Frankfurt School authors, meant to participate in, and thus help to reproduce the very problems they were trying to explain. For them the processes of abstraction, quantification, and deduction, that characterise scientific method, mirrored the same thought principles that governed the capitalist market. The fixity of 'first principles' underlying a theory, were an extension of the reifications that characterise a bourgeois understanding of economic laws. That is, a situation where (capitalist) 'economic laws' concerning production and consumption, are blindly assumed to be fixed universal laws, independent of human history.

Their dilemma was how to sustain a Marxism that had been emptied of its metaphysical pretensions, without adopting alternative theories that suffered from the pitfalls of reified thinking? To adopt the latter would mean a weakening of the power of critique, because it involved forms of thought that tacitly reified the status quo. Whilst avoiding the latter could (and did) lead to dazzling critical analyses, it also would necessarily lack the weight of a (once) well grounded theory like Marxism, with which the Frankfurt School always wished to maintain an affinity. It seems to me that this dilemma left an unresolved tension in their writings, between a need to demonstrate the depth of their critical insight, and the search for some ground or basis, by which these insights could be fully justified. Their work often displays an either/or quality: either ground is minimised for the sake of critique, or critique is held in check for the sake of having firm ground. In broad terms one could say that it was Adorno and Horkheimer's work in the 1940's and 1950's that exemplified the case for groundless critique, while Marcuse amongst the older Critical Theorists, and Habermas amongst the younger, who sought a justified basis for critique.

When Habermas (1967) used Gadamer's hermeneutics as one of the building blocks for a new Critical Theory, he saw it as the most adequate position available to ground the interpretive side of his work. It provided the most carefully worked out justification for a non-objectivist social science. But part of this justification included the conservative idea that the human condition involves us being so deeply immersed in particular cultural traditions, that a radical Marxist critique of them is not really possible. In taking this on board, Habermas brought to the surface the old problem of how to gain ground without losing critique. He then found himself in the odd position for a Critical Theorist, of seeing science as a critical rather than an ideological tool, needed to remedy the more fixed and conservative implications of hermeneutics. Why this was the case will be dealt with more thoroughly in later chapters.

It is now necessary to place these background themes against an account of the development of the two traditions, with particular reference to the role that science and objectivity have played in modern thought. Both traditions, in broad terms, have been critical of this role, yet in the Gadamer-Habermas debate it became the single source of greatest difference between them.

I think it is important to bear in mind that these two traditions have acquired more coherence in being recounted for academic purposes, than is actually warranted by their intellectual unity at any one time. They are made up of very diverse groups of authors whose work shared some common themes, but individually each author speaks with their own distinctive voice. Nevertheless there is some common shape that can be discerned.

Two traditions separated by a common idea

The hermeneutic tradition

In the English speaking world the hermeneutic tradition is perhaps the less well known of the two, though it has received some attention over the years, Robinson and Cobb (1964), Pannenburg (1967), Palmer (1969), Ricoeur (1973, 1977), Bauman (1978), Hoy (1978), Bleicher (1980, 1982), Ermarth (1981), Warnke (1987), all deal with the tradition though in terms of particular themes and authors, while Mueller-Vollmer (1985:1-53) provides the most comprehensive general introduction to it. There are also several collections of essays that provide useful translations for the English reader as well as useful bibliographies, such as Connerton (1976), Shapiro & Sica (1984), Mueller-Vollmer (1985). The position is complicated by the fact that interwoven with the hermeneutic tradition are threads from other schools of thought such as phenomenology, and authors such as Heidegger, whose ideas now speak well beyond the confines of any one starting point.

Nevertheless one can discern broad contours that give shape to the hermeneutic tradition. The term, hermeneutic, is generally thought to have its etymological roots in the activities of the messenger of the gods of ancient Greece, Hermes. Hermes' job was to render 'god-knowledge' intelligible to ordinary mortals. Such knowledge existed, but could only be grasped by mortals when mediated through the ordinary conditions of their lives. There was therefore a tension between truth, and the mundane conditions which constitute the human ability to understand it. Hermes was also a god in his own right, he could bring good or ill luck, sudden gain or sudden loss, he was a ready reminder to mortals of the capriciousness of their lives, and the finiteness of their existence. He was the god of travellers and could guide people on dark roads, he could disclose things at night, he was always on the way somewhere, but had no place of his own to finally dwell. In fact the nightime was very much his element, because it is the time when ordinary perceptions are disrupted, what seems obvious during the day may become much less so at night. The normal relations of distance and proximity between things are altered at night, in the darkness things can be seen in a new light. The tradition of thought that bears his name still bears the imprint of these restless, quicksilver qualities.

In the modern world, hermeneutics can be seen to have gone through three broad and roughly chronological stages. First, it emerged in the form of biblical interpretation, at the time of the Reformation, when the word of God as understood by the Catholic church, became problematic, and subject to an alternative vision by Protestant theologians. Secondly, it appeared in the secular context of the emerging human sciences, *(geisteswissenschaften)* in the nineteenth century, when the concern was to discover a methodology that would supersede local philological practices, and acknowledge the insight that what marked off human nature from physical nature was that human beings were historical beings, beings that formed themselves through their own history. The aim of both Schleiermacher and Dilthey, for example, albeit in different ways, was to establish general criteria for interpreting the human world, that would be equal to, if different from, those being established in the natural sciences. Thirdly, there was a radical shift, largely brought about by Heidegger's *Being and Time* [1927 (1962)], away from the question of correct methods (epistemology), towards an investigation of the ground on which the assumptions of these methods stood. The aim was not thereby to improve our knowledge of the world through better methods, but to uncover the conditions in which human beings 'had their world' (ontology).

This third stage of hermeneutic development, despite being historically the most recent, and including contemporary authors like Gadamer and Ricoeur, remains the most awkward and difficult to blend in with the more familiar concerns of the humanities and social sciences, not least because of the strangeness of its language use. Indeed, I found the effort involved in just reading and making sense of *Being and Time*, was a most formidable obstacle, for although Heidegger uses terms like 'understanding', and 'interpretation', which were also the stock-in-trade of the methodological hermeneutics of the previous generation, he uses them in a strikingly different way. His ambition was to get behind the ontic or (roughly speaking) the empirical realm, to disclose the basic existential structures of our existence, and thence to the nature of Being itself. What made this work so difficult for me was the way it was pitched outside normal reading assumptions. Social science students standardly find themselves faced by a field of empirical 'objects' such as class, race, bureaucracy, and so forth, that are pre-formed in the sense that they are made up of an amalgam of fact, received wisdom, and evaluative projection, and sometimes bear a relation to their lived experience. On this basis, the student, with some effort, can learn to manoeuvre him or herself around in it, but Heidegger's *Being and Time* bypasses these assumptions and provides no familiar guideposts. Even those taken for granted connecting words, such as 'if', 'because', 'thus', and 'therefore', which normally provide the reader with a subtle helping hand, seemed thin on the ground. What Heidegger did was to show that 'understanding' is part of our primordial being-in-the-world, rather than an uncertain methodological technique, which when properly rectified by more objective methods, could give us the correct interpretation of things. This latter view of course, is the lesson sociology students are usually expected to learn from Max Weber's concept of understanding (verstehen) (3). But for Heidegger, verstehen is not a *method* that the unfortunate social scientist is obliged to use, unlike the natural scientist, in order to intuit the motives of others. 'Understanding' in his sense is not one thing we do among others, but what we are. Before we are able to reflect on the lives of others or on our own, we are always already guided and oriented towards things in certain ways by this pre-reflective understanding. He uses the term *Dasein*, which translates as 'being-there', to encapsulate this idea of grasping things and being grasped by them, of finding ourselves already placed in relation to them before we can reflect upon them.

It fell to Gadamer to bring out the radical implications of this analysis of Dasein for the methodology of the social sciences, most famously in *Truth and Method*[1960 (1989)]. Gadamer's case is, that because of this fore-structure of 'understanding', the idea of an autonomous and objective interpretation is mistaken. The ambition of the social sciences to be objective is pre-empted by the way all interpretations are preceded by our (pre-structured) 'understanding' of the world which derives from our historical tradition. When we interpret something we do not escape from our tradition to a place where disinterested objectivity reigns, but rather we interpret what we have already 'understood' by way of the tradition that produced us and it. For Gadamer 'understanding' is what makes interpretation at the empirical level possible; both are woven together in a way that objective methods cannot separate. In fact in a sense, Gadamer reverses the normal assumptions of what a successful interpretation consists of: instead of a brand new understanding emerging, he claims that we amplify and extend what we already know, by disclosing more thoroughly the tradition in which we are immersed.

Such a view seems close to some of the ideas that members of the Frankfurt School developed, in terms of their opposition to a model of knowledge as the purely disinterested exercise of human reason. For them, like Heidegger and Gadamer, this model is not confined to science alone, but is symptomatic of a much wider cultural deception. For example, even given the many differences that exist between the natural and the social sciences, and between different disciplines within those boundaries, there is still characteristically a drive in them towards a knowledge free of pre-judgements, to the point where (true) knowledge is virtually defined by its detachment from any interests outside it.

But there is also here a divergence between the hermeneutic and Frankfurt traditions, in that for the Frankfurt School, objectivistic modes of thought actually concealed implicit forms of social and political domination.

The Frankfurt School

The Frankfurt School is the better known of the two traditions, at least to the sociological community, and has a certain unity which derives from the fact that its early members had a common affiliation to the Institute for Social Research in Frankfurt, founded in 1923. It has drawn inspiration from a wide variety of philosophical sources, but most significantly from Hegel, Marx, Lukacs, and more recently, Kant. Its reception into the English speaking world has been helped by the steady stream of translations of its authors' major works, as well as several collections of their essays, (Connerton 1976., Arato and Gebhardt 1978, Bronner and Kellner 1989, Adorno 1991), but even more so by fairly comprehensive and sympathetic commentaries: (Jay 1973, Held 1980, Feenberg 1986, and Kellner 1989, Wiggershaus 1994).

For the Frankfurt School the pre-structured nature of our 'understanding' has been overtaken by an essentially instrumental orientation. Behind the apparent neutrality of the concepts and techniques of science lies the assumption that objective knowledge depends on our capacity to manipulate objects, be they natural *or* social objects. Moreover these habits of thought are now part and parcel of our social currency, they have been internalised by modern industrial societies and become one of their organising principles. As Marcuse put it :-

> The scientific abstraction from concreteness, the quantification of qualities which yield exactness as well as universal validity, involve ..a specific mode of "seeing" the world ...in terms of calculable, predictable relationships among exactly identifiable units... (thus)... The principles of modern science were *apriori* structured in such a way that they could serve as conceptual instruments for a universe of self-propelling, productive control; (Marcuse :1964:164, 158)

In saying this Marcuse implicitly draws as much from Weber as from Marx, with whom Frankfurt School authors are usually associated. Weber's conception of capitalism is built around the growing preponderance of *zwekrationalitat* or technical reason, over other forms of reason. This process of 'rationalisation' refers to the methodical application of technical and scientific principles to all aspects of life, independent of their value or wider cultural significance. However, for Marcuse the Marxist, this process is also tied in with capitalist economic relations, and is thus an historical project potentially capable of change. The immense success of Western science and technology when utilised by the interests of capital, has led to a kind of 'controlling affluence', where people accept regimentation at the point of production (work) as being technically necessary in a 'rationally' organised society that is geared to meeting people's material needs. Moreover this subjection is carried over into the area of consumption, where even people's free time is structured around the desirability of consuming leisure products. Thus as the circle closes the political character of capitalist society becomes invisible. The manner in which it controls its members and the price they pay in bringing off its endless success, is concealed precisely by the conspicuousness of what it, (and they), define as success. It becomes impossible to imagine an alternative way of doing things: progress comes to mean just more of the same thing.

However, the Frankfurt School tradition, like the hermeneutic tradition is far from being a unified body of thought, its changes in style and content cannot be seen simply as a cumulative development, for they represent ruptures as well as continuities. Indeed there are tensions within individual authors' writings, as themes disappear and reappear in the effort to resolve contradictory tendencies. Marcuse's attitude towards science and technology is a good example.

A basic theme for the Frankfurt School was that science, based upon empirical observation, had originally served the normative purpose of demystifying superstitious illusions about the nature of the world. In the contemporary situation however, science has come to deny, or rather conceal its normative assumptions (instrumentality and control), and is legitimated by its apparent value neutrality. The effect of this has been to turn science into a kind of 'rational ideology'. Scientific thinking, and its social counterpart, technical reason, has come to serve as a model for all rational thinking; the epitome of reason. Indeed the theme that is perhaps common to all of the Frankfurt School authors is that this process of scientization brings about, not reason, but unreason. What passes for reason nowadays is a truncation of its full potential. For the Marcuse of *One-Dimensional Man* (1964) this tension between the original liberative potential of scientific thought, and its current repressive form as 'technological rationality', presents a particular problem. On the one hand he clearly sees technology and the style of thinking from which it is derived, as intrinsically repressive. On the other hand he is no 'Luddite', and as a Marxist, he wants to see science and technology harnessed to meet the real needs of people (1964:231). As Feenberg (1988:227) aptly put it, he seems to want to "have his conceptual cake and eat it too". [The issue is not helped by Marcuse's own writing style which is so densely woven and rhetorical that differences between science, technology, technological rationality, domination, and so forth, tend to disappear.] Certainly the main thrust of his writing at that point, seems to be a tireless drive to negate the (scientific) principles on which modernity is built, but which he intermittently contradicts, in order to retain a progressive (Marxist) impulse, and avoid the charge of being irrationally anti-modern.

However, the question of whether Marcuse is self-contradictory in *One-Dimensional Man* matters less in this context than the fact that his dilemma reflects something of both the different stages through which Critical Theory has gone, and its ambivalent relationship to the similarly anti-positivist thought of Heidegger and Gadamer.

Frankfurt School writings can be split up into three roughly distinguishable phases. First, the relatively optimistic neo-Marxist writings of the early period (1923-38). When Max Horkheimer became the Director in 1929, the tone of the output remained within a Marxist framework but the innovative authors he attracted to the Institute, such as Adorno, Marcuse, and Fromm, meant that the more deterministic elements of historical materialism were jettisoned. Secondly, a period of increasing pessimism from the late 1930's through the 1950's to the early 1960's. The work from this period is highly varied, but the growing 'irrationality' of the world is seen by them to be so intractable, that even 'rationalist' theories like Marxism are inadequate to meet the task. Marcuse's *One Dimensional Man* is the most famous work from this period, though it retained a faint glimmer of optimism in its willingness to try and make sense of the 'totality' of the time, even if it could find no historical agent that might change things. However Adorno's writings, such as *Dialectic of Enlightenment* (1947) and *Minima Moralia* (1951), are characterised by an almost corrosive gloom. In the light of events in Europe in the 1930's and 1940's he sheers away from the very idea of gracing humanity with any general view of the totality, and reflects this in writing mostly short essays, in a terse, impacted, style. It is the point at which groundless critique comes to the fore. Thirdly, there is a reconstructive phase from the mid 1960's to the present time, where a younger generation of authors such as Offe, Habermas and Apel, seek to renew the progressive and interdisciplinary spirit of the first phase.

As a tradition, Critical Theory has always been 'reflexive' in acknowledging that it is a part of the same social historical process which it seeks to analyse. It sought some autonomy from merely local circumstance, but accepted that the effects of history would be clearly imprinted on its work.

Indeed the radicalness of its critical claims are based on the idea that it does *not* have autonomy from history, instead its critical force depends on the indwelling relationship it bears to the historical process. According to Max Horkheimer's programmatic essay *Traditional and Critical Theory* ([1937]1972), traditional (positivist) theory is based upon the formal-calculative thinking of science and mathematics, and works deductively from fixed postulates. By contrast, Critical Theory searches in dialectical fashion for the roots of phenomena in wider historical contexts; it seeks to uncover the relationship between ideas and their social and political environment. Horkheimer argues that with traditional theory the process of abstraction from concrete circumstances, and the use of quantitative calculation, gives the impression of having produced knowledge that is free from the effects of history. However, the historical context in which traditional theory's own formal-calculative style of thinking had developed, was the world-view of capitalism, based on principles of abstraction and quantification for the commercial market.

Frankfurt School writing in the 1930s reflects Horkheimer's (1937) model of Critical Theory in its dialectical style of analysis. The term for the methodological technique which they used, was *immanent critique*. This involved following the lines of trajectory of an idea from the inside, i.e. unfolding it sympathetically on its own terms, and then confronting it negatively, with its opposite implications. This procedure aimed to transform the idea into something more rational. Hence, for example, capitalism understands itself as embodying the best political/moral ideas of freedom and justice, which it sees as the corollary of its free-market economic system. As a free-market is claimed to be best at meeting the economic needs of individuals, so capitalism's social system, based on individualism, is thought to be best at meeting the individuals' needs for justice and freedom. However, one can confront these claims with the reality that 'free markets' are dominated by large monopoly corporations and these are indifferent to such needs. By challenging or negating capitalism's self-understanding with its reality, and by dwelling on the disjunction between its words and deeds, Critical Theory hoped to open up possibilities for a better, more rational life, albeit one still presently concealed. However, here lies the nub of the problem.

The use of immanent critique presupposes that there are forces in society capable of recognising this gap between society's ostensible claims and its contradictory reality. However, the effects of the rise of Nazism with all that entailed for the Frankfurt School authors, and the spurious freedom they found in the 'commodified reality' of post-war industrial society, led them to doubt whether such critical capacities still existed. In the second phase (late 1930s to early 1960s), their pessimism stretched to the belief that the processes of instrumental reason and of commodification, had gone so far as to reach into and change the very structure of the human personality. The result was that they implicitly believed there was now no difference in people's minds between freedom from oppression, and the freedom to choose between different commodities. People had, as it were, learnt to enjoy their own subjugation to the system, believing it to be freedom.

Habermas's writings since the late 1960's can be seen as an attempt to draw Critical Theory away from this kind of intellectual cul-de-sac. There was, as Richard Bernstein (1985:4-8) points out, only a thin line that separated Adorno and Horkheimer's account of instrumental reason as an inescapable vicious circle, from Weber's account of technical reason (*zwekrationalitat*) as an 'iron cage', and Heidegger's analysis of calculative thinking as part of the 'fate of being' of Western metaphysical thought. All of them to some extent saw the 'same' process being virtually unstoppable. Such inevitability of course, did not sit well with the Marxist spirit of Critical Theory.

The changes in Critical Theory wrought by the likes of Habermas, Claus Offe, Albrecht Wellmer, and Karl-Otto Apel are too vast to be easily recounted. Habermas' work on its own has a fresco-like quality which resists easy summary. Many of his essays are programmatic, with their significance only becoming apparent later, as they feed into his wider enterprise. In broad terms his ambition has been to renew the tradition by building a path away from the dilemmas of Adorno and Horkheimer's 'critique without hope', on the basis of his theory of *communicative rationality*.

He shares only in part with his predecessors the idea that the growth of technical or instrumental reason has a deleterious effect on modern life. He argues that the stunning success of science and technology in the West has produced a lopsided form of development, rather than a wholly defective one. He certainly accepts, in continuity with them, that the pervasive technical form of reasoning is a truncated and distorted version of human rationality. In using it we are able to predict and control some aspects of the natural and the social world. We can calculate the outcome of different courses of action and assess them on this basis. But we cannot evaluate the *goals* of such action as right or wrong. In order to do this we would have to invoke values, which from the point of view of technical reason are subjective and arbitrary, and about which it has no answers; because wider questions concerned with the fairness or justice of a course of action cannot be calculated. All that can be calculated is the technical effectiveness of the course of action. And herein lies its crucial and dangerous limitation. In the modern secular world we can find no universally justified moral values, which leaves a vacuum that may be filled with a kind of 'emotivism' and 'decisionism'. Hence a situation can arise where the forces that can orchestrate the emotions of a population, can also arbitrarily decide on goals, and pursue them on a purely technical basis. Zygmunt Bauman in his recent book *Modernity and The Holocaust* (1989), shows in a vivid and disturbing way, how once the Nazis had decided on the goal of eliminating the Jews, the task became a technical-bureaucratic one, of merely finding the method that would be most cost effective. Bauman's case is that the Holocaust was not the aberrant feature of the modern world, but an intrinsic part of the way technocratic rationality transmutes moral issues into technical ones.

Bauman's work illustrates generally the Frankfurt School case, though in seeing modernity itself as culpable, it comes closer to the (pessimistic) spirit of Adorno and Horkheimer's *Dialectic of Enlightenment* (1947), than to Habermas's work. For Adorno and Horkheimer progress and repression had come to be virtually the same thing. For Habermas technical rationality does threaten to "colonise the life-world", but it must still remain a crucial part of any notion of progress. Its very success, not least in the system of capitalist production, has had the effect of squeezing to the margins other forms of rationality, but it has not eliminated them altogether.

What has happened, according to Habermas, is that because of the demands of the modern (capitalist) social system, we have tended to lose sight of important differences between two quite different forms of social action. The first, purposive-rational action, derives from the assumptions of technical reason; it is a form of social action guided by the idea of successfully achieving a goal by using the most technically effective means. In the process of society's modernisation, purposive-rational action has infiltrated and squeezed to the margins a second form of action, communicative action. This second form is action guided by the idea of reaching a consensus through mutual understanding and dialogue. It is Habermas's case that this form of action is just as worthy of being called 'rational' as its technical counterpart. Even though it includes value-laden areas of life such as the moral rules that underpin social life, it is based on a kind of objective knowledge. This refers to the objectivity that can be achieved through an inter-subjective agreement about what is to count as right, proper, fair, and so forth. Moreover this is not something that is just contingent on people choosing to agree about things, it is a possibility built into the very nature of all human communication. When we speak to another person we expect that what we have to say will be found plausible, we expect it to be believed; and if it is not we can set about trying to make the case more convincing. In Habermas's terms, every speech act always implicitly raises 'universal validity claims', which if challenged could in principle be justified by the speaker. If a particular claim is challenged, such as the sincerity of the statement, and this is found wanting, we may adjust or even drop the claim in the to and fro of an ongoing dialogue. We pursue agreement in this way because human communication is about convincing others through the force of better argument alone. In principle, when we communicate with others we assume that what we have to say could be agreed to by *anyone* who is freely capable of understanding it.

Of course he is well aware that what he is describing is a kind of inner model or ideal type, and that in actual empirical situations all kinds of extraneous elements intrude to distort communicative dialogue. His point nevertheless is that every time we communicate with one another, we implicitly and inevitably raise the possibility of a freely achieved dialogic agreement. This is the telos of communicative action. Habermas believes that it can provide him with the firm ground for critique, that the work of the previous generation of Critical Theorists lacked. It can serve as a critical bench-mark, helping us to evaluate the validity of any actual social consensus. The more a consensus can be shown to be based on the force of the better argument alone, the more legitimate it can claim to be. One of his central arguments against Gadamer's conception of dialogue, was that it provided no way for us to distinguish between a legitimate consensus, and one that had been achieved through a 'systematically distorted communication'. This refers to a spurious agreement achieved under the conditions of a deformed dialogue, where the very structure of communication is fixed in such a way that the interests of one group are invariably enhanced at the expense of another. In a patriarchal society, for example, forms of inequality between men and women may be accepted by both sexes, but still be the outcome of assumptions and definitions that preempt any other conclusion than the rightness of male superiority.

Although Habermas does not believe that there are ultimate objective values, such as *equality*, just waiting to be uncovered and applied, he does believe that normative questions about justice, located within particular cultural traditions, are capable of rational solution. The thing he inveighs against is the idea, prevalent in modern societies, that morality must lie outside the realm of reason. This produces a dubious sense of moral relativism, where the local norms of behaviour are arbitrary, in the sense that they lack any wider justification. Whether Gadamer's hermeneutics should be viewed as suffering from this inadequacy, as Habermas claimed, is altogether less straightforward.

The character of the debate

The hermeneutics of suspicion versus the hermeneutics of faith

It is not an easy debate to characterise. At one level it is a debate over the methodology of the social sciences, with Habermas defending the importance of 'scientific objectivity' as a way of gaining adequate purchase on social phenomena. This, he argued, was necessary in order to provide a sufficiently independent kind of knowledge to undertake an adequate critique of society. Yet both authors had already been involved in what could be termed anti-positivist debates, Gadamer with Emilio Betti, and Habermas with Karl

Popper (4). Both Gadamer and Habermas shared an opposition to the way objectivist assumptions underpinned, not only social scientific thought, but Western rationality generally. In the previous debates they had rejected the subjectivistic conception of human understanding, where objective, scientific methods, are thought to be necessary to rectify the vagaries of human interpretation. In this sense, even though there was an important methodological difference between them over the nature of objectivity, their debate could still be placed *within* the boundaries of a broadly hermeneutic outlook; one that was opposed to the insidious way scientific assumptions could undermine the wider validity of human experience. Certainly there is still much in Habermas's work to suggest his continued commitment to this interpretive view of social science (Baynes 1989-90).

The idea that it is a 'hermeneutic debate', is one that Paul Ricoeur, particularly, has constructed, arguing that their dispute was between the two opposing but interdependent poles of understanding that make up all modern interpretation. He uses the terms, the hermeneutics of suspicion (Habermas), and the hermeneutics of faith or the recovery of tradition (Gadamer) to describe them(5). They refer to two competing sets of foundational interpretive assumptions that give rise to two very different kinds of knowledge. The hermeneutics of suspicion takes up an attitude of fundamental doubt and mistrust towards the world. From the outset it is critical of what appears to be the case; from the ground up, as it were, it seeks to challenge the status quo. Within the social sciences, particularly sociology, Marxism would serve as a clear example. It continually casts doubt on what seems to be the good order and open nature of capitalist society. It questions the validity of how social actors perceive the world, arguing that behind their backs is concealed an exploitative structural order quite at odds with its apparent legitimacy. Different 'Marxism's' construe this concealment differently. Habermas, for example, sees the actors own self-understanding as largely deriving from a process of distorted communication. Using the language of sociological systems theory, he argues that this distortion arises from the voracious, but scarcely perceived technical demands of society's sub-systems, such as the economy and the political administration. These, in the guise of increasing their levels of rationalisation, shape and orchestrate a social consensus so as to enhance the technical efficiency of the system; but in so doing subtly undermine the idea that a consensus consists of an unforced agreement between people. Habermas believes that a social consensus could, and indeed should, be based on such a reciprocal discourse, and that this is not mere wishful thinking because it is a possibility built into the structure of human communication. Indeed, he believes it is the core of the inter-subjective nature of the human world. The human subject, as it were, only learns to become human (i.e. social) through a process of communicative reciprocity with other subjects. While the idea that a society based on *perfectly* reciprocal communication is an illusion, he does believe this structure of human communication can be used as a source for the critique of society. He uses it as a normative centre-piece for his renewal of Critical Theory. His aim is to uncover the way the process of system-rationalisation imperceptibly imposes itself upon people's thoughts and actions, by pointing up how it actually distorts what appears as a consensus at the level of human interaction. The rather ominous phrase he uses to describe what has happened in modern industrial societies, 'the colonisation of the life-world by system imperatives', evocatively captures the spirit of his hermeneutics of suspicion.

It is doubtful whether his work is Marxist in any strict sense, in that it shows little concern for the role of social classes, and replaces Marx's 'base-superstructure' model of society with its own account of the tension between system and life-world (6). However, as Ricoeur includes Freud and Nietzsche as well as Marx as the 'masters of suspicion', this rather wider brief would encompass Habermas's work too. He certainly shares with them a view that always casts a jaundiced eye over the world and the claims it has to being 'rational'. It is an outlook that seeks to demystify illusions that keep whole peoples in thrall, especially the illusion that their consciousness of what things mean is the limit to meaning itself.

By contrast, the hermeneutics of faith, or the recovery of tradition, starts not from the desire to break up false consciousness, but the desire to restore or reveal meaning in all its fullness(7). Ricoeur uses the phenomenology of religion as the key illustration of this pole of interpretation. Here, suspicion is replaced by faith. The interpreter takes up an attitude of care and concern towards the object of attention, so as to allow the full weight of the (sacred) message to appear. There is a faith that illumination can follow from such careful attention. Where the hermeneutics of suspicion finds deception the norm, and hunts down the cause of it, or what function it plays in maintaining the status quo, the hermeneutics of faith refuses to reduce these things to cause or function. It insists that the meaning of the message is to be found constituted in and by the message itself, not outside it. It asks for the interpreter not to rush to the circumstances surrounding it, but bracket them off and show a willingness to listen, and allow the meaning to be heard. Although Gadamer's hermeneutics moves well away from the phenomenological idea that one can bracket and apprehend 'pure meaning', it does in an analogous way emphasise the importance of allowing meaning to emerge. He describes the task of the interpreter as one of engaging with a text in the same manner that we engage in a conversation. If we read off what the other person has to say in a mechanical way, as if it were just an illustration of their 'class' or 'gender', as though we were saying to ourselves, "that's just what they would say", we kill the conversation before it starts. A conversation requires us to be who we are, but also to allow the other to speak and be themselves. In fact a good conversation takes off when both partners attend to what the other says, not to what they are. Gadamer puts it this way:-

> To conduct a conversation means to allow oneself to be conducted by the subject matter to which the partners in the dialogue are oriented. It requires that one does not try to argue the other person down but that one really considers the weight of the other's opinion. (Gadamer 1989:367)

It is the meaning of what is at issue between people that draws them forward in conversation, indeed in the best conversations the partners lose track of themselves as they bring new meaning to light. Even when one of the partners is a text, the same model applies, the task of the historian or sociologist is to engage with the text in a questioning but undogmatic manner. From this dialogic process some new level of coherence may be found.

Within sociology, the interpretive tradition, including symbolic interactionism and ethnography, come closest in approximating to these ambitions. Their aims are centred on the task of uncovering the internal coherence of the beliefs and practices of groups of actors. There is often a sheer delight shown by authors here, in revealing how mundane areas of life are actually patterned in unsuspecting, but highly organised social ways. Take for example Jack Douglas' study, *The Nude Beach* (1977). In this ethnographic study of a nudist beach in California, he shows how the removal of clothes, far from simply liberating people into a more 'natural state' away from the demands and constraints of everyday life, actually sets up new arrangements and new taboos. Great care is taken in presenting the body in certain ways, to conceal or reveal it to the best effect. The studied casualness of the most beautiful, the sudden bursts of movement from those seeking an audience, the static poses of those with all-over tans, the territorial demarcations between different groups, all signal that life on the nude beach is as controlled and carefully organised around the principles of status and success, as anywhere else.

It is this concern to draw out the underlying intelligibility of a text or a social reality that characterises the hermeneutics of recovery, and sets it off against the hermeneutics of suspicion. Certainly at a superficial level the spirit of Gadamer and Habermas's work can be located within these two separate frames of reference, although Ricoeur is not suggesting that they are exclusive of each other, but that they represent two limits to contemporary thought. In fact he argues that hermeneutics generally is subject to a double motivation: "willingness to suspect, willingness to listen". His analysis of the Gadamer-Habermas debate is similarly based on the idea that a dialectical relation exists between their two bodies of work. He uncovers a large area of common ground and finds their substantive differences to be mostly matters of emphasis. To some extent I find this view quite plausible, and the examples used above also show signs of this double motivation. Douglas's *Nude Beach* is motivated by a desire to show the coherence of life on the beach, but there is also an element of demystification, a desire to explode the pretensions of the nude-beachers. Likewise, while Habermas's aim is to demystify the apparent good order of the modern world as a distortion of what the good life should be, he is also concerned to restore coherence to the life-world, the world of lived experience.

However, the problem with Ricoeur's account of the debate is that neither Gadamer nor Habermas really accept that there is a 'happy dialectic' between their positions. Certainly both see their own work as embracing that of the other, but also as *exceeding* it in important ways. Habermas (1983,1986) stays aligned to the antipositivist spirit of hermeneutics, but still seeks to establish a vantage point from which a justified, or grounded critique of society can be undertaken. He builds this normative centre-piece around the structure of human communication, the underlying features of which are species-wide competencies. In doing this he apparently accepts Gadamer's 'conversational' model of communication but moves outside it to examine the conditions that make particular kinds of conversation possible(8). From a knowledge of these rules, he believes, one can distinguish between a conversation where a legitimate consensus obtains, and one where it does not, and we may thus have good grounds for critiquing spurious, distorted social consensuses. This capacity is something he claims is beyond Gadamer's model.

But Gadamer (1984), for his part, believes that suspicion is no less a part of his theory of interpretation than faith. The hermeneutics of faith was never that of blind faith, and he traces out a history of hermeneutics, drawing attention to the way it is often informed by an attitude of suspicion. Essentially he rejects Ricoeur's view that there are two poles to hermeneutics which need to be reconciled, regarding authors like Habermas, who want to move beyond 'the conversation that we are', as simply misguided.

However at this stage I think it is more important to engage with the ideas that emerged in the debate rather than trying to prescribe the nature of its outcome.

Notes
1. An assessment of the relation between the two is to be found in Rovatti (1973). Marcuse's early sympathetic attempt to link Marxism with Heidegger's work is to be found in Marcuse ([1928]1969), an essay critical of Husserl's phenomenology in Marcuse ([1936] 1968), and more sympathetic but still critical, in Marcuse (1974). For an assessment of Marcuse's 'misreading' of Husserl see O'Neill (1988). For

an assessment of the influence of Heidegger on Marcuse see Piccone and Delfini (1970), and a view from Marcuse's own side critical of this influence see Schmidt (1988). For a negative assessment of Critical Theory from a phenomenological point of view see Piccone (1975). Adorno's critique of existentialism in general and Heideggers' in particular is in Adorno (1973). For Habermas' critique of Heidegger see Habermas (1977) and (1987:chtVI).

2. Lowith, though no Frankfurt Schoolman, makes the same conceptual connection as Marcuse pointing up the link between what he calls the idea of "pure resolve" which underpinned *Being and Time* and the inner nihilism of National Socialism, in Lowith (1988:121). In that same edition of *New German Critique* there are instructive translations of some of Heidegger's political speeches of the time as well as an account of the recent 'French Heidegger debate' by Richard Wolin.

3. I am referring to Weber's recommendation that sociology should be adequate both at the level of cause and at the level of meaning. This has been subject to a fairly positivistic interpretation by many in Anglo-American sociology where the understanding of meaning is often reduced to the auxiliary role of being a source of hypotheses in need of causal testing. See Abel (1948), Sahay (1971), Parsons (1968:Vol 2 cht XVI). There are contrary views which suggest that Weber did not intend the 'meaning side' of things to be played down, and that it was equal if not more important than the 'causal side' of things. See Outhwaite (1975), Merleau-Ponty (1973). In fact Winch (1958:111-20) criticises Weber for not realising the full weight of his own insight that the understanding of meaning is absolutely central to the nature of social science. Apel (1967) and (1972:15-27) provide a complex affirmation of this thesis by way of a critique of the positivist view, as does Skjervheim (1974). Sica (1988) provides a careful account of Weber's work pointing out the way he brilliantly used his own his own imaginative understanding.

4. The exchange between Habermas and Popper was part of the wider and perhaps misnamed 'positivist dispute' in German sociology, in which the main protagonists were Karl Popper and Theodor Adorno. See Adorno et al (1976), for a commentary see Frisby (1974), How (1980), and Holub (1991). The issue between Gadamer and Betti is more difficult to locate in English, but Bleicher (1982) offers an introduction to and translation of some of Betti's work. There is also a short introduction to and translation of some of Betti's work by Susan Noakes in Shapiro and

Sica (1984). E.D. Hirsch (1967) provides an English language critique of Gadamer akin to that proposed by Betti.

5. Paul Ricoeur develops what he calls these "two fundamental philosophical gestures" in Ricoeur (1970:28-36) and (1974). He applies them to the Habermas-Gadamer debate in Ricoeur (1973b) and (1981:cht2).

6. The question of whether Habermas should be thought a Marxist is affirmed by Jay (1988:cht15) and Ingram (1987:cht1), but denied by Rockmore (1989). Critiques of Habermas from various Marxist(ish) points of view, and expressing varying degrees of sympathy or antipathy for his work can be found in Therborn (1971), Laska (1974), Thomas (1979), Sensat (1979, 1986), Roderick (1986). A comprehensive bibliography of this and other issues can be found in Rasmussen (1990a), collected by R.Gortzen.

7. The title given to this outlook varies slightly according to whether an author is referring to religious meaning or to a more social secular meaning; e.g. the hermeneutics of 'recovery', 'recollection', 'restoration', 'faith', 'trust', or 'respect'.

8. Although Habermas' view of communication resembles Gadamer's view of dialogue one should be wary of seeing them as the same. For Gadamer communication is but one aspect of what he calls 'the linguisticality of being'.

2 The disputed territory: The first part of Truth and Method

Introduction

Before examining the debate in detail it is necessary to look at the substance of Gadamer's ideas as they appeared in *Truth and Method*, for these provided the ground which Habermas sought to appropriate, and it was Habermas's partial use of them that was the starting point for the debate. I shall not attempt to provide a complete commentary on the book, it has already been done superbly by Joel Weinsheimer (1985), but provide a more limited gloss on those elements which seem to me to catch the spirit of his hermeneutics. I shall then move to a more detailed account of those ideas which were the focus of Habermas's critical assessment.

One cannot help being conscious that any gloss on a work like *Truth and Method*, apart from being necessarily selective, will also bear an odd relation to the original in other ways. In both style and substance Gadamer's writing is not immediately amenable to anglophone ears and resists easy summary. His arguments are complicated and woven around a tradition of German thought that includes authors well outside the range familiar to the contemporary reader. The style too, is indirect, and does not consist of formal propositions for which he seeks proof, rather, he tends to circle round an idea, asking questions of it in a quietly probing manner, allowing as it were, the idea itself to answer and throw up new possibilities. In this sense his ideas about the nature of dialogue are built into the style of his writing as well as its substance. There is also a dual momentum in his writing, it is both systematic and heterogeneous at the same time. He works consistently in pursuit of a particular goal but does not give the impression of having decided the outcome beforehand. His analyses open up a terrain of understanding without finalising things for us. As a result one cannot list the formal properties of his ideas and hope that this will meet the bill, as it is the suggestiveness and mutually informing nature of relationships between his ideas that gives them their meaning. All of which means that my gloss on his work cannot in any way match the complexity of his argument. and will at best be, as he put it with regard to translation, "at once clearer and flatter than the original".

Nevertheless, acknowledging the inevitable gap between the two, I shall still seek to show how different themes in his work are interwoven towards what I shall take to be a central emphasis on the way human beings 'belong to the world'. That is, his concern to show how thoroughly we are *immersed* in our historical tradition, and that attempts to establish knowledge that breaks free of it, are deeply misleading. Instead of trying to free ourselves from the effects of tradition, Gadamer argues that we should find ways of immersing ourselves in it more thoroughly. Such a willing submission to tradition was, of course also the theme that jarred most with the left-wing political sensibilities of Habermas, whose aim was to incorporate hermeneutics into his own radical critique of society.

Truth and Method is divided into three related sections and though they are angled in from different directions, all are driven by the desire to uncover the ontological basis of experience that exceeds the remit of controlled, scientific explanation.

On the experience of art

In the First Part Gadamer examines the experience of art as something that cannot be contained or verified by, (scientific) method. Our experience of art shows up more clearly than anything else the limits of using method to grasp the 'truth' of art. It is not that scientific method as such has been applied to the understanding of art, indeed the post-empiricist philosophy of science has successfully challenged the wider truth claims of the more traditional positivistic accounts of science(1). It is rather that scientific assumptions have been unwittingly smuggled into the process with the result that the full import of the experience of art has been undermined. Art tends to be thought of as 'decoration', as something that at its most serious is hived off into museums or concert halls, and at its more superficial is regarded as mere entertainment. In either case it is seen as something battened onto the side of reality, as a distraction from it, rather than as something that is part of our knowledge of reality. Gadamer asks how this state of affairs has come about, such that we do not even consider art capable of telling us any truth about reality; we see it primarily as untruth, as a fiction.

He describes Kant's *Critique of Judgement* as initiating a tradition of thought that split off "aesthetic consciousness" from other forms of thought. In seeking to justify aesthetic judgement as a form of understanding existing separately, and in its own right, Kant marked it off from the kind of knowledge produced by the natural sciences. One of the effects of this separation was to 'subjectivise' aesthetic judgement, and concede the task of producing objective knowledge to the natural sciences alone. Though it was Kant's intention to legitimise rather than belittle aesthetic judgement, and his account is certainly not wholly responsible for the outcome, there is an irony in the ease with which questions of aesthetic taste and judgement can now be disparagingly reduced to matters of personal opinion.

If "aesthetic consciousness" became the mental attitude which filtered out all extraneous matter save that of beauty, it performed this task through an operation Gadamer calls "aesthetic differentiation". This involved a process of abstraction, whereby the work of art is hauled out from its rootedness in the form of life of a particular historical community, in order to purify and reveal its aesthetic qualities :-

> What we call a work of art and experience aesthetically depends on a process of abstraction. By disregarding everything in which a work of art is rooted (its original context of life, and the religious or secular function which gave it its significance), it becomes visible as the 'pure work of art.' (Gadamer 1989:85).

As a parallel to this, the artist too had to undergo a kind of alienation "by losing his place in the world". Where once most art was commissioned by wealthy patrons, such patronage now discredits the artist, the real artist must seek creative inspiration outside such constraints.

> The free artist creates without commission. He seems distinguished by the complete independence of his creativity and thus acquires the characteristic social features of an outsider whose style of life cannot be measured by the standards of public morality. The concept of the bohemian which arose in the nineteenth century reflects this process The home of the Gypsies became the generic word for the artist's way of life. (Gadamer 1989:87-88)

This enforced freedom leaves the artist in the role of romantic hero, but it is a role that makes him or her an ambiguous figure. In a society no longer cemented by its religious traditions the artist takes on mythical qualities, he becomes a "secular saviour" whose creations are expected in a small way to unite an irredeemably fragmented world. The experimental artist tries to discover new ways of reuniting our experience of the world, but in so doing reveals the implicit tragedy of the effort. Artistic success creates a particular community of admirers, but thereby only highlights the fragmentation that is going on all around.

As these processes involve the splitting off of the aesthetic elements in the consciousness of those who enjoy art from the wider meaning of their everyday lives, and also uprooting the artwork's own place in a particular social world, so the appreciation of 'pure art' takes on the character of "simultaneity". What Gadamer means by this is that the real significance of temporal distance has been lost. Aesthetic consciousness purifies the artwork of all non-aesthetic elements, so that where and when it was produced is not decisive in our appreciation of it. A work of art, no matter how historically removed from us can be simultaneously appreciated along with all other works of art. In abstracting the aesthetic from other elements we are able to treat the artwork in a quasi-scientific way, as an object which does not induce us to take up a moral attitude towards it. We can suspend its particular significance to our own temporal milieu, and then make objective comparisons, for example between an 'original' performance of a Shakespeare play, and contemporary reproductions of it. Purely aesthetic appreciation enables us to disinterestedly consume art from any time or place. Such an attitude of course bears a resemblance to the purely observational outlook of the scientist, who in following scientific method must bracket off all wider cultural significance.

The effect the purified aesthetic attitude has on art, is to sidetrack it into having a merely decorative uncommitted place in our understanding of the world. It denudes art of its real power to move us, and denies its capacity to provide us with knowledge of our world. Against this Gadamer argues that there is something more recalcitrant and less domesticated in the experience of art, something that draws us away from this refined observational attitude. We can be caught up in the experience of art in ways that bypass such abstemiousness, as though drawn into a game that exceeds the consciousness of the players. Gadamer uses the concept of play as the clue for uncovering "the ontology of the work of art", before moving to the wider significance of the experience of art for the project of hermeneutics.

On the importance of play

In order to find a way of dislocating the assumptions of modern "aesthetic consciousness", he describes an underlying structure that is common to both the experience of art and the nature of playing games. Where aesthetic consciousness is concerned to control the purely aesthetic by excluding all extraneous material, in an authentic experience of art it is we who must lose control, and as when we play games, submit to the to and fro of the experience. In playing games we, as subjects, do not have priority over the game; quite the reverse, we must submerge ourselves as participants in the open-ended nature of the game, allowing its own natural bouyancy to bear us along :-

> Play fulfils its purpose only if the player loses himself in his play....The players are not the subjects of play; instead play merely reaches presentation through the players. (Gadamer 1989:102-3)

The paradox is that play is one of those things that must exceed the control of players for it to be play, and yet must also have their wholehearted commitment to be effective as play. Only when players are serious about play do they play properly. The player who is not serious but only makes a pretence of it by taking up the 'attitude' of being serious, or who 'behaves towards play as if it were an object, is a spoilsport', and will break up the game. We as subjects never finally master the game, for even the most skilful of players must risk themselves in play. Indeed if one party controls the game too much, and wins too easily, we say that it was no game at all. There is truly no point to a game where one party is certain to win, for though winning may be integral to the game, the purpose of playing is not winning as such, but the play itself. If you master the skills of a game, this does not primarily enable you to win more easily, for you immediately have to play players of comparable skill, and you will be challenged just as thoroughly as before; what it does is to deepen the game itself, by making play more subtle and varied. The purpose of the game is simply the playing of it. When games are played it is the players who are 'being-played' as they are absorbed in the movement of the game, indeed the attraction of games is that they tend to master the players. There is always a sense of unpredictability or 'riskiness' in games, in that there can be no guarantees that our best efforts will bring something off, even though we have succeeded at it before. But Gadamer's case is dialectical, even though players must accede to the movement of the game, games in their turn only have their real existence in being played. However much a game is repeated it is always different, such that its identity as a particular game, depends on it being endlessly re-newed.

The features that unify Gadamer's very nuanced phenomenological description of play, also characteristically open out towards other areas of his project. He is certainly trying to show that the experience of art can overcome the debilitating effects of aesthetic consciousness. But he also wishes to bring to light an ontological arena that will link this account with the other parts of *Truth and Method*, notably with the accounts of historical understanding, tradition and language. In each of these, which were the areas that bore much of the brunt of Habermas's critique, there are important echoes of his account of play. For example, in the area of language Gadamer emphasises in an ontological fashion, that it is the playful and dialogic qualities of conversation that have priority over any rules that may structure language use. This is because human beings could only ever learn what a 'rule' is through their prior immersion in the dialogic field of a living language. Similarly with regard to historical tradition, it is our sense of growing into the open-ended, living qualities of a tradition, that has priority over any subsequent critical judgements we may make about its 'structures of domination'. Indeed it seems to me that it was Habermas's non-inclusion of any material from the First Part of *Truth and Method*, where the concept of play is emphasised, that make his comments seem too obviously targeted for critical purposes. It is therefore appropriate to dwell a little longer on the central ontological status of the concept of play (2)

There is a certain obvious way in which the experience of art and the idea of play are linked, in that when we enjoy an artwork we find ourselves freely submitting to it, and welcoming the sense of being borne along by it. As with play, so also when reading a novel or listening to music, we become immersed in the ebb and flow of its meaning. But in Gadamer's account this analogy is not to be mistaken for human *subjects* submitting to an art *object*. The experience of art is not a contemplative one undertaken by disinterested observers. The point is that in engaging with art, we as subjects are surpassed by the way it plays us:-

> When we speak of play in reference to the experience of art, this means neither the orientation nor even the state of mind of the creator or of those enjoying the work of art, nor the freedom of a subjectivity engaged in play, but the mode of being of the work of art itself." (Gadamer 1989:101)

Gadamer constantly moves his reader's attention away from *subjects* and *objects* and towards the spaces between and behind them. The nature of games are not to be found in the subjective intentions of the players, nor in objects like the rules of the game, but in play itself. The enigma of a game is that it claims some authority over the players yet has no existence independent of the instances when it is played. Similarly, while an artwork may claim authority over us, and turn us this way and that, it needs us for completion. It is not a thing in itself, but has its being, or more accurately comes into being, when it is viewed, read, or listened to by us. Hence both games and artworks have the odd quality of gaining their identity by being different on every occasion. There are thus no 'pure original' works of art, only a living, ongoing, tradition of their interpretation. He therefore describes his concept of play as a "medial" one, one that is used to describe the ongoing transfer of meanings. We speak of "the play of light, the play of waves, the play of gears or parts of machinery, the interplay of limbs, the play of forces, the play of gnats, even a play on words" (Gadamer 1989:103). In each case it is the movement between things that matters and by which they may be understood. When we speak of the play of colours we do not mean "one colour plays against another, but that there is one process or sight displaying a changing variety of colours". Play, as it were, is part of a much wider condition, where the work of art is but one variation "on the infinite play of the world".

But even if the experience of art is best described in terms of its closeness to play, and play is described in an ontological fashion, rather than in a subjective fashion, we still do not yet know what kind of knowledge art brings us ? Gadamer does not answer this question directly, for he has not formulated the question in anticipation of a pat answer. He is nevertheless concerned with it (3). What he does is to ask how a work of art manages to make any serious claim to our attention? How is it that something which is often thought of as no more than a beautiful illusion, something to distract us from reality, actually holds our attention so completely that for a while we experience no distance between it and ourselves?

Art and truth

In the same way that a game surpasses our willed intentions, the work of art makes a claim upon us that outruns the control of our personal tastes. The work of art is not something that we experience subjectively, i.e. something which is just a private and temporary enjoyment, it has its "true being in the fact that it becomes an experience changing the person experiencing it". It changes our usual relations to the world, it transgresses our customary ways of observing, evaluating, knowing and acting in the world. In short, in a more than subjective sense, we are *moved* by it, and as a result we no longer know ourselves or the world in the same way. In giving ourselves over to the play of art we do not remove ourselves from reality but find ourselves absorbed into it more deeply. There is a continuity of meaning "which links the work of art with the world of real existence", and it is this which enables us to be gripped far more exhaustively than by a mere illusion. We are required to bring ourselves into play more thoroughly than usual, we must cease to be disengaged observers and allow the fundamental features of our lives to be played out against the meaning we find in the work of art:-

> Since we meet the artwork in the world and encounter a world in the individual artwork, the work of art is not some alien universe into which we are transported for a time. Rather, we learn to understand ourselves in and through it, and this means that we sublate the discontinuity and atomism of isolated experiences in the continuity of our existence. (Gadamer 1989:97)

It is through this process, one that is both ontological and dialogical, that art provides knowledge, and makes a claim to telling us a truth about the world.

But what does truth mean in these circumstances? Despite the title of his masterwork being *Truth and Method*, several authors have pointed out (e.g. Bernstein 1983, Wachterhauser 1986), that one will search in vain for a singular and systematic account of what truth means to Gadamer. He invariably speaks of it tangentially and in connection with other concepts, as though declaring it too openly, would somehow undermine its elusive character. Certainly when he argues that truth is an event, something that happens to us, rather than something that always results when we follow the correct methodological principles, he implicitly confirms this idea by allowing it to appear only briefly in his own writing before letting it recede in the face of other discussions.

Nevertheless, the issue of what he means can be broached from two directions that are not usually thought to be complementary, viz Hegel and Heidegger. Perhaps because Gadamer was Heidegger's student his work is sometimes seen as an exemplar of his mentor's ideas, which is really quite misleading. Certainly there are also echoes of Hegel in Gadamer's dialectical account of the experience of the work of art, where art speaks its truth to us through the living context of our historical tradition. But equally, Gadamer's case, that the power of art can jolt us into the recognition of something, draws on the Greek concept of truth as *disclosure* or *unconcealment*, (aletheia), where his debt to Heidegger is plain. I will discuss this latter account first, and then show how the idea of the resonance of art blends into the living context of historical tradition (4).

The view that truth involves bringing something out of concealment involves a break with the more familiar (social) scientific concept, in which truth is found where there is a correspondence between hypotheses and facts. Truth in this other sense refers to 'an event of dis-closure', an occurrence that reveals something in a new light, that opens something up to show it in its true coherence (5). Gadamer's 1960 essay: On Heidegger's Later Philosophy (Gadamer 1976), may illustrate the point. In this, Gadamer explores how Heidegger, in his 1935 lecture(s): The Origin Of The Work of Art (Heidegger 1978), addresses the question of truth. The work of art does not provide us with a copy of the world, it does not simply present us with a "recognisable and familiar surface contour", even though the world is present in it and is disclosed by it. Rather works of art have a kind of self-sufficiency, they "stand in their own being" by bringing forth what is essential and leaving out what is not. Their brilliance lies in being able to bring something, that, as it were, already has a factual existence, out of its usual hiddenness and into the light of its true being. In a way this reverses our normal assumptions that a proper account of reality should consist in the correct factual and literal descriptions of it. What Gadamer draws attention to, here and elsewhere, is the idea that reality has as much if not more of a metaphorical status, than a factual-literal one. For Gadamer art involves an amplification of the ordinary, which, far from being a distortion of things and their proper place in the empirical world, is actually what allows the truth of reality to appear. Art does not involve a break with reality in order to produce a mere copy, but rather it heightens the (metaphorical) truth of it by showing us what is essential in it. Heidegger drew on Van Gogh's painting of a pair peasants shoes to illustrate the point :-

> From the dark opening of the worn insides of the shoes the toilsome tread of the worker stares forth. In the stiffly rugged heaviness of the shoes there is the accumulated tenacity of her slow trudge through the far spreading and ever uniform furrows of the field swept by a raw wind. On the leather lies the dampness and richness of the soil. Under the soles slides the loneliness of the field path as evening falls. In the shoes vibrates the silent call of the earth, its quiet gift of the of the ripening grain and its unexplained self-refusal in the fallow desolation of the wintry field. (Heidegger 1978:163)

In Van Gogh's painting the peasants shoes are not the passive objects of an 'aesthetic consciousness', they make a much more unmistakable claim upon us, by allowing the truth of the peasants world to come to light in them.

Of course we might still ask whether or not it is contradictory to talk about the truth of an artwork emerging in this way, when every experience of art, like every game that is played, is supposed to be different? The idea of truth seems to imply something more fixed than is possible with an experience that is new each time it happens. Likewise, when he talks of the self-sufficiency of artworks, this seems to resemble the idea of art as 'the eternally beautiful', which is precisely what he opposed in his critique of aesthetic consciousness. These doubts, I think may be answered by directing our attention to the more Hegelian motifs in his work, and reaffirming two related themes.

(1) Gadamer's attitude towards the truth of art must be distinguished from any suggestion that he sees it as a documentary copy of a fixed reality in-itself.

(2) His ideas about the truth of art must also be meshed in with the importance he places upon the role of play in the understanding of art.

With regard to the first theme, for Gadamer even abstract, non-representational painting, which seems furthest from the reality of everyday life, can be seen as speaking the truth about it. If the modern world is dominated by a system of mass-production and consumption the nature and value of "things" necessarily changes. The sheer availability and disposability of commodities means that "objects" generally cease to have any substantial weight or significance about them. As such the nature of the reality they inhabit also changes, and the manner in which art speaks the truth of this situation cannot remain the same :-

> ...the only "things" we know are mass-produced in factories marketed with intensive advertising, and finally thrown away when they are broken..can any thinking person expect the visual arts of today to give us the opportunity of recognising things that are no longer real, that we can no longer encounter around us, that mean nothing to us, as if that could deepen familiarity with our world. (Gadamer 1986:103)

As I understand it, what Gadamer is getting at is that precisely in order to deepen our familiarity with the reality of the modern world, art addresses its instantaneous and kaleidoscopic nature through abstract and dislocated forms of representation. In much the same way one might say that in the novels of writers such as Proust and Joyce, there is a break with the familiar and fixed forms of 'time' and 'personhood', which brings out the truth of the fragmentary nature of these things in the modern world. It has to be remembered that for Gadamer reality is not a firm, substantive phenomenon, that exists independent of those who live it. As a result, truth for him, in following reality, must have a necessarily relative, historical quality. This is something that Habermas tended to minimise when he criticised Gadamer for the conservative implications of his concept of tradition. Habermas objected to the way, as he saw it, Gadamer's account overplayed the reality of tradition by seeing it as a cultural limit on those who lived under it. But this attributes to Gadamer a too substantive and determinate view of tradition, and one that is at odds with the more relative account of truth and reality found in part one of *Truth and Method*.

With regard to the second theme, it must be remembered that for Gadamer the question of the truth of art is always relative to the *living* context in which it is played out. Georgia Warnke (1987:56-72), points out the importance Gadamer places on the audience engaging their own lives with the artwork, of being drawn into it, and finding a truth that speaks to their current concerns. For example, in terms of drama, the same play can be represented quite differently in different productions and at different times. In Shakespeare's Hamlet the prince may be played heroically as one faced by intractable decisions of state, or anti-heroically as one driven by scarcely concealed feelings of oedipal anger. There is no true original Hamlet, it exists neither in the intentions of the author nor in the fixed words printed on the page, but in what happens on the occasions it is played. Its truth lies ultimately in what its audience finds there when they are part of the play. Moreover, audiences at plays, (unlike academics), do not find they have a problem with the 'relativism' of there being more than one possible truthful interpretation. They are well able to evaluate one interpretation as better or worse than another, without having to find fixed, timeless criteria, by which to judge the play. The reason being, that an audience which experiences the artwork truly, does so, not by being aloof and applying their "aesthetic consciousness", but by being drawn into the play and finding themselves in it. For Gadamer, the living of life eliminates relativism. In fact Gadamer uses tragic drama to make the point that the truth art provides us with in the end, is true knowledge of ourselves. The tragic emotions experienced by audiences at such plays are not to be thought of as a subjective pity for those undergoing bad luck, or a sense of indignation at the injustice of things, but as manifestations of a far more profound sense of distress, an overwhelming sense of 'shuddering apprehension' at the prospect of the fateful outcome. For it is an outcome we all share in that we also are subject to overwhelming forces, it is our common lot to find ourselves overtaken by events, and shaped by history. As the tragic hero is brought low by forces quite outside his volition, so the audience may recognise the finiteness of their own existence in the face of such forces, and find some cathartic value in seeing that "this is how it is" :-

> The spectator recognises himself and his own finiteness in the face of the power of fate. What happens to the great ones of the earth has an exemplary significance. Tragic pensiveness does not affirm the tragic course of events as such, or the justice of the fate that overtakes the hero, but rather a metaphysical order of being that is true for all. To see that 'this is how it is' is a kind of self knowledge for the spectator, who emerges with new insight from the illusions in which he. like everyone else, lives (Gadamer 1989:132)

This same kind of account is echoed later in the Second Part of *Truth and Method*, where Gadamer describes in an analogous way the nature of the truth generated by the human sciences. Truth in the human sciences is also conceived of as having an event-like quality which deepens self-knowledge, so that the great texts are not the ones that espouse eternal verities, but are those in which subsequent generations are able to find a living significance for themselves. Thus what Gadamer finds in the experience of art in terms of the status of play, truth, and knowledge, he gradually absorbs into a more general concern for the nature of understanding, interpretation, and history. In short, in the second part, he merges his concern for the meaning of art into a wider concern for the nature of hermeneutics and the human sciences.

Notes

1. I am of course referring to the various debates that followed from the exchange between Karl Popper and Thomas Kuhn. Joel Weinsheimer, in the introduction to his *Gadamer's Hermeneutics* (1985) makes the valid point that Gadamer tends to assume a too unified view of scientific method, a view that was already being successfully challenged from within the philosophy of science camp when *Truth and Method* was being published.

2. Richard Bernstein (1983) concurs with the importance of 'play' in Gadamer's work generally. Georgia Warnke (1987) is more critical, not so much in terms of its centrality but of its adequacy as a concept to account for the experience of different kinds of art.

3. Gadamer is one of the few authors still concerned with the truth disclosing power of art. Weinsheimer (1985:101) points out just how provocative and unusual is the the link he makes between art, truth, and play.

4. One point of difference between Gadamer and Heidegger may lie, according to Vattimo (1988:122), in the way Gadamer reduces the radically disruptive quality of art by meshing it with a more Hegelian notion of historical experience. This may be so, but Gadamer is not unaware that he has emphasised, contra-Heidegger, the assimilative power of the past over 'Dasien', and therefore does not follow Heidegger fully down his "radical path", (Gadamer 1989:XXXVII). Where *Being and Time* emphasises the pull of the future, *Truth and Method* emphasise the power historical tradition has in assimilating the autonomy of our best laid plans. I do not see why this should be considered non-radical when compared with Heidegger. See also Bernstein (1983:152-3) who rightly warns against reifying the way Gadamer relates truth and history.

5. I am not here suggesting that Gadamer holds to a coherence view of truth, though there are are some elements of such a view in his work, rather that for him truth happens when things are seen in a comprehensive light. There is an important difference here between him and Habermas: for Habermas truth is the outcome of dialogue undistorted by external force, i.e. a consensus theory, for Gadamer consensus is a goal of dialogue but truth is more elusive. It is tied in not only with dialogue but also with the nature of the subject matter that comes to light. David Hoy (1994:189) puts it well: "Whereas a consensus theory suggests that agreeing to something makes it true, Gadamer's sense is that we agree to something because it is true. So truth is not the result of agreement, but agreement the result of truth".

3 The second part of Truth and Method: Understanding and the human sciences (a)

Understanding and historical consciousness

The same habits of thought Gadamer found to be defective in our understanding of the experience of art, he also finds present in modern thought generally. For example, the tendency to regard human understanding as naively subjective and therefore in need of remedy through the use of objective methods, has dogged the human sciences since their inception. The human sciences have found themselves compelled to trail after the 'objectivity' of natural sciences in order even to claim they are producing something that stands up as 'knowledge' at all. To be sure they have retained some elements opposed to this tendency, such as an awareness of the significance of meaning, and the relevance of feeling and empathy and so forth, but these are often seen as obstacles to be overcome in the process of their maturing into full-blown natural sciences. Gadamer's task then, is nothing less than a complete reorientation of things away from these habits of thought that identify the subjective with the private and the ephemeral, and the objective with knowledge only obtainable through the use of disinterested observation. Indeed, he sees it as measure of the lopsidedness of our current thinking that we have come to see truth as the outcome of such restricted methods, even to the point where we are unable to 'think truth' in any other way.

Gadamer traces out the way this misleading ideal of disinterested objectivity was incorporated into the history of the hermeneutic tradition in the nineteenth century. One might expect that the German tradition of 'the sciences of mind' (geisteswissenschaften), with their emphasis on the distinctions between social and natural sciences, would be most in tune with Gadamer's ideas. It was after all their ambition to highlight their own special character in terms of the fact that they dealt with a qualitatively different kind of phenomenon to that dealt with by the sciences of nature. The human world was thought to be different in that it was the product of the creative human will, and had its own self-created history which was not explicable in terms of the laws of nature. It was appropriate therefore that the human sciences would take history as their distinct domain using its artefacts, such as documents, registers, artworks and so forth, in order to reconstruct the aims and ambitions of their creators. The problem for the human scientist became one of how best to empathise and re-live the intentions of his or her predecessors, something that was possible because both shared common features of humanity (Dilthey in Mueller-Vollmer 1985). Paradoxically, this is the point where Gadamer believes the rot set in.

He does not reject the views of Schleiermacher and Dilthey outright, but aims rather to peel back the misplaced assumptions by which they unwittingly incorporated elements of the very outlook of the natural sciences their work seemed to challenge. The effect of incorporating these 'positivistic' assumptions has been to leave the human sciences under a misapprehension about the real nature of the knowledge they produce. They have been left with the debilitating feeling that the constraints of scientific method invariably leave their 'knowledge' seeming like an inferior version of what the natural sciences produce. However, he does share with them a belief that the human condition is a deeply historical one. Our historicalness, (or historicity), refers not just to the fact that we experience our lives as being in time, but that we are caught up in the pulls and shoves of history in a way that constitutes who we are. History makes *us* at least as much, if not more, than we make it. Where Gadamer differs from his predecessors is in pursuing the implications of this in a far more radical way. Indeed for Gadamer the very term - the human condition - would be misleading in these circumstances, because that condition is not unchanging but is historically mutable. For Gadamer there is no fixed human essence at the heart of our condition, we have become who we are via the changing historical features of our lives, through the way the particular beliefs and social practices of our tradition have evolved.

As a result the knowledge we have of the world and ourselves, the issues we find significant, the things we find acceptable or unacceptable, rational or irrational, those that seem desirable and those that raise our ire, are all generated from within the changing historical field of our tradition. This claim entails more than just the idea that history provides an external context for our lives, it means that we and our knowledge emerge only through, and by virtue of, the ideas and practices that make up our historical tradition. It does not mean that different traditions are necessarily sealed units cut off from other traditions, but it does challenge by relativising, the universal pretensions that often accompany the Western idea of knowledge. In Western thought, knowledge, almost by definition is something that has risen above the contingencies of history and can claim to be universally true (1). Against this, Gadamer claims that all knowledge is woven in with the historical situation of its production, and importantly also, with the historical situation of its reception. It does not imply that there is a progressive impulse to history, no happy dialectic exists between past and present, such that the present provides us with a superior vantage point from which to look down on the past. We may in a sense know more now, but we cannot arrogate any superiority to ourselves on this basis, for the present is as finite and conditioned as the past. Indeed it is the ongoing articulation of a mutable past and present, for which he uses the term "the fusion of horizons", and which marks off his ideas about the nature of historical knowledge from those of his nineteenth century predecessors.

Hermeneutic understanding versus psychological understanding

What he finds generally mistaken in their approach is twofold. First, he finds problematic their reduction of the interpreters own historical situation to being that of a problem, one that at best can be controlled by the use of an adequate (scientific) method. Secondly, he challenges their assumption that the meaning of a text, and by implication the meaning of a social action, can be grasped through understanding the subjective intentions of the authors or the actors involved.

For nineteenth century hermeneuts such as Schleiermacher and Dilthey, the interpreters own horizon is seen only in a negative light, and the desire to make this invisible, or at least bring it under control, is based on the misleading ideal of achieving an objectivity that will parallel that of the natural sciences. History and its effects, which he agrees are constitutive of our human lives, are paradoxically seen by the 'romantic hermeneuts' of the nineteenth century as something to be avoided, something that needs to be suspended in order that we may apprehend things correctly. Schleiermacher, writing in the early part of the nineteenth century, extended the scope of hermeneutics beyond being 'an aggregate of observations' with only localised textual concerns by bringing the general importance of language and understanding to the fore. But in so doing he conceived the *problems* of understanding to be general too, so general that :-

> ...from now on we no longer consider the difficulties and failures of understanding as occasional but as integral elements that have to be prevented in advance. Thus Schleiermacher even defines hermeneutics as 'the art of avoiding misunderstandings'. (Gadamer 1989: 185)

This seeing of *mis*understanding as the first condition we always find ourselves in has considerable implications. We have so learnt to mistrust our initial orientation, and to see our current horizon as a barrier to accurate understanding, that we feel obliged to seek ways out of the situation. Like the natural sciences, where nothing can be accepted at face value and where everything must be doubted until proven, the human sciences also find themselves pushed into devising methods that will perform the same kinds of task. They must seek to purge from their practitioners all those 'subjective' assumptions that get between them and the objects of their attention, all those 'prejudices of consciousness' that distort the correct apprehension of things.

The second and related mistake that Schleiermacher and Dilthey make, according to Gadamer (2), is to identify the meaning of historical documents and social actions with the intentions of those who wrote or performed them. This error rests on a distinction Gadamer makes between two kinds of understanding, his own hermeneutic account of understanding and psychological understanding. Hermeneutic understanding refers to that primary set of agreements we achieve with others about some subject matter. It implies that to understand means to find common ground with others over the validity of some substantive issue. Gadamer puts it thus :-

> We begin with this proposition: 'to understand means to come to an understanding with each other'. Understanding is, primarily, agreement. Thus people usually understand each other immediately, or they make themselves understood with a view toward reaching agreement. Coming to an understanding, then, is always coming to an understanding about something. Understanding each other is always understanding each other with respect to something. From language we learn that the subject matter is not merely an arbitrary object of discussion, independent of the process of mutual understanding, but rather is the path and goal of mutual understanding itself. (Gadamer 1989:180)

By contrast psychological understanding does not mean arriving at an agreement with someone over the validity of something, but separately deciding what they mean, usually in terms of some cause or origin. It means bypassing any engagement with the validity of *what* they say for the sake of establishing an explanation of why it is being said. This usually involves moving to some 'objective context' be it sociological, economic, or even biological, which is thought to account for what has been said. The distinction between hermeneutic and psychological understanding is a rather elusive one mainly because we often seem to accept the latter, psychological version, as definitive in modern thought. Even in the fairly well developed areas of interpretive sociology, such as symbolic interactionism and ethnomethodology, where no move is made to explain situations by reference to more 'objective contexts' outside of the way the actors define their own situations, the psychological definition of understanding remains in place. The truth of situations is still found through a neutral description of the intentions of actors (symbolic interactionism), or in the mechanics of how they generate meaning (ethnomethodology), but not through an engagement with the validity of what they say. The social scientist stays out of the picture as a matter of methodological principle. It seems to me that Gadamer's critique of the nineteenth century attempt to use 'objective methods' in order to glean the 'subjective intentions' of actors, applies as readily to contemporary sociology; even in those approaches where the intersubjective validity of meaning has replaced the traditional concept of objectivity.

But is Gadamer right to deny the relevance of human intentions for analysis in the human sciences? Certainly Georgia Warnke (1987:15) suggests that he has exaggerated the case against them, and may have overstated their role in Schleiermacher's work. She points out that insofar as there are two separate definitions of understanding, this does not provide us with an automatic reason for choosing one over the other. There may also be good reason to be concerned with what an author or an actor intended, as well with the truth-content of their writings or actions; that is, "one still needs to know what an author intended so that one knows that the claims one adjudicates are in fact the author's claims".

Gadamer's point I think though, is not so much that the accurate reconstruction of intentions may not occasionally be useful, when the normal movement of the processes of understanding have broken down, but that in the end it is a secondary and derivative activity. For example, one may fall into this detached psychological way of viewing things, when one cannot achieve consensus in a conversation. One party may be so mystified at the ideas being expressed by the other that they move away from the living, reciprocal process, of coming to a mutual understanding about something, and start to think what motives the other person could have that produces such views. This draws one down the path of reifying the other's views as merely the product of external circumstances. The problem is that this psychological concept of understanding does not simply complement the hermeneutic one as Warnke would wish, for once we fix the other's views in this way we seem to have no use for a return to the question of their validity. Use of this psychological version of understanding does not lead to the re-establishment of shared understanding, because it fixes the truth of the views solely in terms of being objects explainable by reference to some outside factor. For, Gadamer if you start from the assumption that misunderstanding is the basic condition, as Schleiermacher did, and carry this through into a method based on the reconstruction of alienated intentions, you do not overcome the problem of alienated understanding, you reproduce it.

Larmore (1986) makes a similar though slightly stronger claim than Warnke, arguing against Gadamer, and in support of Schleiermacher and the contemporary literary theorist E.D. Hirsch, that the determination of a text's meaning has a logical priority over the particular ulterior goals for which we may want to use it, such as evaluating the truth of what it says. I will dwell on this issue a little longer because it seems to me to bring in to focus still more sharply what Gadamer means. Larmore claims that :-

> We cannot enter a conversation with a text about its subject matter except to the extent we believe we have reconstructed its perspective on the subject matter; otherwise, there is absolutely no sense to talking about agreeing or disagreeing with the text; carrying it further; or applying it, as Gadamer says to our own situation. (Larmore 1986:162)

For Gadamer this statement does not describe what actually happens when we come to understand a text, it puts the cart before the horse. We cannot reconstruct the meaning perspective of a text prior to and independent of the significance it has for us. We only come to grips with meaning in terms of the contrasts and similarities it bears to the assumptions we have about the significance of things. We cannot, or rather do not, appropriate the 'pure original' meaning of what the author intended through a process of neutral observation, and then use it for contemporary (value) purposes. When Gadamer speaks of the fusion of horizons he does not mean that there are two horizons, the original meaning of a text, and the current significance it has for us, which are separate but can be subsequently joined together in a final interpretation. He specifically means the fusion of horizons as something which goes on at an ontological level, independently of our volition, and in all understanding of historical phenomena. He sees these horizons as ideal constructs which only putatively have a separate existence. Like competing players in a game they are not subjects and objects set over against each other, but are elements fused together in an ongoing process that exceeds the subjectivity of both parties. To give priority to the reconstruction of a fixed, original meaning, is misleading because it means regarding understanding as something passive and neutral, it means putting ourselves 'in brackets' and being disinterestedly receptive to given data. We know that when we are engaged in a conversation if we want it to be successful we have to give ourselves over to the topic, to what the conversation is about, and not try to pin down the subjectivity of the other person. So also in the understanding of texts :-

> ... it is not a matter of penetrating the spiritual activities of the author; it is simply a matter of grasping the meaning, significance and aim of what is transmitted to us...In one move we find ourselves in the dimension of the aim [la visee], already comprehensible in itself and without so much as a second look at the subjectivity of the partner. The meaning of hermeneutical inquiry is to disclose the miracle of understanding texts or utterances and not the mysterious communication of souls. Understanding is a participation in the common aim. (Gadamer 1979:147)

But what if we don't find ourselves participating in the common aim of the historical text because its meaning is so far removed from our horizon that it makes no sense to us? Surely then we need to reconstruct what the author's intentions were in writing that text at that time. Gadamer seems to accept that in these circumstances we must seek to understand "the author's entirely personal use of words", but he places that process *within* the wider hermeneutic frame of understanding. He points out that we only come to spot the disjunction between horizons because the normal expectations we have in engaging with the aim of the text, have been disrupted. That is to say the need for psychological understanding is always preceded by our awareness of an impasse present in our (normal) hermeneutic understanding. Moreover even when we have to seek out what an author specifically meant, in practice we do not suspend our own opinions for the sake of an 'objective reconstruction', but in the ongoing process of anticipation and revision of sense, we constantly re-situate ourselves in relation to what we find. The problem with the psychological concept of understanding is that it overlooks the participatory and projective nature of all understanding, something that Gadamer drawing on Heidegger will call the fore-structure of all understanding (3). It ignores the ontological conditions which underpin understanding as something which enables us to engage with the living traditions through which intentions are constituted.

In certain respects Gadamer's critique of Schleiermacher parallels some of the responses he made to Habermas's Marxist critique of his work. Indeed

Weinsheimer (1985:137 note 3)) points out that Habermas's own programme is not far removed from Schleiermacher's, in that he too wants to insert a universal "content-free" or disengaged method (Habermas' 'universal pragmatics'), between the social scientist and the world, one that will filter out the ideological misunderstandings that beset us. Gadamer's response to that was also to argue that such a method would not straighten things out for us, but would actually confirm just how far removed we are from our own living historical tradition.

We can perhaps usefully summarise what Gadamer establishes in his critique of nineteenth century hermeneutics before moving on to his quite provocative reorientation of the concepts of prejudice, authority and tradition.

(a) He accepts along with his nineteenth century predecessors that human beings are deeply historical beings, and that because this characteristic is distinctively human, it has methodological implications for the human sciences which cannot be avoided. However, he radicalises the significance of the historical dimension by drawing the knower's own horizon into the picture of how we understand and interpret things.

(b) In doing this he denies the validity of a concept of objectivity for the human sciences that could be based on method, and which would parallel the equivalent to be found in the natural sciences. And despite their claim to be clarifying the autonomous nature of the human sciences, the efforts of Schleiermacher and Dilthey are still thoroughly entangled in the objectivistic assumptions of the natural sciences. Their mistake is to pursue a method that tries to eliminate historical distance, when what makes the human condition distinctive is its conditioning by history.

(c) He sees their psychological version of understanding as similarly based on a misapprehension, namely that (historical) understanding requires us to step out of our own shoes into those of others so as to re-experience their subjective intentions, as though they were fixed entities. By contrast his case is that when we understand others, prior to anything else, we engage ourselves with what they have to say about something, not with their subjective intentions. Meaning does not have its source in the interiority of individuals but in the interdependent historical horizons that condition individual experience. To use method in order to fix truth in the intentions of others does not lead us towards it, but away from it. It obliges us to objectify the other party, be it a person or an historical text, and bypass any engagement with the claim to truth that they are making. As Weinsheimer (1985:155), aptly puts it, "there is no method of reconstructing or returning to the past, and none is needed. We already belong to history".

The circle of understanding and the value of prejudice

Having undermined the misplaced assumptions of nineteenth century hermeneutics, about the nature of understanding and the need for subjective empathy, Gadamer sets about the task of replacing this concept with a much less neutral and far more pro-active account. In doing this one becomes aware that he is not just tackling methodological issues within the human sciences, but in a quite provocative way is addressing ideas that embrace a whole range of moral assumptions normally concealed by modern ways of thinking. In support of his reorientated concept of understanding, for example, he brings into a positive light the usually negative concepts of prejudice, authority, and tradition - three features of modern life from which social science has often sought to liberate us.

Gadamer's initial move in his reconstruction of the concept of understanding is to invoke the relevance of the hermeneutic circle. For his predecessors this was a methodological principle to be followed in different ways in the interpretation of texts. In general it involved the interpreter in a circular process of moving between understanding the parts and the whole of a text. In understanding a single sentence a reader will tack back and forth between the meaning of individual words and that of the whole sentence. The individual words only have meaning in terms of the sentence in which they are placed, while the sentence in its turn only means what those individual words allow it to mean. In the same way reading the chapters of a novel involves us in constantly revising our understanding of the book. What we find in chapter one will lead us to anticipate a certain kind of development in chapter two, but when we read chapter two we may well have to revise our understanding of chapter one, and also our anticipations of what we will find in subsequent chapters. For Schleiermacher the art of hermeneutics had two sides to it, a grammatical and a technical (or psychological) side; the grammatical side was concerned with identifying the precise meaning of the linguistic terms used in the text, the technical with the motives the author had at that point in his life in writing that text. In both cases the hermeneutic circle was the key methodological principle to be adopted, indeed subsequently the two sides of the interpretive process were to be linked together in a similar dialectical and mutually revising way.

What is provocative even today is the fact that such circular forms of reasoning seem to have no secure, unequivocal basis on which one could found a finally correct interpretation. If we can only understand the parts of a text in terms of our knowledge of the whole, and we can't get that until we have understood the parts, we seem to have a recipe for quite arbitrary interpretation. It seems irrational that we have to presume we already know a text when that is just what we are undertaking an interpretation for! Schleiermacher's solution to finding an accurate way into the hermeneutic circle was to posit the possibility of 'divining' the subjective life of the author. But for Gadamer the hermeneutic circle is not primarily a methodological principle based on subjective empathy, but an ontological principle that constitutes our being.

The problem with the methodological outlook is that it places the text before the interpreter as though it were an object in history with which we had no intrinsic connection. We suspend the historical claim to truth that the text makes, (which should be our connection with it) and concern ourselves only with what the text meant then. This leads to a kind of moral relativism, even nihilism, such that the meaning of things, be they good or evil, become merely relative to the conditions in which they were produced. To Gadamer this is a distortion of the authentic nature of the hermeneutic circle which has to be understood as enveloping the knower as well as the known. To bring out the real significance of this he draws on Heidegger's account of it in *Being and Time*. There, it is not seen as a methodological principle which a free-standing subject applies, but as something that describes the very process through which understanding goes on prior to any particular interpretation. It describes the process by which we have a 'world', or in the language of Heidegger it describes our being-in-the-world. 'World', does not refer here to a situation made up of empirical objects set before a human subject, but the fact that human subjects always find themselves *already* placed in relation to things. We find ourselves thrown into a world we did not create, and yet this *is* our world in a strong sense. We cannot ultimately detach ourselves from it in that we live in it by projecting the possibilities that we find there. In fact these possibilities constitute who we are before we can reflect upon them. As Gadamer puts it :-

> In fact history does not belong to us; but we belong to it. Long before we understand ourselves through the process of self-examination, we understand ourselves in a self-evident way in the family, society and state in which we live. The focus of subjectivity is a distorting mirror. The self-awareness of the individual is only a flickering in the closed circuits of historical life. *That is why the prejudices of the individual, far more than his judgements, constitute the historical reality of his being.*
> (Gadamer 1989:276-7)

The form that understanding takes is still the circular one of the projection and revision of meaning, but unlike the methodological account, this (ontological) one refers to a process that guides and exceeds the deliberate acts of understanding and interpretation which are the normal stock-in-trade of the historian or sociologist. Understanding is not to be seen as one of the psychological faculties that we possess, but what we are.

In following Heidegger's ontological description Gadamer is arguing that the embeddedness of understanding and interpretation is not an exceptional thing but part of our normal condition. In our everyday lives we do not come across a world of pure data waiting to be interpreted, but always find ourselves already part of an ongoing tradition, making automatic sense of what we find, placing what is unfamiliar into a familiar context. There is in fact nothing that we do not make some sense of, even if it is the incomprehensible sounds of an alien language, we will still place what we hear in a field of meaning. In fact hermeneutics, or the art of interpretation, only really comes into its own when there is a clear rupture in the good order of this process. That is a situation where our assumptions are disrupted by something, so we have our own most basic understanding of the world challenged, and in the effort to make it comprehensible again are forced to see our own tradition in a new light.

The most obvious implication is that because all understanding is prestructured in this way, the possibility of gaining 'objective', in the sense of, presuppositionless knowledge, is fatally undermined. And certainly this is Gadamer's case, but it is not the end of it, for he does not identify this inability as a weakness. We fail to understand the hermeneutic circle, (as well as ourselves), if we see it as a vicious circle from which we need to escape.

But if understanding is automatically led by our prejudgements, is there any way Gadamer can avoid the charge that all interpretation is merely relative to those prejudgements, and that no one interpretation can be finally judged better or worse than another? His response is akin to the one he makes to the problem of relativism in the judgement of art - that is, in practice our understandings are simply not arbitrary. When we carefully attend to what a text has to say to us we cannot understand it arbitrarily, we cannot wilfully invent any interpretation and say this is what the text is about. It does not mean that we should try to efface ourselves, our prejudgements, in order to neutrally receive the message; in the light of the ontological description of understanding, this would amount to self-deception. What Gadamer says is that :-

> Just as we cannot continually misunderstand the use of a word without its affecting the meaning of the whole, so we cannot stick blindly to our own fore-meanings about the thing if we want to understand the meaning of another. (Gadamer 1989:268)

That is to say, when we seek to understand a text or another person we are faced with the relative coherence of a field of meaning. If we misunderstand the use of a word in a text, for example, we will find that we are pulled up short by the disjunction that appears in what we anticipated to be the meaning of the whole text, and this will oblige us to revise what we thought the word meant. We can thus regard as arbitrary and misguided those prejudgements that come to nothing when they are worked out against what we find in the text. Understanding consists in projecting a meaning based on our cultural biases but allowing it to be played out against the otherness of the text. This requires that we avoid two 'method' extremes that are both familiar in modern humanities and social science disciplines. First, there is a reductive attitude where we blindly superimpose our own conceptual concerns upon a cultural field, thus denying the specificity of its meaning; secondly there is an attitude of self-effacement where we deny our own interests by trying to step into the shoes of those who inhabit the field. Both attitudes can be seen as misguided attempts to solve the problem of objective knowledge by holding either the subject or object in check, when the truth of our condition is that we belong in a more primordial way to a process that surpasses the subject-object relationship. Gadamer is not recommending a new method, only that we should guard against "arbitrary fancies" and keep our attention fixed on the subject matter, so that :-

> ...we remain open to the meaning of the other person or of the text..(and that) this openness always includes our situating the other meaning in relation to the whole of our own meanings or ourselves in relation to it. (Gadamer 1989:268)

It should still be emphasised that when we project a meaning towards something, Gadamer does not see it as a subjective act, a particular methodical procedure that we have deliberately chosen to use, as though there were others that could have been chosen instead, though clearly he sees methods that break with this account as mistaken (4). The circular model is the form that all understanding and interpretation takes, but it is the form only, and his description reminds us that the reality of understanding and interpretation is thoroughly embodied. It is something we undergo, something that cannot be finally controlled by us because our prejudgements are not our possessions. They are not things that, as it were, we could get round the front of us in full view. They are what we are before we know it, and in being so are also the positive prerequisites for all our actual understandings and interpretations. We don't really know our own prejudgements till we bring them into view in the process of furthering our tradition.

The German word - *Voruteil* - can be translated equally well as 'prejudgement' or as 'prejudice'; both catch elements of Gadamer's meaning. Perhaps in English the word - prejudice - captures the provocative intent best, as he is challenging the now deeply rooted assumption that prejudices are by definition a bad thing, and since the eighteenth century Enlightenment our proper task has been to try and clear them from the scene once and for all. Such an ambition, he believes, is both misguided and arrogant.

A prejudice, Gadamer points out, is only a judgement made before all the elements of a situation have been ascertained. In German legal terminology it refers to a provisional verdict, one that has to be worked out positively before there are negative consequences. It is a measure of how much modern thought has corrupted this sense, that we now identify a prejudice with an entirely false judgement. Prejudices are not the subjective distortions of truth that are misguidedly held by people, they are rather the stock of our common understanding which structures the anticipatory way we live our lives, and they are entirely in line with the finite nature of our historical condition.

> Prejudices are not necessarily unjustified and erroneous, so that they inevitably distort the truth. In fact the historicity of our existence entails that prejudices, in the literal sense of the word, constitute the initial directedness of our whole ability to experience. Prejudices are biases of our openness to the world. They are simply conditions whereby we experience something - whereby what we encounter says something to us." (Gadamer 1976:9)

Prejudices then, in the first place are neither right nor wrong. they are the ground of our knowledge. Upon having them depends our capacity to have the world address us in particular ways. We can't in the first place distinguish between blind prejudices and those which are justified, as both equally constitute our being. This distinction can only be made secondarily through the dialogical process of projection and revision, and in terms of whether we find such prejudices to be blind and unjustified, or a productive source of insight. But in either case they will remain within the range of our finite historical horizon. Gadamer is in effect criticising all those theories that claim to have risen above the prejudices of everyday life, and thence to look back and see prejudices as invariably a distortion of truth. This is something he will level against Habermas's claim that everyday life is riven with ideologies just waiting to be dissolved by Critical Theory.

Gadamer then extends this rather unnerving rehabilitation of prejudice into a challenge to the Enlightenment's denigration of authority and tradition. His argument is that in the modern world knowledge (and freedom) have become opposed to authority. To gain knowledge it seems we have always to exercise our own reason against the force with which authority presents things. But this excludes the possibility that authority may be a source of truth. Gadamer argues that one of our justified prejudices may be to accept authority, and that the essence of authority is based not on enforced obedience, but on recognition. That is, a recognition which sees that someone else's judgement is superior to ones own, and on this basis accepting that it should have precedence over one's own. This idea does not sit well with modern sociological sensibilities where taking up a critical and disbelieving attitude toward authority is seen as almost a moral and intellectual necessity. It was certainly an area of Gadamer's thought that roused Habermas's ire. Nevertheless Gadamer's case is not that authority cannot be abused, only that it has its source in our capacity to recognise the superiority of another's judgement. He notes that Descartes, a forerunner of the European Enlightenment, specifically excluded morality as a subject that was open to reason. This was because the truth or validity of morality cannot be seen to depend on our own autonomous judgements, but on the authority of the prejudices of our tradition. That is, our moral reaction to things is to a large, though not overwhelming extent, governed by the tradition that precedes us. But given the role of prejudice in the structure of understanding, there is no reason then to see 'moral' authority as irrational. Gadamer has in mind the kind of authority exercised by the teacher, the parent, or the expert, where the prejudice in favour of their authority is validated by their being able to reveal things to us. Even the anonymous authority of a superior has its validity in the recognition that they have a wider view of things. In Britain during the second world war, for example, Winston Churchill seems to have ruled in a distinctly anti-democratic way, and perhaps even as an autocrat and a bully. Yet the affection that many held him in was, from a Gadamerian point of view, not thereby irrational, but something that flowed from the free acceptance that in those dire circumstances, his unbending attitudes had a rightful authority. Again this was an idea that grated on Habermas's left-wing sensibilities, for it seemed to provide a dangerous moral justification for blind obedience to the authority of tradition.

Both prejudice and authority are in their turn woven into the nature of tradition. If we accept that we are placed in a finite historical situation and this means that we are always bringing unreflected ideas into play in our daily lives, then these unreflected ideas are no more or less than our tradition. The mistake the Enlightenment made was to believe that a simple antithesis existed between tradition and reason, so that tradition became identified with superstition and unreason, an obstacle left over from the past that had to be overcome. It was seen as a dead weight that held us back from the freedom that would come from our living fully rational lives. Even the nineteenth century Romantic reaction to the Enlightenment, which sought to affirm the authority of tradition, still saw tradition as opposed to reason. Gadamer's claim is that both positions failed to recognise that all reasoning happens *within* tradition, and that locating these positions as polar opposites is mistaken whether preference is given to reason (the Enlightenment) or tradition (Romanticism). Both attitudes are wrong because they have thought of tradition as "something historically given, like nature", when in fact it is not an object at all, but the ongoing outcome of our historical lives. It cannot therefore oppress us in a naturalistic way, as Habermas was to argue, not least because the very capacity to see ourselves as oppressed is something that happens to us while being part of a tradition. Our immersion in a tradition of social customs, attitudes of mind, even moral dilemmas, is the positive enabling condition of all our aspirations for the future. Traditions then are not something we can divest ourselves of, for they are the very historical environment through which we know ourselves. They constantly and subtly inform our lives through the fore-structure of our understanding and the specific prejudices or prejudgements that make it up. They are never static but are changed and sustained through the ongoing circular process of interpretation and reinterpretation. Even after revolutions, much more continues than disappears, and what is new is necessarily created out of the old.

In arguing this Gadamer is drawing out what he sees as the central importance of the concept of tradition for the humanities and social sciences, something that in spite of their trying to overcome it through the use of 'scientific method', is its real distinguishing feature. His aim is not to demonstrate how much we are at the behest of tradition, but to reveal the real productiveness of it for our self-understanding. He is asking the humanities and social sciences to recognise the nature of their enterprise, and not see themselves as the poor relation of the natural sciences. To highlight this he asks why, in the face of increasing levels of empirical research, do we still return to 'the classic texts' of our tradition?

On why the human sciences have 'classic texts'

The idea of something being classical can denote two things. It can denote that has its origins in the historical period of ancient Greece, but it can also denote something more evaluative, something that arrests our attention through its exemplary qualities. It is this latter meaning that Gadamer focuses on to show that the "great achievements in the human sciences almost never become outdated", (Gadamer 1989:284). As usual he starts off in a quizzical (or perhaps phenomenological) fashion. He is struck by the idea that in spite of the advances made in historical research we would, on the whole, still rather read a classic text - he cites the German historical writers Mommsen and Droysen, as authors that fit the bill for him. The arguments for and against the continued relevance of classic texts to social science, is one that still rumbles on, not least because it goes to the heart of how the social sciences define themelves, and ultimately to how human beings should regard themselves. Roughly speaking those who see the social sciences in positivistic terms, regard the classic authors as providing at best, interesting hypotheses that ought to be tested, at worst mere fictions supported by unscientific moral values. In both cases the work of the classic authors should either have been verified and incorporated into contemporary theory, or booted out altogether. In sociology the role of the works of classical authors has in fact expanded in proportion to a growing disenchantment with positivistic modes of investigation (Alexander 1987). But their role has remained contentious because sociology itself is split in having a certain scientific ambition, and alternatively recognizing the qualitatively distinct nature of its 'objects'. Gadamer's ideas on the nature of the classical have an application to all the social sciences, though he addresses the study of history in particular.

His case is that because we are immersed in a living, ongoing tradition, it is the way a text speaks to us from within it that gives it its significance. Merely accumulating more research data may be informative, but it will not be decisive in enlightening us about a particular historical phenomenon. This is because history is not something that is set before us as an external object before a subject. The historical 'object' is not an object for the historian in the same way that an object in nature is for the natural scientist. The historian belongs to a tradition and must engage with the 'object' by allowing the prejudices of his or her tradition to be played out against it in the most productive way possible. In a sense the purpose of history writing is not to gain complete knowledge of the 'object' in the manner of scientific research, but to attain for a tradition a greater level of self-understanding. As Gadamer points out there is no 'object' in-itself, against which we could test the validity of different historians' accounts. Historical 'objects' are what our tradition makes them, they emerge through the mediation of our historical horizons, and will continue to do so with each subsequent historical generation. Historical 'objects' gain their validity by being "described properly", that is in a manner whereby their significance for us is most clearly brought to light. Of course we must control our prejudices to the extent that we do not misunderstand the past by naively imposing our current understandings, but in the end the significance of historical 'objects' is determined by the interests of our current horizons, and the manner in which they illuminate the tradition that we are. In a sense the classic texts are timeless, but not because they have risen above history. The classic achievements of historical scholarship do not appear credulous or outdated, because they "always preserve something of the splendid magic of immediately mirroring the present in the past and the past in the present"

(Gadamer 1976:6). Hence, classical texts are timeless, but only in the sense that they repeatedly speak to our new historical horizons, in fact "timelessness is a mode of historical being" (Gadamer 1989:290).

Because the purpose of history writing is not to gain total knowledge in the scientific sense, "we can easily make allowances for the fact that, a hundred years ago there was less knowledge available to a historian who made judgements that were incorrect in some details". This is also the case because understanding for us in the present, no less than for the classic historian, involves the engagement of our prejudices with those of others, not their suspension. The classic historians of the past would not be better historians if they disowned their prejudices, any more than we can or should do ours. This is quite in line with the nature of the subject matter :-

> We accept the fact that the subject presents different aspects of itself at different times or from different standpoints. We accept the fact that these aspects do not simply cancel one another out as research proceeds, but are like mutually exclusive conditions that exist by themselves and combine only in us. (Gadamer1989:284)

Moreover, the prejudices that constitute classic histories not only tell us something about the historical horizon that informed the work, but more importantly they tell us something real about the historical 'object' itself, something that could only have become apparent by virtue of a subsequent horizon of prejudices being brought into play. Historical 'objects' unlike the objects researched by natural science, are potentially inexhaustible in that the prejudices of new horizons constantly bring out novel, but real features of them. These 'new features' are still part of the 'object' even though they are contingent on events and ideas that happen afterwards, and thus are seen only with hindsight to shape it. In fact historical 'objects' only really come into being when their effects are being understood. Hence temporal distance should not be seen as a gulf needing to be traversed by objective methods, but as a productive field of of meaning.

Henri Lefebvre (1975), in a review of Albert Soboul's history of class struggles in Paris between 1793-94 (Soboul 1964), draws surprisingly Gadamerian conclusions from an explicitly Marxist account of an historical 'object', the French Revolution. Soboul's case is that the Jacobins were swept to power on a wave of radical class fervour by the Parisian masses, the Sans-Culotttes. But where the Sans-Culottes were driven by the pressures of daily life such as the need for food, their Jacobin 'leaders' were increasingly concerned with stabilising state power in their own hands, and were faced with other pressing concerns, such as national defence. A gulf soon opened up between the language of the Sans-Culottes who called for 'food', and a Jacobin leadership that called for 'patriotism'. In Marxist terms, Soboul identifies the Jacobins as bourgeois revolutionaries who were prepared to use the support of the masses for their own more limited ends. They were prepared to accept political democracy, but turned away from the idea that this should lead to direct democracy, and thence to social and economic equality. Soboul sees the manner in which politics were conducted in this period as the emerging model for bourgeois democracy, where all manner of manipulative political devices are used to legitimise certain economic ends, and where dictatorial power may be exercised under the banner of freedom and democracy. Lefebvre draws attention to the fact that Soboul does not deny the validity of previous histories of the Revolution, but like them is able to reveal something new about it, precisely by bringing his contemporary Marxist prejudices to bear on it. That is, in seeing the French Revolution as being at the start of an emergent capitalist society, where the interests of a bourgeois social class will come to hold sway, he can use a Marxist understanding of these developments to make greater sense of that initial historical 'object'.

> The French Revolution made a certain number of events possible, through a 'process' of which it was either the origin or a decisive element. Each time one of these possibilities is realized, it retroactively sheds a new light on the initial event. Thus the revolutionary event...belongs to a deeper historicity, which reveals itself slowly with the realization of such possibilities..(and thus)..when historians take into account their own experience in their research into the past, they are profoundly right to do so. They do not mistakenly project the present on to the past...(because)..the introduction of the concept of the possible should not be confused with any merely philosophical interpretation of history......(it is)......in no way an external importation into historical method, but the formulation of a principle hitherto absent yet inherent in it. (Lefebvre:1975:34)

I do not know whether Gadamer would share Lefebvre's admiration for Soboul's history of the Sans-Culottes (5), but it seems to me that it displays an awareness of both the situated and projective nature of human existence, and incorporates this into the practicalities of writing history. And whilst our understanding of capitalist society may change, this does not preclude our recognizing the validity of Soboul's case. In the world he describes we can find traces of our own, and in ours an understanding that we still belong to it. The historical 'object' is coextensive with what our tradition has made it, and the classic history is the one that decisively illuminates how our tradition may still best understand itself through it. I have drawn attention to this case to illustrate the fact that Gadamer's account of the way history continually furthers tradition is not automatically conservative, as Habermas has claimed, but can equally accomodate Marxist accounts of a revolutionary challenge to tradition.

In sociology the renewal of interest in the writings of Weber, Marx and Durkheim has brought similar issues to the surface. From a positivistic point of view their work should be outdated, and there are many sociologists who regard the habit of repeatedly combing through it as uncritical and foolishly reverential. Yet its substantive results are not what is at stake, but rather the capacity to illuminate our present world through, what C. Wright Mills termed the 'sociological imagination'. Indeed our recognition of the ability of certain authors to open up whole new vistas of (self)understanding has increased rather than diminished. One could without embarrassment add names such as Michel Foucault, Norbert Elias, and Herbert Marcuse to the classical list. What we perhaps intuitively recognize and Gadamer makes explicit, is the idea that in social science empirical 'objects' do not exist independent of our descriptions of them. Their meaning as objects depends on how we describe them, and these descriptions are embedded in the living traditions of which we are a part. For example, Max Weber's The Protestant Ethic and The Spirit of Capitalism seems to have remained a classic text for sociologists in spite of its doubtful validity as an empirical-causal thesis (6). This has happened, I believe because Weber was able to render intelligible a relationship between parts of our living tradition that at first sight seem incompatible. The voracious appetite of capitalism for economic success appears to have little to do with the religious asceticism of early Protestant beliefs. Weber, by tacking back and forth between descriptions of them, is able to show how the spiritual anguish of the Calvinist provides the impulse to work methodically and unstintingly for the glory of God. He then weaves this into the fabric of a capitalism based on the unceasing application of rational calculation to the material world. Weber fully recognized that modern capitalism had broken free from its religious antecedents, but I suspect that what we recognize in his thesis, what makes it classic for us, is that a certain driven, puritanical quality persists even amidst the luxuries of contemporary society, and thus we can still find ourselves in his thesis. There is, as it were, a normative claim built into a classic text, in that it brings out a truth for us that precedes our assessment of factual data.

It seems likely that for sociologists as for historians, what sustains the clasic text is its striking capacity to be able tap into a particular nexus of taken for granted understandings, and reveal something that was unwittingly known, but never realized before. If this is true of course, the idea that reality is made up of fixed, empirical phenomena, becomes less convincing. We tend to think of tradition as something external that stretches out behind us, to which bits are added as time goes on.whereas for Gadamer its full reality will always elude us because we belong to it before we know it, and are constantly reconstituting it whether we want to or not.

For us to use objectivistic methodologies as though social or historical 'objects' were the same as the observable data of a natural science, conceals what Gadamer calls their effective-history and our effective-historical consciousness of them. The consequences or effects of an historical event are part of that event itself, the event is what our tradition has made of it. And in the same way that there is no historical 'object' in itself, so also the historian is not a subject in itself, but an effect of the prejudices of tradition. Our tradition determines in advance of us what appears worthwhile enquiring into, and how it will appear to us. To describe the manner in which we inhabit tradition Gadamer uses the German phrase - wirkungsgeschichtliches Bewusstsein - which is almost untranslatable into English. It has often been rendered as - effective-historical consciouness - though Hoy (1978:63) describes it as meaning "the consciousness of standing within a still operant history". Weinsheimer in the recent revised translation of Truth and Method (1989:xv), adopts the phrase "historically effected consciousness", to try and capture the sense that our consciousness of history is itself embedded in, and helps to further our tradition of history. What they are all trying to capture adequately in English, is the rolling, enveloping relationship, that Gadamer believes exists between us and our historical tradition. What he is opposing is the false immediacy of approaches to history that seek to eliminate the efficacy of history itself. He is suggesting that we need to become aware of historical effects, not because we can ultimately overcome them in the sense that we could eliminating them as intellectual impurities, but for the opposite reason; we need to bring them into play precisely to avoid misunderstanding. If we naively fail to recognize that behind such immediacy "there is also another kind of inquiry in play", the play of our tradition, then we will be misled into generating distorted forms of knowledge. To play more thoroughly as historical agents we need to recognize that we also are also being played.

When Gadamer refers to our consciousness of the effects of history he is pointing again to the fact that all our understandings and interpretations are fundamentally laden with background assumptions. These assumptions can be seen to form an horizon insofar as they form a general outlook which "includes everything that can be seen from a particular vantage point". He introduces the concept of the horizon in order to emphasize the fact that becoming conscious of the effects of history is itself a situated activity, and can never be an act of complete reflection, it will never enable us to escape from, or rise above history. This is because all self-knowledge, all reflection, arises from issues found within the finite boundaries of a particular historical horizon. In other words achieving a greater degree of historical self-understanding will enable us to immerse ourselves more thoroughly in our tradition, though not to take up an all-knowing position beyond it. But if both past and present are bound by their respective horizons, how can we expect to understand anything satisfactorily ? The answer is that horizons, despite the apparent contradiction in claiming so, are both binding and open. In fact being bound by an horizon is what enables us to have a history and know ourselves as historical, for it enables us to recognize ourselves as different from others, and to distinguish our present horizon from that of the past. If we eliminated these things we would eliminate our history and our identity.

Gadamer overcomes any sense that we are merely restricted by history, (and would therefore naturally look for a way to escape from its effects), by describing the process of the fusion of horizons. For an historical interpretation to be adequate and the productiveness of temporal distance to come into play, we must avoid two familiar outlooks. First, we must avoid the habit of blindly superimposing our present conception of things onto the 'objects' we wish to interpret, and which are alien to them. Secondly, we must avoid the pretence of self-effacement in the effort to empathize with those in the alien situation. The task of historical understanding is analogous to the way we understand and participate in everyday conversations. We must recognize the full weight of the other's point of view, but to do this honestly we have also to engage with their views wholeheartedly; from there a widening horizon embracing both points of view can emerge. So also by acknowledging a dialectical relation between past and present, a fusion of historical horizons can take place.

Gadamer though, is cautious not to leave us with the impression that this process is a straightforwardly harmonious one. He is at pains to point out that what is being described is not the production of a single, fixed, new horizon, one that is the result of a happy reconciliation between two diverse horizons. Rather our capacity to know ourselves in a proper hermeneutic fashion depends on us being attentive to the tension between the past and the present, being aware of the moment of difference between the familiar and the alien, never trying to subdue one in favour of the other. In fact the present horizon itself is not a set of fixed opinions, but something that is in an ongoing process of formation and revision. What Gadamer is trying to evince is the sense that horizons exist separately only in a relation to each other, they are imputed parts of an ongoing process or fusion :-

> There is no more an isolated horizon of the present in itself than there are historical which have to be acquired. Rather, understanding is always the fusion of these horizons horizons supposedly existing by themselves.(Gadamer 1989:306)

However, the charge might be brought that while he has successfully challenged the naiveties of the subject-object relationship, upon which much work in the social sciences and humanities is based, he has replaced it with a very sophisticated form of relativism. If the standards of the present horizon are not automatically appropriate to the past, and the standards of the past are at odds with those of the present, what standards are we to employ in fusing the two horizons ? How are we to avoid a confusion of horizons ? To amplify why this is not the problem it seems, Gadamer looks to the concept of application and its relationship to understanding and interpretation.

Notes

1. Opposition to such a view of knowledge is far from unknown in contemporary sociology via the work of Peter Winch (1958) and Michel Foucault (1975). However, Gadamer does not challenge it on the basis of linguistic cultural limits (Winch) or historical ruptures (Foucault), but on the basis of the effects history has on our understanding of things.

2. I am not adopting a critical attitude towards Gadamer's interpretation of the history of hermeneutics, but one should be aware that his account has not gone uncontested, particularly with regard to his interpretation of Schleiermacher, see Mueller-Vollmer (1985:8ff,39), Frank (1989), Warnke (1987:10-15), and Larmore (1986).

3. The historian of ideas, Quentin Skinner (1975) shares along with Hirsch and others the view that authorial intention is the criterion to use to establish correct interpretation. But even he notes (p227) that when we reconstruct the context in which an author meant a particular thing we already have to know which context to investigate. Thus he seems to admit that the reconstruction of historical contexts is not a neutral process but one that presupposes prior understanding.

4. Gadamer makes it quite plain that his analysis is not to be seen as the outline for a new method. But he does shift from the pre-personal ontological level of Heidegger's work to the ontic (or roughly speaking empirical) level of the practising interpreter. This leads to the belief that there are some normative implications in his ideas for those working in the human sciences.

5. I suspect he would find Soboul's account acceptable in that it avoids the crude imposition of a Marxist economic concept of class onto a pre-capitalist society. He is partially critical of Horkheimer and Adorno in

their *Dialectic of Enlightenement* (1975) for applying the word 'bourgeois' to describe Odysseus in Homer's story (Gadamer1989:274 note 198). I think he would be much less sympthetic to another Marxist historian, Daniel Guerin, in his *Class Struggle in The First French Republic* (1977). This is a translation of the French edition published by Gallimard in 1973, which in turn is a shortened version of an original two volume edition dating from 1947. Guerin fairly explicitly identifies the warring groups as prototypical bourgeois and proletarian classes. Merleau-Ponty (1973:211ff) is critical of this claim along Gadamerian lines.

6. Because Weber himself sought to show that there was a causal relationship between religious asceticism and capitalism, his thesis is open to criticism when empirical evidence runs counter to it, e.g. Tawney (1978), Marshall (1980), Trevor-Roper (1967). Useful discussions can be found in Eldridge (1971), Parkin (1982), and Anderson et al (1987). Weber's defence of the case was that the connection represented only one possible causal chain and that there could be many more. In fact he swings between bringing a strong and a weak causalist case. Neither position makes his work Gadamerian, but Merleau-Ponty (1973:9-30) sees Weber's description of the "elective affinity" between Protestantism and Capitalism in a hermeneutic light.

4 The second part of Truth and Method: Understanding and the human sciences (b)

To understand is to apply: the concept of application

In contemporary usage the term - application - has an instrumental ring to it, we talk of having knowledge and then applying it for particular purposes. These purposes are thought of as being separate from the knowledge itself, which exists prior to and independent of the ways it may be used. Gadamer argues that ultimately no such separation exists and that application is internally bound up with understanding and interpretation. For example, (though not Gadamer's example), if one tries to translate a foreign language joke into English in a literal fashion, one is likely to be met with mute incomprehension. An English audience will have no idea why a foreign audience should laugh at such words. For the joke to be understood it needs an English application, it needs to be understood in the light of the norms and values of the living culture that is receiving it. In other words we do not first understand and then apply something, rather, we understand in applying something. Understanding happens at the moment when we know how something applies to our contemporary circumstances. It is that moment when something is crystallised within the horizon of meanings that constitute our lives. Robert Holub (991:59) describes it as being "akin to what Roman Ingarden has called 'concretion', an actualising or making present for the interpreter". Given the fluid and temporal nature of our horizons, understanding repeatedly involves us in making new interpretations, which actually only make explicit what we have understood at the moment of application. For Gadamer the three elements, understanding, application, and interpretation, must be seen as internally linked aspects of the one process of knowing things. By contrast the instrumental usage has its clearest illustration in the field of science, where the uses to which scientific knowledge are put are seen as quite separate from the knowledge itself, and marginal because they are value-laden too. Gadamer does not address the question of the relation of scientific knowledge to application, but is concerned with the central importance of application to the humanities and social sciences. He uses the examples of legal and theological hermeneutics to make his point. He claims that in both of these, there is an important tension between the meaning of the fixed text and the sense arrived at in concrete interpretations of it. Written laws cannot be applied in a purely instrumental fashion without an injustice being done. Applying them justly involves understanding how they fit in with the circumstances of particular cases, and interpreting them in this light. Similarly

> ...the gospel does not exist in order to be understood as a merely historical document, but to be taken in such a way that it exercises its saving effect. This implies that the text, whether law or gospel, if it is to be understood properly - i.e. according to the claim it makes - must be understood at every moment, in every concrete situation, in a new and different way. Understanding here is always application. (Gadamer 1989:309)

But does the fact that the comedian, the judge, and the preacher, all need to find an application to make their understanding effective, mean that the understandings of the historian or sociologist requires the same thing ? Surely the task of the legal historian in discovering the meaning of the law in the past, is quite different from the task of the judge who must actually apply it in court in the present ? Gadamer responds to this query, which originates with Emilio Betti (Gadamer 1989:325-330), by pointing out that the legal historian's task of reconstructing the original meaning, is never a simple one. In order to understand the original historical meaning of a law, the historian must be aware of the difference between the law then and now. This requires an applicative moment in understanding if only to discover the lack of fit between the present and the past. One cannot know the past without knowing how it differs from the present, which means tracing out the applicative transformations a law has undergone in its history.

But supposing one was dealing with the legal history of a society other than one's own, where there was no historical continuity with our present; in order to understand that history, should we drop the idea of there being an applicative moment in relation to our present ? Gadamer does not believe that we can drop the applicative moment if we want to understand the truth of anything. His argument is ontological rather than methodological, and we must avoid a tendency to slip into the mental habit of thinking that application is an instrumental procedure that we follow after we have understood something. To apply, in Gadamer's sense, is not to impose, but to find and be found by a common sense of significance. Even when cultural discontinuities cut across and add to the historical distance of meaning, the same ontological process is going on. One of the fundamental conditions of understanding in the human sciences is that of belonging to a tradition. The way we are conditioned by that tradition provides us with a forestructure of understanding through which we inevitably project meaning. We anticipate that our projected understanding will be vindicated when brought into conjunction with the 'object', but at the moment of application will find these anticipations meet with varying degrees of success. Thus in order to achieve an appropriate level of coherence, we will revise the applications until the meanings are aligned satisfactorily.

My rather formal description of the process can again misleadingly imply that application is a series of deliberate acts undertaken by a human subject, when in fact Gadamer is breaking with traditional notions of subjectivity and objectivity. In his account of an equivalent term - appropriation - Paul Ricoeur (1981:191) amplifies Gadamer's idea of application in relation to literary texts. He points out that paradoxically "relinquishment" or "letting go", is a fundamental feature of appropriation. What he means is that as we read a novel and gradually make it our own, we allow our horizon to expand by submitting to the 'world' or horizon of the novel. To appropriate or apply things to our 'world', we also must allow ourselves to be taken over by the other's 'world', such that both horizons are embraced by something larger. Gadamer and Ricoeur challenge the arrogance of knowledge based on the assumptions of a subject-object relationship, where the subject takes possession of an object. They highlight the way we, as subjects, are preceded and exceeded by horizons of meaning, and where application is that moment when we recognise the possibilities of our own lives in some unfamiliar horizon.

Of course if the cultural backdrop of what we want to understand is quite alien to that of our own culture, any simple translation will be difficult, perhaps a perfect fusion will be impossible. For example our conception of legal hermeneutics depends upon the law being binding on all members of the community. Studying the law in a society governed quite differently, by an absolute ruler who is above the law, means that we cannot find a way of applying the law that is comparable to its applications in our society (Gadamer

1989: 329). But the point remains, both continuity and discontinuity presuppose application.

In terms of their debate, Habermas offered arguments both for and against Gadamer's concept of application. He initially sided with Gadamer against the likes of Dilthey, and those that naively sought to reproduce the experience of people who lived in the past. He accepted that understanding the past involves an applicative moment in the life-practice of the present. However, he subsequently built in a reservation, akin to the one he levelled against the conservative implications of the concept of tradition. To him, the account of application seemed to smack of an acceptance of things built into the concept of understanding itself. To understand an historical phenomenon may mean concretising it within our current life situation, but it should not mean that we also uncritically accept its validity (Habermas 1984:133-34).

Perhaps one of the most familiar examples for the sociologist, of what Gadamer means by the concept of application is to be found in the way Peter Winch (1958, 1964) talks of understanding the practice of witchcraft in a primitive society. In order to bring out the significance of this example, it will be useful first to consider some of the key ideas that Winch developed in illustrating what he saw as the distinctiveness of social reality. These also bear a notable resemblance to some of Gadamer's ideas.

There are other reasons too for considering Winch in tandem with Gadamer. In order to challenge the conservative implications of Gadamer's concept of application, Habermas (1984:133-34) invoked the anthropological approach to tradition. He contrasted what he saw as Gadamer's 'subordinate' attitude to tradition, with the more critical and evaluative approach of the anthropologist; he had in mind Evans-Pritchard study of Azande witchcraft. Winch's work is pertinent here because he too uses Evans-Pritchard's account of Azande witchcraft, but to affirm what I take to be an essentially Gadamerian approach things. To complicate matters further both Habermas and his co-worker, Apel, included a critique of Winch's ideas as propaedeutic to their critique of hermeneutics. In the end Habermas sees Gadamer's account as superior to Winch's by virtue of its more reflexive and historical view of things, but this I believe, underestimates Winch, and underplays important points of convergence between him and Gadamer, which are more apparent in the essay, Understanding a Primitive Society (1964). A discussion of Winch also conveniently opens up onto the final area in part two of Truth and Method I want to discuss, namely, Gadamer's use of Aristotle's ethics.

Excursus 1: Peter Winch and Gadamer's concept of application

Peter Winch's book *The Idea Of A Social Science And Its Relation To Philosophy* (1958) has had a persistent, if chequered influence on sociology, mainly in the area of social theory. Its most substantial contribution is probably to be found in Anthony Giddens' development of structuration theory, where Winch's account of social action as 'rule governed behaviour', is used, not uncritically, to support a non-deterministic view of social structure. (Giddens 1976, 1979, 1984a, and summarised 1984b, see also Cohen 1989, Held & Thompson 1989, Clark, Modgil & Modgil 1990, Bryant & Jary 1991, Cohen 1989, and Craib 1991). More generally for social theory, the problem initiated by Winch of how to compare different standards of rationality has produced a small glut of publications including, Apel (1967,1980), Bernstein (1976,1983), Gibbons (1987), Habermas (1984,1988), Hollis & Lukes eds. (1982), Mattick (1986), Turner (1980), Wilson ed. (1974).

The success that the *The Idea Of A Social Science* has had in stimulating debate amongst very different kinds of social scientists and philosophers is surprising, because the style of writing is digressive and the argument in the end, quite sketchy. What Winch has done, I suspect, is to touch not just on foundational issues of how the social sciences should proceed, but also by implication, on the much more troublesome issue of how we, as men and women, should properly understand ourselves. The social and intellectual arena in which the book appeared in the late1950's, was heavily dominated by the prestige that the natural sciences had gained in transforming the material world. It was felt that their success could be duplicated in all areas of life, including those that were the concern of the social sciences, if the principles of scientific thinking were duly adopted. The often unstated, but worrying implication, was that human beings belonged to the object domain and should therefore think of themselves in the same way that they thought of physical objects. Against this Winch argued that the central concepts needed to understand the social world, were logically incompatible with those needed to predict things in the natural world. No amount of statistical evidence could be decisive in validating an interpretation, even the ability to predict things with some accuracy would not make a wrong interpretation right (Winch 1958: 111-120). One might be able to predict the likelihood of a game of cricket being played, for example, against the occurrence of particular levels of daylight and rainfall. However, unless you have correctly understood the way these things are tied in with the very nature of what it is to play games in general, and cricket in particular, the accuracy of your predictions will not enable you to say that something has been explained. The correlation between weather conditions and the playing of cricket is parasitic upon our correctly understanding the meaning of how they are related.

Winch develops two basic themes:- (1) that social regularities cannot be explained adequately in terms of the causal mechanisms found by the natural sciences, but must rather be thought of in a qualitatively different way, as 'rule governed behaviour'; (2) that different societies have different regimes of rationality, which can make simple comparisons between them extremely problematic. In Winch's work these two themes are linked together in that failing to appreciate that social behaviour is rule governed leads to mistakes in understanding the nature of the rationality of a primitive society. Both of these concerns bear on Gadamer's conception of application.

As is well known Winch draws on the ideas of Wittgenstein's later work, Philosophical Investigations (1968), particularly in relation to the way language and reality are entwined, one with the other. They argue against the deeply ingrained assumption of empiricism and positivism that reality exists independently of any particular linguistic description of it. By contrast, their case is that the reality of our social practices are embedded in the kinds of description that make things meaningful for us. And in a reciprocal way, those kinds of description 'live' for us by being intrinsic to our daily life-practices. The way we speak and the way we live are two sides of the same coin. The linguistic concepts that we use shape the kind of experience of the world we have, in fact "the world is for us what is presented through those concepts". Hence it follows that, as the relation between language concepts is an internal one of 'meaning connectedness' rather than one of cause and effect, so also the regularities of our social world must be understood in the same way. In other words, participating in social reality, or in Wittgenstein's terms - a form of life - is analogous to the way we participate in a conversation, it involves us in knowing 'how to go on' in certain circumstances, of what it is appropriate to say, and by extension, to think, feel, and do. Such a view bears a striking resemblance to one presented by Gadamer in section three of Truth and Method.

Central to Winch's account of social regularities is the distinction he makes between their positivistic misconstrual as natural laws, i.e. as chains of cause and effect that determine human behaviour, and the correct understanding of them as 'rule governed behaviour'. The regularities of our social world have the quality of being rule governed, in that the force they exercise over social actors is a normative, not a causal one. Indeed one of the characteristics of social rules, according to Winch, is that the following of them is logically tied in with the possibility of making a mistake with them (Winch 1958:31-32). If one cannot assume the possibility of getting it wrong, that the rule could be contravened, then it loses all purchase as the guide to a particular social regularity. To break a social rule is, in extremis, a kind of moral violation which may have the effect of reinforcing the rule, whereas a break in the laws of nature would have the effect of falsifying them, i.e. if they got broken they would no longer hold true. Rule following in a specifically social sense is one that involves more than the mere repetition of a verbal or physical act. It entails the idea that we know how to apply the same rule in appropriate, but different circumstances. Indeed like Gadamer, Winch uses the example of the application of the law to illustrate the central importance of application to social understanding generally :-

> It is only when a past precedent has to be applied to a new kind of case that the importance and nature of the rule become apparent. The court has to ask what was involved in the precedent decision and that is a question which makes no sense except in a context where the decision could sensibly be regarded as the application, however unselfconsciously, of a rule. The same is true of other forms of human activity besides law, though elsewhere the rules may never be made so explicit. It is only because human actions exemplify rules that we can speak of past experience as relevant to our current behaviour. If it were merely a question of habits, then our current behaviour might certainly be influenced by the way we had acted in the past but that would be just a causal influence...whereas I know the right way to go on the basis of what I have been taught. (Winch 1958:62)

The role that the concept of application plays in Gadamer and Winch is remarkably similar. For Gadamer it is the process whereby an historical or legal interpretation is concretised in a current situation, for Winch it refers to our ability to know what was involved in a (legal) situation such that we know the right way to go on in other applicable situations. The language they use is different but their point is the same: the peculiarity of the social world is that it is sustained by our ability to interpret situations on the basis of knowing how to apply previous understandings in new, and different circumstances. As such, the standard criticism of both Winch and Gadamer, that their outlooks are relativistic in not providing a fixed criterion for judging interpretations, is misleading. Our interpretive capacities cannot be thought of as arbitrary or relativistic in the first place, without the very idea of the social world breaking down. In everyday life there is no fixed criterion that we can apply in a mechanical, formulaic fashion to understand things. Indeed those that try to do this are thought to be dogmatic, and incapable of the flexibility necessary to proper understanding. What we do in practice is to participate in an ongoing process of interpreting things within a framework of given, but essentially open ended meanings.

Of course, it might then be concluded that the task of the sociologist is to interpret the meaning individual actors give to their practices. Indeed they might then use this as the objective data for a scientific approach to society, one that incorporates human beliefs and intentions, in the manner suggested by Max Weber. Certainly much interpretive sociology and social psychology has been based on this assumption, but for Winch it is wide of the mark. Individuals are not the locus of meaning in the social world, and should not therefore be the focus of our attention. Like Gadamer he believes that the individual is preceded by a matrix of meaning of which he or she is often only barely conscious. Where for Gadamer it is the prejudices of our tradition that precede us, for Winch it is 'linguistically patterned' rule governed behaviour that makes up our form of life. In fact the motives of individuals, for both Gadamer and Winch, always presuppose a wider matrix of meaning, and this must be the real basis of an adequate interpretation of what is going on. As Winch (1958:82) points out, to say (for example), that someone murdered his wife from jealousy is intelligible to us only in terms of the social rules of our society, where there are particular convention that guide how we feel and act in relation to being displaced in someone's affections. How jealousy works in a particular society should be the primary focus of our attention, not the motives of human subjects. Indeed Winch like Gadamer, though sometimes accused of 'subjectivism' or 'idealism', has little time for the supposed powers of human consciousness (1). Following a rule, for Winch (1958:58), does not depend on whether the actor can formulate the criterion for the rule's use, but on the ability to distinguish between right and wrong ways of going about things. In other words people can be said to act meaningfully in following rules, even when they are not fully aware of the criteria they are using in following them. In a similar fashion Gadamer insists that the meaning of a text is not dependent on what its author's intentions were, but on what emerges when we participate in its subject matter. For both of them the consciousness of the human subject is de-centred, and 'subjective meanings' have no substance outside the public arena of social discourse.

Certainly there are important and subtle differences between Gadamer and Winch, as Smith (1979) and Hekman (1986;117-129) have pointed out, but these have frequently been amplified at the expense of highlighting common ground (2). Gadamer's account of understanding and interpretation is very much based on the possibility of mediation between different frames of meaning, and seeing this as a process that draws both text and interpreter up into it. By contrast Winch and the Wittgensteinian position is often pejoratively characterised as monadic, in that so thoroughgoing is its sensitivity to the uniqueness of linguistic meaning that it seems to rule out the possibility of 'translation' between the meaning of different 'language games'. There is some truth in this, in that Winch does see understanding in a rather too 'cognitivistic' light, i.e. as learning how to go on correctly in different situations, or of getting things right or wrong according to rules. This implies that the more we efface our own position for the sake of understanding the other's rules of meaning, the more technically accurate our knowledge of them will be. Put like this the contrast between his and Gadamer's more dialectical account is sharp. Habermas (1988:136) saw their differences in this light, arguing derogatively that Winch's work provided the linguistic equivalent of Dilthey's historicism. History, for Dilthey, was made up of unique and incommensurable epochs, and thus the task of the historian had to be one of finding a way to suspend his own current assumptions in order to accurately bridge the meaning gap. While there are similarities here with the way Winch emphasises the uniqueness and unity of a society's beliefs, the analogy with Dilthey unfairly plays down other elements in work that brings Winch closer to Gadamer, such as the way he utilises the idea of application to translate between life in an alien society and life in our own.

Excursus 2: Applying *the alien* in our own society

In Understanding A Primitive Society (1964) Peter Winch sets out to develop some of the ideas he introduced in *The Idea Of A Social Science*. He uses E. E. Evans-Pritchard's famous anthropological study, *Witchcraft, Oracles and Magic Among The Azande* as a vehicle to discuss the way deep seated Western assumptions about the rationality of science, negatively colour the way we regard other forms of rationality. He argues that Evans-Pritchard went a long way towards recognising that our disparaging attitude to apparently irrational beliefs, such as Azande witchcraft, is no less a function of our scientific culture than is the Azande's belief in magic a function of theirs' However, despite this apparent sensitivity, Winch believes that in the end Evans-Pritchard falls back on the idea that it is our views which are "in accord with objective reality". In so doing he slips into the mistaken belief that reality exists independently of the different ways that different societies conceive it, and that the Western scientific conception of it is the most accurate one.

At first sight Winch's claims seem to lead towards the kind of relativism of which he is standardly accused, namely that as there is no 'real world' independent of the particular descriptions that different societies have, then there is no way to check the adequacy of one version as against another. But he inverts this criticism by pointing out the significance of the fact that we could not conceive of a society that did not distinguish the real from the unreal. Although the concept of reality has therefore a kind of 'universality' about it, what it means in any actual situation is dependent on the way it operates within that society's language. As Winch puts it :-

> Reality is not what gives language sense. What is real and what is unreal shows itself in the sense that language has. Further, both the distinction between the real and the unreal and the concept of agreement with reality belong to our language... we could not in fact distinguish the real from the unreal without understanding the way this distinction operates in the language. (Winch 1964 in Wilson ed. 1974)

Hence what is real for the Azande cannot be read off simply from our assumptions about reality without misunderstanding the various distinction they make between things. Our understanding of magic and witchcraft, for example, is invariably bound up with the assumption that it either entails a perversion of Christian beliefs, or is irrational in being non-scientific. In both cases it is negatively valorised and seen as rightly marginal to everyday life. Winch follows Evans-Pritchard in pointing out that for the Azande witchcraft is an entirely normal part of life, and is woven into the very fabric of their beliefs and practices. As such, for them it belongs in the realm of the real, not the unreal, and if we wish to understand it we must seek a foothold in a place other than where our society first suggests.

For the Azande, witchcraft is a power by which an individual may damage the interests of others. It is also an inherited organic condition that in fact all members of the tribe may possess. When misfortune strikes, the victim will consult oracles of various kinds to find the source of it. If an elephant charges for no apparent reason, if the termites undermine someone's house, or if crops fail, witchcraft may be suspected, an oracle consulted and the malevolent individuals can thereby be discovered. The most important oracle is the 'poison oracle', which the Azande consult when major misfortune befalls them. The ritual of consultation is fairly elaborate, but in our terms it involves administering a poisonous substance called benge to a fowl. The survival or the death of the fowl is then taken to be either a 'yes' or a 'no' answer to an already specified question about the origin of the victim's misfortune. To confirm the result benge is then administered to a second fowl with the question turned round the other way. For example :-

> Is Prince Ndoruma responsible for placing bad medicines in the roof of my hut? The fowl DIES giving the answer "yes"..(then)..Did the oracle speak truly when it said that Ndoruma was responsible ? The fowl SURVIVES giving the answer "yes"". (Winch in Wilson 1974:86)

Such a system seems to us plainly irrational, yet Winch sets about showing how in reaching that conclusion we have slipped into misapplying the assumptions of our reality. At first sight a system of ideas that allows for the possibility of a 'yes' and 'no' to the same question appears to fly in the face of the most elementary requirement for a rationality that is consistent. Similarly the possibility that the oracle's pronouncements may be contradicted by later experience, ought to show to the Azande just how futile this system of ideas is when it comes to explaining empirical events.

What happens in practice is that the Azande have a variety of explanations for an oracle that produces contradictory answers, and these are built into the concept of an oracle and thereby the fabric of their lives. It may be that the benge was bad, the operator ritually unclean, perhaps the oracle itself was influenced by witchcraft, or the question so loaded that it could not be straightforwardly answered. These kinds of reason may also serve when subsequent experience apparently contradicts what the oracle claimed. To us, this may well sound like spurious rationalisations for a system of beliefs that are fundamentally incoherent, but Winch queries the kind of question we are asking of Azande beliefs. The Azande do not consult the oracle in at all the same way that we undertake scientific experiments, and its revelations are not hypotheses to be tested against a 'neutral' empirical reality. They are not seeking the confirmation or refutation of propositions, and therefore to press their ideas in that direction is to mistake what they are actually about.

If we consider the role of the inheritance of witchcraft, here too the Azande seem to be holding to contradictory beliefs. Given that all Zande are ultimately related to one another, and that 'witchcraft-substance' is biologically passed on, then all Zande are ipso facto witches. If all members of a clan are witches, then the idea of witchcraft having any specific relevance to things is undermined. The Azande are not unaware of this, but see no contradiction in it. They do not press things toward what we would call their logical conclusion, because they simply have no interest in doing so. It is us who try to press what we see as the contradictoriness out of things, in the name of our scientific rationality. By contrast :-

> Zande notions of witchcraft do not constitute a theoretical system in terms of which Azande try to gain a quasi-scientific understanding of the world. This in turn suggests that it is the European, obsessed with pressing Zande thought where it would not naturally go - to a contradiction - who is guilty of misunderstanding, not the Zande. The European is in fact committing a category mistake. " (Winch in Wilson 1974:93)

In fact in the context of his discussion of language Gadamer makes the same point in relation to Western beliefs, which at a formal level may be contradictory, but at the level of them being lived ideas are not. He gives the example of the seemingly contradictory habit we have of talking about 'the sun setting', which since the Copernican explanation of the universe became an accepted part of our knowledge, should no longer be how we think of things. It is not the movement of the sun that makes it set, but the rotation of the earth. He notes that in spite of this we feel there is nothing arbitrary about the phrase, for it expresses what really appears to be the case :-

> It is the appearance presented to a man who is not himself in motion. It is the sun that comes and goes as its rays reach or leave us. Thus to our vision the setting of the sun is a reality (it is "relative to Dasein"). (Gadamer 1989:449)

We can, as it were, try to mentally liberate ourselves from the evidence of our senses and see the world only from the viewpoint of Copernican theory, but the latter model will not supercede the former. This is so not only because we live what we see, what we see constitutes our reality, but because the truth of science is relative to a particular orientation, and cannot claim to be the whole truth. What does open up *the whole* is language, the suppleness of which allows these apparently contradictory views to exist together and be recognised for what they are. The mistake is to try and impose a (scientific) language that privileges one view and seeks to eliminate those that contradict it.

If we want to understand Azande magic, Winch argues, we will have to look outside the language of science to find some more adequate category in our self-understanding that will approximate to it. This is not an easy task, and he freely admits that there is no category that can be applied unproblematically. The Azande do in fact have a working distinction between the technical and the magical, and they do perceive cause and effect in an empirical way akin to our own. A Zande perceives how things happen much the same as we do, if the granary roof collapses it is not a witch that brought it down but the termites that ate the posts away. But whereas we would content ourselves with that explanation of how something happened, the Azande supplement this, they want to know why it happened. They want to know why that particular event happened at that particular time affecting those particular people sitting under that particular granary roof. In short, those areas of life that we leave at the margins of our rationality, by resignedly referring them as 'luck' or 'fate', are for the Azande at the heart of daily life, and dealt with by reference to witchcraft.

Winch's claim is that through their magical rites the Azande are trying to come to terms with those contingencies of life that fall outside their technical control. He suggests that though the application is inexact, there is a parallel between this and aspects of religious belief in our Judeo-Christian tradition. In Christian prayer there is an important element of supplication that does not, indeed should not, seek to control empirical outcomes, but instead seeks to "free the believer from what he is supplicating for" it is expressed in the Christian attitude of submission to God's will. In other words, Zande rites find an application in our culture by bringing to concretion an attitude comparable to that taken by Christians in prayer, an attitude which recognises that life is subject to contingencies beyond their control.

It seems to me that at this point Winch's work is at its most imaginative and closest to Gadamer's in offering an interpretation that is hypothetical and circular in character. However, some authors such as Mattick (1986:47) are less convinced that the connection Azande witchcraft and Christian prayer is as Winch claims. Mattick makes the point that according to Evans-Pritchard, the Azande in using their oracles are trying to control the contingencies of life not submit to them. They check for witchcraft before major decisions are made or plans are executed. As such, Winch himself is making a category mistake in finding common ground between such rites and Christian prayer. However, this view may involve an overestimation of the degree to which Christian prayer involves only supplication or submission to God's will, and ignores the fact that it can also entail pleas for particular outcomes. Certainly it plays down how both sets of practices can be seen as attempts to give shape and significance to people's lives. As Winch argues, the growing of crops for the Azande is not just the technical affair it is for us, success in this is intimately bound up with the moral and social relationships they share with others. Magical rites therefore are an expression of how these things may be contemplated and reflected upon - and perhaps also thereby transformed and deepened.

Whatever the case, Winch's aim is clearly to open up areas of our culture to a dialectical relation with an alien culture. In taking this attitude he veers away from the pure 'cognitive fit' model of which he is sometimes accused, and towards the more actively mediating view that Gadamer presents. The fit between Azande rites and Christian prayer may not be exact, but like Gadamer he emphasise that understanding is an active process involving more than the absence of intellectual contradiction; it is a process that engages a person's life-practice. In coming to understand an aspect of Azande life we inevitably find ourselves searching for an appropriate application of it in our own. The effect of this may be to disturb some of the assumptions we hold about ourselves, for what we can learn in studying other cultures is not merely other techniques for doing things we already do, but "different possibilities of making sense of human life", (Winch in Wilson 1974:106). What Winch is driving at is that in coming to properly understand the complexities of an alien culture we learn more about ourselves, something he links to the concept of wisdom.

Like Gadamer, Winch advocates neither imposing our own assumptions on those we wish to understand, nor effacing them and trying to take the part of the other. His critics have mostly emphasised the latter, which they see as springing from the importance he places on the internal standards of rationality of other cultures. His rejection of any universal standards of rationality has, they claim, made it virtually impossible for him to find any way of marrying up our standards with theirs. It leads in short, to an unsatisfactory cultural relativism. However they have claimed this by ignoring the other, more Gadamerian side of his work (3) where he emphasises the potentially unsettling, projective effort required to understand an alien culture, and the fact that this may involve more than making the right intellectual match, but of revising and extending our own ways of seeing things. For both he and Gadamer it is in the effort required to find an application for something unfamiliar, that brings most sharply into the open our own cultural assumptions, that is, the nature of who and what we are, the nature of our being.

Winch does not use the language of 'being' as does Gadamer. Nevertheless, there is a striking similarity in the way he leans towards the idea that being human involves having one's life shaped by certain "limiting notions", and the way Gadamer (1981:69-87) describes the essential features of social practice. For Winch these notions are specifically 'birth', 'death', and 'sexual relations', which he regards as inescapable features of all known societies, and which can therefore provide us with clues about the meaning of alien systems of institutions. His critics, for example Giddens (1975), have seen this move as a rather glib attempt to establish an Archimedean point independent of any particular social belief system. Thus 'limiting notions', Giddens claims, are cultural universals meant to guarantee some reliability in interpretation, and designed to rescue Winch from the relativism he created for himself. This view is itself too glib, for Winch is trying to describe what is presupposed by the very idea of 'human life', not latch onto sociological or psychological features that are the same in all societies. This is an important distinction, and not merely a hedging of bets, as Giddens implies. Certainly it brings Winch once more into conjunction with Gadamer's ideas, in that he broaches the issue of the ontological nature of social life, which is of course also central for Gadamer.

Winch's claim is that human life, unlike animal life, is not merely lived, for human beings "also have a conception of life". Moreover this difference changes the "very sense which the word 'life' has when applied to men". It is no longer equivalent to 'animate existence' in that human beings ask moral questions about the right and wrong ways to live, about what things are important in life, and whether life has any significance. In ontological terms Winch is saying that because humans have their being in a particular mode, they are able to ask questions about the meaning of being. The limiting notions that he refers to provide the ethical space in which people work out their fundamental possibilities for doing good or evil. Death is one of these limiting notions, and of course animals die too, but the idea of animal death argues Winch, entails something rather different from the way we think of our own human death.

> My conception of the death of an animal is of an event that will take place in the world; perhaps I shall observe it - and life will go on. But when I speak of my 'death', I am not speaking of a future event in my life; I am not even speaking of an event in anyone else's life. I am speaking of the cessation of my world. That is also a cessation of my ability to do good or evil. It is not just that as a matter of fact I shall no longer be able to do good or evil after I am dead; the point is that my very concept of what it is to be able to do good or evil is deeply bound up with my concept of my life as ending in death. If ethics is a concern with the right way to live, then clearly the nature of this concern must be deeply affected by the concept of life as ending in death. One's attitude to one's life is at the same time an attitude to one's death. (Winch in Wilson 1974:109)

Winch means that because we live knowing that one day we will cease to be, we attach a significance to our lives, and that this awareness of our finititude leads us to have a moral concern with how best to live life. If we compare this with Gadamer's views on the relevance of death, as expressed in his essay What is Practice ? The Conditions Of Social Reason, we find a notable similarity between the two :-

> This special human dimension is the in-built capacity of man to think beyond his own life in the world, to think about death. This is why the burial of the dead is perhaps the fundamental phenomenon in becoming human. Burial does not refer to a rapid hiding of the dead, a swift clearing away of the shocking impression made by one suddenly stuck fast in a leaden and lasting sleep. On the contrary, by a remarkable expenditure of human labour and sacrifice there is sought an abiding with the dead, indeed a holding fast of the dead among the living. We stand amazed before the wealth of mourning gifts that continually flows up towards us from the graves of every ancient culture. Gifts of mourning are a way of cherishing human existence. They do not let death have the last word. We have to regard this in its most elementary significance. It is not a religious affair or a transposition of religion into secular customs, mores, and so on. Rather it is a matter of the

> fundamental constitution of human being from which derives the specific sense of human practice; we are dealing with a conduct of life that has spiralled out of the order of nature. (Gadamer 1981:74-75)

Gadamer, like Winch, believes the peculiarity of being human lies in the fact that the awareness of forthcoming death structures human life. We find meaning in our common life, and are not indifferent to those who have died, but seek to affirm the significance of their lives by abiding with them. Human social practice is specific in that it is not merely the product of nature, we choose common goals and evaluate their worth, indeed he regards as amongst our greatest achievements "the stabilisation of norms of conduct in the sense of right and wrong". Hence he, like Winch, sees social practice as fundamentally moral practice, something that has loosened its connection with nature. They both believe that being human means to share a common ontological ground, even though quite clearly social practices, including those relating to death, vary highly from one culture to another. Indeed it is this common ontological ground that is the source of our capacity to interpret between what is familiar and what is alien to us. In the light of this Winch again draws attention to the way we may find an application in our society for something that at first sight makes no sense at all.

Winch also addresses the attitude of incomprehension adopted by the philosopher Alastair MacIntyre when faced by the fact that some aborigines carry a stick or stone around, as if it embodied the soul of its owner. Apparently if the sick or stone is lost the owner will anoint himself in the same way that the dead are anointed. MacIntyre confesses that although he can see how the rules of this social practice work, he comes up against a blank wall as far as the meaning of them is concerned. But if we follow Gadamer's account of the internal connection between understanding, application, and interpretation, we must accept that as we interpret how the rules of a strange practice work we also necessarily come to understand their meaning or significance by finding an application for them in our own arrangements. This is just what Winch does. He asks why MacIntyre finds the idea of carrying one's soul about in a stick so thoroughly incoherent, when there are comparable and entirely coherent practices going on in our own society. He argues that because the soul for us is not a material object, MacIntyre has assumed there is no comparability of meaning whereas in fact in our society a lover may carry a picture or a lock of hair of the loved one, and in this is to be found, if not their soul, then at least the symbolic embodiment of a non-material relationship. If the lover loses the token through carelessness this may be felt to be an act of betrayal, and result in feelings of intense guilt, which can only be assuaged by the forgiveness of the other person. The need for such forgiveness parallels the way the aborigine anoints himself in order to re-establish the integrity of his life in the face of losing his soul. The loss of a wedding ring in our culture can similarly evoke acute distress, perhaps undermining the very sense of purpose someone attaches to their life. Winch claims that both practices express a need for atonement, based on a concern for finding significance in the living of a human life; and in this also lies the recognition that such a life is bound by a forthcoming death. There is nothing irrational or mysterious in the aboriginal practice, for we also live our lives in non-material ways, we also imbue physical objects with quasi-spiritual, but nevertheless real qualities.

Again it must be remembered that in Gadamerian terms the fact that the fit between the two practices is inexact, in the sense that life in our society is quite different from life in Azande society, does not represent a weakness that needs to be overcome. We are not looking to obliterate difference by using a method that will subsume one under the other. The 'text' of Azande, or aboriginal life, is not a fixed entity, any more than the 'text' of our Western life is given in a once only way. Application does not consist in first understanding a text and then applying it to some particular aspect of our situation, but of bringing our own cultural self-understanding into play in such a way as to enable us to make sense of alien social practices. Indeed, if we were different to what we are, we would understand their practices differently too. As Gadamer put it: we understand differently where we understand at all. The idea that there may be no final correct interpretation of another society's social practices, is something that is made explicit by Gadamer, but not by Winch. The temporal quality of understanding, and the historicality of our cultural horizons, are central for Gadamer, and do mark a difference between his and Winch's outlook. My guess is that if Gadamer were to challenge Evans-Pritchard on his analysis of the Azande, it would take a slightly different form from the one given by Winch. Gadamer I think would be interested in the historical context in which Evans-Pritchard views arose, and would also relativise in historical terms, the (Winchean) application of our present assumptions. That is, Winch would be thought right to bring into play current applications, but wrong if he is suggesting that these are permanent features of our life. Gadamer might argue for example, that our own view of Christian prayer has changed, and will continue to change over time, and therefore its present application, while perhaps currently appropriate, will not always be so. We may. as it were, just have reached a stage in our history where precisely that application is most apt.

Winch does not thematise history as such, but whether the stock criticism that his work is ahistorical should stand is less clear cut. It does not seem to me, at least in principle, that his account rules out the relevance of historicality, but rather that he just does not address it as a question. If we take the study of an historical situation to be analogous to the study of an alien culture, then the common ground he shares with Gadamer, would suggest that the absence of history in his work, is an omission rather than something endemic to the position (4).

To summarise, I have dwelt on Winch's work in these excurses for two reasons. First, it has provided a good way of illustrating how Gadamer's concept of application is tied in with the very nature of understanding. Gadamer believes that the nature of understanding only truly shows itself when a real hermeneutic effort is required to make sense of the unfamiliar. Making sense of Azande witchcraft provides an excellent example of just that. Secondly, from Winch's side I have been concerned to show that his work has been seen in too limited a light, and that when mediated through Gadamer's hermeneutics, its interpretative possibilities are opened up. That is to say, one of the standard criticisms of Winch, that his emphasis on the uniqueness of internal standards of rationality leads to a hopeless relativism, is wrong. Rather his approach, like Gadamer's, involves extending our prejudgements in an engagement with unfamiliar ideas and practices, thus altering the way we see things. From this a new perspective can emerge, one that was hitherto available neither to us, nor to the other culture.

Winch, no more than Gadamer, accepts mere relativism. In fact Winch explicitly claims that rationality is something we assume anyway, in our dealings with alien cultures. However they both reject the primacy of any overarching, universal criteria of rationality. There is no free-standing, 'rationality-as-such', that could be separated from the particular social practices in which it is inscribed. But they also both agree that these practices are not sealed units, there is something common in human being, that is, in what it is to live a human life. In relation to this I have drawn attention to the way they both describe death as structuring human life, in the sense that an awareness that one's life will cease inflects it with an ethical significance, which is something peculiar to the human world. (I will deal in the next section with Gadamer's views on the relevance of Aristotle's ethics). But underlying this, and central to our being able to 'assume rationality' in dealing with others, is their joint recognition that human beings are language users. I shall return to the importance Gadamer attaches to language when I deal with Part Three of Truth and Method. Suffice to say at this point Winch strikes a similar note to Gadamer, insisting that rationality is not just another concept found in language, but is intrinsic to all language use. To say that a society "has a language is also to say that it has a concept of rationality" (Winch in Wilson 1974:99). Because language cannot be used arbitrarily we have to assume that it has a rationality that shapes the way its users see the world.

The assumption that rationality is built into the nature of language was seen by Habermas as an open gate to ideological deception, but for Winch and for Gadamer it is at the heart of human social life, and therefore must be at the heart of the human sciences and not something that can be suspended to allow a scientific or more ideologically sound method to be interposed. Gadamer argues that the human sciences must recognise this moment of application in their understandings and interpretations if they are not to fall into the trap of producing "knowledge as domination". That is knowledge blind to how the meaning of something affects us in being applied to present circumstances.

Gadamer and Aristotle's *Ethics*

Gadamer does not develop an ethical theory as such, and seems to suggest that to pursue a theory of ethics would be to misunderstand the mutable nature of morality (Gadamer 1989:312ff). Yet he clearly finds Aristotle's Nichomachean Ethics to be congruent with his hermeneutics. Moreover, he utilises Aristotle's account in his critique of Habermas and his aim of developing a quasi-transcendental communicative ethics, as the basis for the critique of society. Certainly there are clear echoes of the issues that separated Gadamer and Habermas, in the recent resurgence of interest in philosophical ethics, between 'communitarians' (Gadamer), and 'universalists' (Habermas). See the collections edited by Kelly (1989-90), Rasmussen (1990), and Benhabib and Dallmayr (1990), also relevant is Kelly (1988) and Kelly (1989).

The analogous nature of Winch and Gadamer's ideas with regard to the concept of application, and to some extent language, is also reflected in the central importance they attach to ethics. When Winch declares :-

> ...through my birth ethical limits are set for my life quite independently of my will: I am, from the outset, in specific relations to other people, from which obligations spring which cannot but be ethically fundamental. (Winch in Wilson 1974:110)

he is expressing the same attitude towards the role of morality in social life, as Gadamer. Moral beliefs are not something that is superimposed on social life, they are intrinsic to it. To live socially is to be oriented towards each other in a moral way, that is, in a way which is concerned with right and wrong ways of going about things. Gadamer, like Winch in the quotation above, emphasises that we have no choice in the matter, in that our social and moral solidarity precedes us in such a way that we are always already oriented towards things, in accord with the ethical norms of our tradition. These though, are not objective systems set over against the subjects that believe them, controlling them like a natural force. Certainly they are a source of social solidarity, but one that is constituted in the dialectical fashion indicated by Aristotle.

The common problem hermeneutics shares with Aristotelian ethics is how one and the same thing, such as a text or an ethical norm, can be endlessly understood and applied in different ways ? It is the problem of the relation of the general to the particular. Using Aristotelian concepts such as praxis, techne, and phronesis, Gadamer reinforces his view that the human or social sciences are different from the natural sciences, by virtue of the specific nature of their 'object'.

He points out that we always encounter the (moral) 'good' in the form of the practical requirements of particular situations, not as detached observers, hence in opposition Platonic and Socratic ideas, we cannot, and should not, expect moral knowledge to have the same exactness as mathematics. But he follows Aristotle in arguing that moral knowledge (phronesis) is not only to be distinguished from pure theoretical knowledge (episteme), but also from the technical knowledge of the craftsman (techne).

This latter distinction became an important one, as it not only was at the centre of Gadamer's description of ethics, but also was a point of fine difference between Gadamer and Habermas in their debate. Both recognised the fact that the nature of social practice (praxis) had become distorted in the modern world, being overtaken by technical ways of thinking. That is, our capacity to think and reflect about what might be a desirable collective destiny is constantly undermined by instrumental habits of thought, which are orientated towards what is most technically effective. Indeed, so far has the process gone, that the word - practical - is virtually synonymous with - technical - in Western society. Thus we identify a practical problem as one that has a technically achievable solution, quite independent of moral values. Human life-practice, and the formation of what is to count as 'the good', has been reduced to the strategic issue of how things may best be manipulated, of how the administration of society and the economy may be perfected. Habermas believed that what was needed to break the spell, was a theory that would categorise different kinds of knowledge and reveal their particular qualities and limitations. He even claimed that a quasi-objective theory of moral development, that of Lawrence Kohlberg, could function to make clearer what was more or less morally adequate. By contrast, for Gadamer, moral knowledge based on prudent judgement (phronesis), is at the heart of human praxis, and theories claiming to be independently objective will never usurp this fundamentally 'lived' quality. Such theories will always be secondary to, and derivative of, the essential features of phronesis. But what are these features ?

First it has to be said that Gadamer regards episteme, techne, and phronesis, as forms of knowledge. They make a claim upon us, they make a difference in how we see the world. Moral knowledge, basic to the modern human sciences, is mutable knowledge, but knowledge nonetheless. In being mutable it is distinguishable from the unchangeable knowledge of the natural sciences, but it seems to bear some resemblance to the knowledge and skill of the craftsman, who knows how to make some specific thing. Gadamer ponders the idea that perhaps "man learns to make himself what he ought to be, in the same way that the craftsman learns to make things according to his plan and will", (Gadamer1989:315). Certainly both involve applying some prior knowledge to a practical situation, and in both there is a general idea of what is to be achieved. But the differences are sharp and not to be overridden They can be summarised :-

(a) The technical skill of the craftsman is one that can be learnt, but also forgotten. Because it stands apart from us we can choose to learn it or not. By contrast moral knowledge cannot be learnt in the same way, nor is it forgotten. We do not acquire moral knowledge as a matter of choice, as it does not stand apart from us as an objective skill. Rather, we are always already embraced by it, as the conduct of our lives is constantly informed by ideas of what is appropriate behaviour. For the craftsman the correct technical course of action is given separately, by the use for which the object is to be put. The design of a chair, for example, is given by its use as an object to sit upon. But with moral knowledge the right course of action is not fully given ahead of time, but is co-determined by the situation in which the course of action is chosen. What will be considered, for example, 'decent' or 'courageous', emerges in and through a particular practical situation. Gadamer uses the example of the judge applying the law to illustrate the point that there is a necessary tension between the law as written, and its application in particular cases. The judge that sticks to the letter of the law, and imposes it in a mechanical fashion, without prudently taking cognisance of how it should apply in this particular case, actually inhibits, rather than furthers justice.

(b) This means that the relation between means and ends, as far as moral knowledge is concerned, is a radically different one to that found in technical knowledge. Because moral knowledge is not an object, we cannot know it in advance, for "there can be no anterior certainty concerning what the good life is directed toward as a whole". Thus we cannot know prior to the event, the right means for achieving an appropriate end. Where we have learnt a technical skill we can without great ado find the correct means, but with moral knowledge we have to consider the appropriateness of the means carefully on each occasion. A moral situation has an evocative force of its own. In fact we have to constantly weigh up anew just what the appropriate moral means are, as the means that we use, will signal the kind of moral ends to which we are committed. Moral knowledge in effect embraces both means and ends, they 'happen' at the same time, and mutually determine each other.

(c) Moral knowledge also requires us to have a sympathetic understanding of others in a way quite at odds with the detached application of technical knowledge. The importance of shared understanding underpins the central role Aristotle gave to friendship in the Nichomachean Ethics. The sophisticated man of the world may know plenty about the ways of the world, but that is insufficient, what is really required for moral insight, is the sense of sharing a common human bond. In fact the seeming moral 'expert', one who treats moral knowledge in a manipulative way, and who with technical skill can turn everything to his own advantage, cynically debases real moral knowledge.

These differences mark off the essence of phronesis from that of techne, but do they thereby present us with any thing other than a highly relativistic form of knowledge ? Gadamer finds the same kind of 'truth' capable of emerging in moral knowledge, as he found in the understanding of historical texts. It hinges on the relation between the particular and the general as mediated by the concept of application. We know for example that the moral virtue of courage is highly relative to particular situations. What takes great courage for one person to do, requires no effort at all for another. In fact diametrically opposite behaviours can be identified as one and the same thing. As Joel Weinsheimer (1985:190) puts it, "there is courage that avoids the fight as well as one that engages in it". The odd thing is that we can recognise both courses of action as examples of courage, so long as we know the details of the particular circumstances that lie behind the action. In other words, understanding the moral virtue of courage requires that we engage with it in terms of the meaning of that situation, we cannot judge it to be present or absent against some fixed universal definition of courage. Yet equally oddly, we must already have some general notion of what it means to be courageous if we are going to be able to spot it in particular situations. However these general notions, importantly, are not general or universal in the same way that scientific laws are. With moral knowledge the particular is not something that is submerged under the general. Each application of the general idea of courage to a particular situation, involves the particular situation redefining the general idea of courage.

One of the reasons that Gadamer is drawn to Aristotle's work is, I think, because of what might be called its phenomenological qualities. Aristotle describes the nature of ethical phenomena from a range of different points of view, gradually revealing the essence of the moral. Certainly in his debate with Habermas, Gadamer baulked most at the pretensions of a Critical Theory that, as he saw it, had forgotten this 'essence of the moral', and was seeking to make itself the moral expert for society.

Experience and the structure of openness

Towards the end of Part Two Gadamer starts to draw the elements of his previous discussion together around the idea, that the common direction to which all the analyses are pointing, is language. He presents this via series of interwoven arguments that lead the reader from the concept of experience, with its essence of openness, to the structure of that openness, which he models on a dialectic of question and answer. The common denominator that allows this, and all that has preceded it, to be, is the conversational nature of language.

I shall not deal in great detail with these final arguments as they were not central to his dispute with Habermas. Nevertheless, there are elements that justify attention here, as they are directed in part against what he believes is the dogmatism of 'reflection philosophy'. By 'reflection philosophy' is meant those outlooks which attribute a transcendental power to consciousness, and thence often assume that once people reflect upon their real condition, they will act to change things in a rational way. Gadamer's claim was to be that Habermas's critical theory, harboured the grandiose ambition of wanting to inform people just what their real interests were.

During the course of Part Two Gadamer described the failings of what might be called a positivistic consciousness of history, one that sees history as an object laid out behind us, and where we, in the present, are tacitly assumed to be separate from it, and thereby to have escaped its effects. He used the concept of 'historically effected consciousness' as a counterpoint to it. However, he is also concerned to describe the nature of an alternative form of consciousness based on genuine hermeneutic experience. This is experience that is aware of the effects of history on it, i.e. one that is aware of its own finitude. He is critical of the contemporary conception of experience, which he sees as being demeaned by the prevalence scientific assumptions. We all get caught up in the idea that because much of our experience is not verifiable in a scientific sense, it cannot be accepted as valid knowledge. Scientific method requires that we extinguish all mutable, historical elements from experience. Both natural science, and the social sciences that base themselves on it, only accept one kind of experience as valid: an experience that is set up in a formal way, such that it can be repeated again and again, by anyone, anywhere; in short, experimental method. The historicity of those experiencing it, and the historical traditions of which they are a part, are altogether irrelevant. Hence, experience that is not verifiable in this way, seems to consist only of a series of arbitrary perceptions. Against this, Gadamer provides an account of the dialectical structure of experience that meets the requirements of his previous analyses, and challenges the modern diminution of it at the hands of science. Indeed, he argues that experience is actually a condition for the possibility of doing science (1989:350).

The dialectical structure of experience is akin to the dialectical structure of understanding, but in addition carries with it the sense of a cumulative, background understanding. In a genuine experience we encounter something whereby we, and it, are dialectically transformed into something new. But Gadamer also wishes to avoid following Hegel too far down a path that suggests experience moves in the direction of progressively increasing levels of self-knowledge. For down this path lies the dubious idea of experience being conceived in terms of something that surpasses it, i.e. a state of complete (self-) knowledge, where experience ceases to be needed (1989:355). Against this he argues that real experience is always finite, and stands in opposition to the claims of any absolute form of knowledge, be it Hegelian, scientific, technical or theoretical. Thus he emphasises the negative aspect of the process. That is, the fact that 'lived experience' entails contrary elements of discomfort, in that when we encounter something new, our familiar expectations are thwarted, and pain is experienced in coming to terms with it. Experience of this kind is clearly not scientific, for we cannot use the knowledge gained in one situation to avoid suffering in another. Parents may wish to save their children from suffering certain experiences, but Gadamer (1989:356) maintains, no one in the end is exempt from this kind of experience. In effect it is as much part of our real condition, as is the projective nature of understanding. He is not advocating the value of painful experiences as such, nor providing a sophisticated justification for slogans such as 'no pain no gain'. Rather, he is claiming that what we acquire through suffering is not knowledge of this or that, but self-knowledge.

What we discover through painful experience is the nature of our own finitude, as we come to see the limits of our being. The experienced person is one who recognises that they are masters "neither of time nor of the future". What he is referring to, is close to what we commonly call - wisdom. It involves acknowledging how limited our capacity to control the future is, and knowing how fragile human plans are generally. Yet ironically, bound up with being able to have such an experience, is the capacity to be open to other, new experiences. The truth of this kind of experience, in a sense confirms our existence and leaves us with an orientation that is open to similarly real experiences. Because experience, in the sense that Gadamer is trying to describe, implies that we have relaxed the grip on our "planning reason", we are well equipped to have new and demanding experiences, and to learn from them. The truly experienced person is not the one that claims to know everything better than everyone else, but quite the opposite, it is the one who is "radically undogmatic" because he is aware of the finite limitations of all understanding. In fact Gadamer believes that this insight is the same religious one that gave birth to Greek tragedy. Namely, that there is an absolute "barrier that separates us from the divine"(1989:357). Hermes was the messenger of the gods, who brought to human beings intimations of what the gods were like and what they were thinking, but they did this because finite, mortal beings, could never possess god-knowledge themselves.

Needless to say, becoming aware of such limits brings us into contact with our historical tradition, and thus Gadamer blends an account of experience in general, with hermeneutical experience in particular. Genuine hermeneutical experience involves us in what he terms an "I-Thou" relationship. When we encounter our tradition in this "I-Thou" way we do not perceive it as an object, but as something that "relates itself to us". We are connected with it through language, in fact the tradition that we are is language. However, even though our relationship is a living one, and also a moral one, and even though it expresses itself as a Thou, we should not mistake this as meaning a relationship with a separate person, as it is not pitched at the epistemological level of the subject-object relationship. In the same way that he previously described understanding in an ontological, rather than a psychological way, so he now reinforces that by emphasising again, that we are not trying to penetrate the mind of some historical author, but to experience openness toward the meaning that addresses us. Failure to be open to the dialogic requirements of this kind of thing, means detaching ourselves from the tradition which is our reality, and flattening out the full nature of the hermeneutical experience. We may come to know more and more about our tradition at a factual level, but we will understand the significance of everything less and less. If we reflect ourselves out of the mutuality of this I-Thou relationship, what might seem to be the garnering of objective historical knowledge will turn out to entail a distortion of truth, and provide us with a peculiarly ahistorical, half-knowledge.

The logic of question and answer

The dialectical structure of experience with its emphasis on negative qualities as the basis of authentic experience, is linked to a similarly structured view of questioning. Both are fundamental features of human being. Indeed being open to new experience necessarily implies a willingness to question, and be questioned by things. :-

> We cannot have experiences without asking questions. Recognising an object is different, and not as we first thought obviously presupposes the question whether it was this or that. From a logical point of view, the openness essential to experience is precisely the openness of being this or that. It has the structure of a question. (Gadamer 1989:362)

Hence to be open to new, genuine experiences, means that we are involved in a fundamental, ongoing life-process of question and answer. But also to ask a question means to bring something into the open. There is thus a reciprocal relation here: to be open requires that we find something questionable, to question things means that something indeterminate is being brought out into the open.

What Gadamer is getting at is that the structure of experience has a similar form to the dialectic between question and answer. This similarity extends to the negativity that prevails in both, where coming to know things does not result from the flat accumulation of information, but of finding oneself affected by something questionable. That is, of knowing that one does not know, and realising that one must question things in a certain way that goes beyond ones' familiar assumptions. Indeed, in the same way that the experienced person is one that becomes painfully aware of his finite limitations, so the logic of question and answer also leads to "a radical negativity: the knowledge of not knowing." This also means, ironically, that the knowing person is the one who recognises the limitations of his knowledge. Knowledge is not boundless, in the sense of being totally complete, it is not the culmination of a process of moving from ignorance into the light of absolute truth. Rather, it is structured by the kinds of question that have been asked. Questions always come from a particular vantage point, and the answers to them will have to come from the same direction as the question. A certain kind of question implies a certain kind of answer. Gadamer gives this fairly familiar idea, a particular resonance, for the opening up of something by questioning it, he argues, simultaneously leads to a closing down of other possibilities. "Posing a question implies openness but also limitation". Lighting up a space for knowledge through questioning, also means leaving what is outside it in darkness. Knowledge like experience is finite, and has a restless, probing, and always unfinished quality about it.

Gadamer then, has linked the structure of experience through the importance of openness, to the logic of question and answer. In this, he alerts us to the importance of the medium in which these things take place: language.

Notes
1. Susan Hekman (1983) even draws a parallel between Gadamer's decentring of the subject and the radical anti-humanism of Louis Althusser.

2. For example Outhwaite (1987:69-70) and Outhwaite in Skinner (1985:33-34) elides this distinction entirely, placing Winch alongside symbolic interactionists such as Herbert Blumer and phenomenological sociologists such as Berger and Luckman. This quite misses out Winch's rejection of any approach based on subjective, mental events, which he regards as

intelligible only in terms of the social format in which they are located. Outhwaite also accepts the monadic 'sealed unit' version of Winch as set down by Habermas and which bypasses any reference to Winch's (1964) article 'Understanding A Primitive Society'.

3. Two authors that do not underestimate the projective and dialectical outlook developed by Winch in his 1964 article are McCarthy (1973) and Gibbons (1987).

4. Hekman (1986:127) makes a similar point with regard to both Winch and Louch, and that other authors who could be called Wittgensteinian render history compatible with their approach. She has in mind the historian of ideas J.G.A. Pocock (1971), but Quentin Skinner would also fit the bill. The problem as I see it though is that they both take historical texts to have a fixed primary meaning; that being roughly what that particualar author meant in saying that particular thing to that particualar audience on that particular occasion. This leads to the idea that the historical text has a meaning in-itself independent of how we presently understand and apply it. This is quite different from the way Gadamer conceives of the way historical tradition determines the meaning of a text.

5 The third part of Truth and Method: On language and reality

Hermeneutics and language

I have previously drawn attention to what I see as the underestimation of Peter Winch's work, particularly when it it is more positively refracted through Gadamer's hermeneutics with which it bears some notable similarities. However when it comes to language the issue is more complicated, for though both of them regard it as constitutive of the human world, how it constitutes that world is rather different.

There is an obvious similarity between Wittgenstein's idea of the language-game and Gadamer's ontological notion of play. Both are based on the idea that 'the world' comes to us through language, and that meaning is determined in the to and fro of everyday life. The language we use does not represent, or 'stand for' things, but actively shapes the very meaning these things have, so that how we talk about them is the way they are for us. This contrasts with the more orthodox view that the empirical world exists independently of our descriptions of it, and is directly available to us through our senses. The task of of the social scientist then is to gather sufficient 'brute' or independent data, to discover causal connections, or elicit functional relationships, between different parts of it. For both Gadamer and for Wittgensteinians like Winch, there is no brute data that can exist independent of the vocabulary in which particular social practices are grounded. Social practices have their reality in the language used to describe them, they are constituted by it (1). The idea of a language-game, like the concept of play, is meant to capture the open-ended nature of language. It also signals the fact that the players determine the meaning of expressions, and thereby the reality of things, through the moves they make in the game. But subtle differences become apparent if we look at Gadamer's opening gambit in Part Three of *Truth and Method*

> We say that we "conduct" a conversation, but the more genuine a conversation is, the less its conduct lies within the will of either partner. Thus a genuine conversation is never the one we wanted to conduct. Rather, it is generally more correct to say that we fall into conversation, or even that we become involved in it. The way one word follows another, with the conversation taking its own twists and reaching its own conclusion, may well be conducted in some way, but the partners conversing are far less the leaders than the led. (Gadamer 1979:383)

Gadamer is making the point that with language, it is not so much we who play the game, but we who are played by it. For Wittgenstein and those whose work proceeds from his, there is a residual sense in which language-games, despite revealing that language does not consist of neutral propositions which correspond to an independent reality, do still involve players who could take control of such games. As Smith (1979) has most ably argued, Wittgenstein still sees the meaning of things as springing fron the human subject who does the playing. Whereas Gadamer's account emphasises that we are not so much agents, as participants. The implication is that for the Wittgensteinian tradition the ambition is still therapeutic, i.e. to sort out what is going on in language, albeit by learning the rules of its games better. Whereas for Gadamer words are not like tools we can draw out of a box and then return, they cannot be used as if they were pieces in a game, they are always with us, and embrace us with their meaning before we are aware of it. They make a call on us, before we use them. Thus there can be no 'final sorting out', because there is no position outside language from which such sorting out could be undertaken. Any sorting out happens within language and as part of its play, for "in all our knowledge of ourselves and in all knowledge of the world, we are always already encompassed by the language which is our own", (Gadamer 1976:62). Smith's point is that for the Wittgensteinians, there is still a residual (Platonic) distrust of language and the rhetorical power it has to deceive people. Though Habermas was critical of Wittgenstein and Winch, he was also suspicious that language could involve a kind of fabrication, one that could distort reality in an ideological fashion, from the ground up. However for Gadamer, the ontological status of language as "the house of being", makes any such judgement impossible. Language cannot be seen in the first place as a barrier to understanding, one which fabricates the true nature of the world, because only through it does the world have its being.

Language is no tool

I have emphasised the importance Gadamer places on the enveloping nature of language, because he believes the fundamental mistake being made in modern thinking is to conceive of language in an instrumental way, i.e. the tendency to conceive of language as something neutrally available for human subjects to use for communication and so forth. Obviously one of the functions of language is to permit human communication, but this functional-instrumental way of conceiving it, serves to rob language of its more primordial 'apophantic' quality, its fundamental capacity to let something be seen, or show up in its own right, rather than just be used to point out things that are already familiar to us. It is the quality, found at its most intense in the language of poetry, which lets something shine out from the poem. Indeed it is this capacity of language to bring something out into the open in the first place, that enables us to point to familiar things, to manipulate, and make judgements about them (2). This is not to say that language creates things, but that things have their being, and can be known by us, only by coming-into-language.

In the social sciences, discussions of language often start with a model of language as an objective system of signs, as though we could separate ourselves from the system, and were able to bring it round the front for a full inspection (3). Such an outlook wrongly assumes that linguistic signs can exist separately from the subject matter they bring to light, as though we were familiar with the meaning of their subject matter from some other source. Being able to conceive of language as a system of signs is an abstraction, one that in fact depends upon a world already having been disclosed to us through language. It is only through living our language that we know what 'signs' and 'systems' mean in the first place. The enigma of language is that it allows us to distance ourselves from it, and treat it as just another object in the world, yet will not allow the breach to be final, for all thinking about language happens within language (Gadamer 1976:62).

Paul Ricoeur (1976:82-86), provides an example of this point in his discussion of Claude Levi-Strauss's structuralist approach to the study of the Oedipus myth. Using the basic unit of myths, the mytheme, Levi-Strauss draws up a formal system of combinations and oppositions, akin to the ones used in structural linguistics, to explain how the meaning of the myth is generated. The details of this do not concern me here, but Ricoeur's point is that the system Levi-Strauss devises, presupposes that we have already understood the meaning of these units in a more primordial way. We must have already have grasped the meaning of such combinations and oppositions as birth/death, blindness/lucidity, sexuality/truth, in such a way that makes the structuralist explanation possible. If these units were merely a system of signs without significance for us, then the particular arrangement of units would have no explanatory power at all. We would be able to find no sense of opposition between birth and death, etc, and we would see no purpose to the myth as a way of dealing with the conflicts that arise in relation to them.

Gadamer believes that with modern instrumentalist habits of thought focusing on the structure of language, and thus on seeing words as mere signs with no intrinsic relation to the thing they designate, the cart has not only been put before the horse, it has been mistakenly separated from it (4). As a result, authors as diverse and sophisticated as Cassirer and Saussure, who take their starting point to be the concept of language, have been led into false positions. In conceptualizing language, both tend to isolate it from what is said in it, so they can objectify it satisfactorily. Cassirer does this by seeing it as the external symbolic form taken by the inner human spirit; Saussure goes much further by describing it as a system of signs that generates meaning through the internal differences between the signs themselves, something it does without reference to the dialogic world of 'lived language', i.e. speech. Even Habermas, who shared many of Gadamer's views on language, slipped into an instrumentalist assumption, when he claimed that language could be seen as an objective system of ideological distortion. This implied that language was externally imposed on the human subjects that 'lived it', though they could bring it under their rational control with a little help from Critical Theory.

So what is the relationship between language and reality ?

Gadamer traces out the origin of the peculiar reversal, whereby the world and its objects are thought to exist (logically) prior to, and separate from the language used to describe them, in terms of Greek philosophy. Despite his repeated rejection of this modern separation between word and thing, he does not attempt to simply reverse the reversal, by suggesting that word and object are exactly the same thing. Such a belief would smack of a primitive word-magic that was rightly dissolved by Greek philosophy. Nevertheless there is something valid to be found echoing in such an idea.

It is in Plato's Cratylus that Gadamer finds two arguments concerning the relation between word and object, which Plato himself never quite accepts, but Gadamer finds worthy of further attention (1989:405ff).The first is the conventionalist theory which regards the connection as one established by common practice, i.e. where objects are given names and the accuracy of these is established through social agreement. The second is the similarity theory where certain words are seen to have a natural sympathy or agreement with their objects. Here words are selected by users according to their aptness in describing particular things. A cursory reflection on these two theories reveals them to be not mutually exclusive, in that the aptness of a word could be the product of a common agreement. Nevertheless they do represent two polar views which entail quite different accounts of language.

The strength of the conventionalist view is that it seems to accurately reflect the sheer variety of words that can be used to describe something, as well as the mutability of language over time. Its weakness is that it suggests that word use is so radically situational, and language thus so malleable, it can be made to do anything at will.

By contrast the strength of the similarity theory is that it seems to reflect accurately the sense we have, that particular words are entirely appropriate to describe particular things. They have a force in themselves which brings those things alive. Its weakness is the opposite of the conventionalist theory's strength, in that it does little justice to our sense that words can mean different things at different times and in different situations. It seems to rule out of court what Saussure called the arbitrariness of the sign.

On the basis of these weaknesses Plato does not finally accept either theory. Gadamer, however, finds it significant that each theory seems to express something true about the language-reality relation, and that the strengths and weaknesses of one, balance out the strengths and weaknesses of the other. He also notes that both assume the object (i.e.reality) comes first, in the sense that it is presumed to be known already, and language is placed in a secondary role, as though the only issue was how it gets superadded to reality. In one theory language is agreed upon through daily practice, in the other it is selected by users on the basis of its aptness for the situation; but 'daily practice' and 'the situation' are thereby assumed to be in play before language gets started. In both theories language starts too late (1989:406). Because of this, he sees Plato as the precursor of modern instrumentalist approaches to language.

Against this, Gadamer of course points out that we never come across reality in a wordless state, but always find language right there with reality. If we change the misleading, basic assumption, of Plato's Cratylus, and substitute the idea that there is a unity between language and reality, then the reason why we find elements of truth in both theories, becomes more apparent. That is to say, language cannot be too arbitrarily changed if we are to have any clear sense of common reality.On the other hand, words, in showing their appropriateness for reality, cannot be seen to merely copy the things they refer to, in that they gain their meaning in the ongoing process of dialogue (5).

Gadamer freely admits that it is difficult to specify exactly what the relationship is between words and what they refer to, and even suggests the value of using a religious analogy. He claims that the relationship between elements in the Holy Trinity mirrors the way language discloses the being of things (1989:421). As the purpose of Christ's life was to reveal the nature of God, so language has no other task than to reveal the nature of things. Like Christ and God, language and reality are not identical, but they are inseparable. One cannot be known without the other.

James Hans (1978:18) makes the point that such a metaphor depends for its effectiveness on its audience being a Christian one, and in shifting from philosophical to theological discourse, Gadamer is obscuring rather than clarifying the relationship. Gadamer himself seems aware of this problem, when he asks "whether we are not here using the unintelligible to explain the unintelligible". However, it seems to me what he is ultimately saying, is that both relationships are fundamentally mysterious, and that's just the way it is. What he is trying to do is describe, through a certain kind of metaphor, what is virtually undescribable. It is ultimately undescribable because we cannot accurately objectify the very medium which allows objects to be for us in the first place.

Nevertheless, we can amplify things a little by looking at the the basis on which language and reality always happen together; why both are mutually dependent, and why neither one can take precedence over the other. Moreover, we can look look at the same relationship from different ends. First, at how Gadamer conceives the essential nature of language to be one of 'world disclosure'. Secondly, how he conceives the world as only and always, disclosing itself through language.

Language as 'world-disclosure'

Gadamer is certainly not the first to point to the way language shapes the way things are for us. He acknowledges the importance of the work of the nineteenth century writer, Wilhelm von Humboldt, as being among the first to reveal how different languages form the different cultural experiences we have of the world. In short, he described the importance of what is now commonly termed - a world-view. Von Humboldt nevertheless though, worked on the basis of the same logical dichotomy existing between language and the world, that Gadamer regards as mistaken. Such an assumption is mistaken, not only because it suggests that language is an instrument at our disposal, but because it gives rise to cultural relativism. The world-view is seen as one perspective on an independent world; different world-views represent different perspectives on the world, each one closed to the others, none finally better or worse than any other.

What Humboldt did was to place the particular cultural form of language in front of its worldly content, which had the effect of giving a kind of reified primacy to language over its living relation to the world. This outlook involves a spurious abstraction in that in its actual operation, language does not draw attention to itself, its structure vanishes behind what is being brought to light in it. In fact the more effectively language does its job, the less we are aware of it, because of the way it enables us to attend so thoroughly to what is being said (6). Language has no other purpose than to bring the world to light in it. Gadamer puts it like this :-

> The more language is a living operation, the less we are aware of it. Thus it follows from the self-forgetfulness of language that its real being consists in what is said in it. What is said in it constitutes the common world in which we live and to which the whole great chain of tradition reaching us from the literature of foreign languages, living as well as dead. The real being of language is that into which we are taken up when we hear it - what is said. (1976:65)

What we learn from being socialized into our world-views then, is not one, merely relative view of the world, but what the world is, as it comes into our language.

Gadamer uses the example of how we learn a new language to illustrate his point. We do not, as Humboldt suggested, discard our native language and its world-view as something that will distort the new one. If we did, not only would our first language disappear, but so also would our 'world', and we too with it. In practice we actually need it in order to appropriate the new one, for it is the source of the world for us, and thus also the source our capacity to learn new world-views. The world has an insistent presence in language that cannot be doubted, so that when we encounter a new language, we inevitably relate it to the world we already know through our native language. The process involves a recognition of the porous nature of language, and thus that world-views expand in the process appropriating new ones.

This analysis can also be seen to reaffirm, from the angle of language, the significance of the previous analyses of prejudice, application, and the fusion of horizons. Their emphasis on the projective nature of understanding is echoed here in the way language does its work.

World-disclosure as language

Language may have its real being in letting the world come to light, but the reverse is equally true, for "language is not just one of man's possessions in the world; rather on it depends the fact that man has a world at all" (1989:443). Gadamer is not trying to suggest that the existence of the (empirical) world depends on humans language-users living on the earth. Patently this is not the case; we can easily imagine the world without humans on it. But rather, when we imagine it so we automatically and inevitably do it, in language.

For Gadamer, language gives us a 'world' in a very particular sense. He contrasts the way animals inhabit their world with the way we relate to ours. Where animals are wholly immersed in their world, in that they respond to its stimulii, humans have some distance from theirs, because they can take up an attitude towards it. Animals are embedded in their environment in such a way that their behaviour can be seen as a function of it. Humans, on the other hand, because they can take up an attitude towards their world, and indeed have more than one attitude towards it, have a certain freedom from the force of their environment.

This capacity to take up an attitude towards the world rests on the nature of human language, as that which mediates the world. It enables us to be both a part of the world and yet apart from it. Gadamer (1976:59) draws on Aristotle once more to heighten this distinction. He (Aristotle), points out that animals too can communicate with each other, indicating what in their immediate world "excites their desire so they can seek it, and what injures them, so they can flee from it". However, the point about human language is that it is able to refer, not just to what is immediately present, but to things that are distant, or absent, or things that lie in the future. Indeed, human language is so variable, and permits so much freedom, that the same thing can be described in quite different ways. Human language enables the real nature of things be known to us, and in a way that is quite different to the way animals understand things :-

> Animals do not have this variability when making themselves understood to one another. This means ontologically, that they make themselves understood, but not about matters of fact, the epitome of which is the world...Whereas the call of animals induces particular behaviour in the members of the species, men's coming to a linguistic understanding with one another through the logos, reveals the existent itself .(Gadamer 1989:445)

Gadamer means that language reveals the world in its factualness. Facts are things that bear different relationships to other things, and recognizing something in its factualness means acknowledging its "independent otherness". That is, we see its separateness from us, and its relatedness to other things, rather than just automatically responding to it as an animal does. It means that a certain distance exists between the thing and the speaker, such that particular facts can be brought to the foreground of our attention, and become part of an assertion that is commonly understood.

This 'linguistic distance', which enables something to stand out in its own right, and be seen by all for what it is, also means that human language is orientated towards common understanding. It enables a common ground to appear between people, and as such is the basis of human sociality. This does not mean that language has to be purposefully willed in this fashion, it is not a tool that we can choose, or not, to achieve common understanding. Rather, common understanding, in the human sense, happens because the nature of language lets things stand out in front of people :

> ..human language must be thought of as a special and unique life-process since, in linguistic communication, "world" is disclosed. Reaching an understanding in language places a subject matter before those communicating like a disputed object set between them....All kinds of human community are kinds of linguistic community: even more, they form language. For language is by nature the language of conversation; it fully realizes itself only in the process of coming to an understanding. That is why it is not a mere means in that process. (Gadamer1989:446)

Gadamer describes this quality of language as its I-lessness. By this he means that a common sense of the world always exists through language before any particular use is made of it by a human subject. Language thus has its real being in linking the I and the Thou to a common world.

It can be illustrated by comparing natural language with artificial languages such as mathematical, or computer languages. These are introduced specifically as tools of communication, and actually presuppose natural language. That is, the consensus about what things mean in an artificial language, is reached by the prior agreement of its creators, in natural language. In a natural language, as opposed to an artificial one, we do not first decide to agree what the elements in it mean, but always already find ourselves sharing the common ground disclosed by it. This does not mean that consensus is always available, clearly disagreements are very much part and parcel of natural language, but it does mean that when disagreements occur, they happen within the shared remit of a common linguistic world. Feminist sociologists, for example, draw attention to the way patriarchal structures pervade modern society, to the detriment of women. However, what they sometimes overlook is the fact that our capacity to discern such inequality, and display its invalidity, actually depends upon the prior, shared recognition in our society, that such a pattern should be thought illegitimate. To put it in

Gadamerian terms, the issue is able to appear before us as an issue, not in spite of, but because of the way our society's 'world' is structured. We recognize the illegitimacy of this state of affairs, because it contravenes our 'natural' sense that people should be able to achieve their utmost without constraint. Ultimately it is dependent on a sense that the integrity of the individual is being compromised. To be sure, most societies do have a sense of how important their individual members are, but it is no coincidence that feminism has found its most fertile ground in Western societies, where individual autonomy is most highly valued.

Summary of the relevance of the language-world relation

Gadamer is claiming that language and reality always happen together, and while they are not one and the same thing, they are only really knowable to us in terms of each other. Take one away and you've lost the other. The effect of this account is to avoid the pitfalls of two positions that underpin opposed approaches in sociology. Expressed rather baldly, the first argument mistakenly assumes that language 'creates' the world. The second mistakenly assumes that the world exists independently of the way we describe it in our linguistic tradition. Each, according to Gadamer, latches on to a part of the truth, but this partiality also leads them both astray.

Gadamer's account can be summarized in terms of the way it challenges both of these positions; viz, the tendency to give priority either to language or to reality. He finds value in both arguments, but does not let one cancel out the other. Instead he insists on the mutual dependence of both :-

1. First, Gadamer challenges the relativism of any purely language centred approach in sociology that bases itself on the assumption that language 'creates' reality. Ironically this was one of the accusations levelled against him by Habermas (1988:173), when he declared :-

> An interpretive sociology that hypostatizes language as the subject of forms of life and of tradition binds itself to the idealist presumption that linguistically articulated consciousness determines the material being of life-practice.

The accusation being that sociologies which fix on language as the key to the whole of society, lose sight of the fact that other non-linguistic dimensions are equally important. They thereby fall prey to the idea that what social actors believe to be the case about society, is really the case. In effect, social actors and the linguistic descriptions that make up their tradition, are mistakenly seen to be the source and the limitation of what things can mean in that society.

However, Gadamer's case, in part, is precisely the opposite; viz, that language has no autonomy from the real world. It can have no real existence outside its primordial task of letting the world come into being for us, and it is the world that is there for us, not language. It is the world that brings language to life, and to conceive of it without the world, would effectively reduce language to being an empty shell. Language would consist of arbitrary signs that could be made to mean anything at all by their users.

When Gadamer states that things have their being in language, he means it fairly literally. A tree, for example, *is*, ie. it gains its factual status as a tree, by virtue of there being a language in which there is a verb to be through which it can have its being. If there were no such verb the tree in an important sense would cease 'to be'. Whatever it was it would have lost its quality of being a tree. In other words, whatever can be, will always have its being for us in language.However, because the 'real' is always mediated through the 'linguistic' it does mean that there is no real world with which language is engaged. Gadamer expressly claims that language is what enables us to know the world, and the real one at that.It is language that allows things to be understood in their independence from us, as well in there relatedness to us and to other things. In effect language offers us a kind of objectivity towards things, although this is not to be confused with the objectivity of science :-

> The distance and factualness of language, of course, are also genuine achievemnts and do not just happen automatically. We know how putting an experience into words helps us to cope with it. It is as if its threatening, even annihilating, immediacy is pushed into the background, brought into proportion, made communicable, and hence dealt with. Such coping with experience, however, is obviously different from the way science works on it, objectivizing it and making it available for whatever purposes it likes. (Gadamer 1989:453)

In ordinary language the objectivizing attitude of science is not possible, because the 'objectivity' of ordinary language includes us as part of what is there. What this other kind of 'objectivity' allows us to do is to put things, including our experience, into perspective.

This is not an arbitrary affair, in that we cannot wilfully make the world what we want it to be, it is much more like getting things into a perspective that shows them to be what they are. In fact it is language that unfolds the structure of things, but just so - *the structure of things* - not the structure of language. Gadamer's claims are clearly quite different from those presented by some of the more fashionable post-structuralist and post-modernist authors (7). He does not see language as a self-referring system in which the world is but an internal creation of language. Language may unfold the nature of things but in doing this it is tempered by the things themselves, which have a weight that language must recognize if it is to avoid mere hyperbole. From the side of language, unfolding the structure of things consists :-

> ..in not interfering arbitrarily - latching onto this or that ready-made notion as it strikes one - with the immanent necessity of the thought. Certainly the thing does not go its own course without our thinking being involved, but thinking means unfolding what consistently follows from the subject matter itself. It is part of this process to supress ideas "that tend to insinuate themselves", and to insist on the logic of the thought. Since the Greeks we have called this dialectic. (Gadamer 1989:464)

Hence Gadamer is claiming that however important the role of language is in shaping the real world for us, the process is not one sided. Language is not something that arbitrarily creates, or indeed restricts what the real world can be for us. Language, he believes, is capable of expressing whatever we are capable of understanding; it cannot be constrained by apriori ideological limits. If our understanding is limited, which in any actual situation it always is, this is not because of a weakness in language itself, or because language has been colonized by outside forces, but because understanding is the product of the entirely finite, and ultimately historical nature of our existence.

However while language does not go its own sweet way without the world, nor does language merely reflect reality, in the sense of mirroring a given state of affairs. It has an important role in constituting that state of affairs too, it brings certain possibilities to light. Gadamer thus brings the opposite case to bear, making a second challenge, this time against the orthodox social scientific view.

2. This side of Gadamer's dialectical argument about the language-world relation entails a challenge to the objectivistic assumption that the empirical world exists separately from the language we use to describe it. Social data is often treated in a quasi-scientific fashion as existing in-itself. On this account language gains its meaning from the things it is used to designate, be they physical objects or non-physical states of affairs. By contrast Gadamer's case is that things are the way they are described in particular linguistic communities. Things don't exist first for those communuties and then get allocated names, rather, it is through language that they come into being. It is in their linguistic descriptions that things have their meaning, and are made manifest to a

community. Shouting abusive words and shaking one's fist in our culture, is not a sign of anger, it is anger made manifest. The implication of this for sociology is that if you reduce words and actions to being an expression, or function, of some other extra-linguistic parameter, you nullify the essence of what is social for that society. The way something is described by a society, is absolutely constitutive of what it is for that society, and as such these descriptions must play a primary, not a secondary role, in any adequate sociological account.

To say that things have their being in language while giving due weight to the things themselves, does not mean that language describes them by flatly reproducing given states of affairs. Rather, language itself has a restless, open-ended quality, one that endlessly reaches out to meet what needs to be thought and said in a changing world. Indeed Gadamer describes language not only as being the medium of our experience of the world, but also as having a speculative structure in its own right (Gadamer 1989:456ff). By this he means that when language is being used to say something, even something apparently unproblematic about the empirical world, it is always pregnant with implied meaning. There is a backwash of implied meaning that always comes alongside and invites a speculative extension to what was first said. What is unsaid, as it were accompanies what is said, so that fixed, final statements, are anathema to the way living language actually works.

Take for example the way 'gendered language' features in everyday life. The use of the term - man - to refer to both the male and the female of the human species is sometimes justified on the grounds, that in practice it has long been accepted as an accurate and neutral statement. Thus, while it may refer in particular circumstances to just males, in other circumstances it just as accurately refers to the whole of the species. Its meaning depends upon the situation in which it is used. However, while Gadamer's account does emphasise that language is situational, in the sense that meaning depends upon the reality of our tradition, he reminds us that language always carries within it a speculative aspect too. What is unsaid, but nevertheless present in the use of the term - man - to describe both sexes, is the implication that the male is definitive of the species as such. This implicit loading is for the most part invisible, but does become apparent if we try to use the word - woman - in a similar way to refer to both the female and the male of the species (8). The speculative nature of language allows the implications of what is in being to become apparent. It is the task of hermeneutics to be aware of the creative negativity that is intrinsic to language, and thus to be open to the unstoppable possibilities of meaning.

We tend to think that if we describe something as being speculative, it means that it is vague or probably untrue. But when Gadamer describes language as having a speculative structure he is deliberately calling into question this habit of thought. Language, he believes is not occasionally speculative, but always so, and it is those who seek to eliminate this quality by making final, definitive statements, that are the ones who actually distort the truth. Anyone who has attended a formal meeeting and then read the minutes of what went on, will know how little they reflect the meaning of what was said. This happens not because of any deliberate intention to falsify things, indeed writers of minutes usually strive valiantly to produce what they see as absolutely objective accounts. The disparity between the two arises because 'the unsaid' has been excised from the minutes in an effort to report the pure sense of statements. If you have not attended the meeting but are nevertheless familiar with the issues and the people involved, you may be able to understand the minutes by mentally supplying 'the unsaid' yourself. But without 'the unsaid' being available at all to buoy up understanding, the minutes would be virtually incomprehensible; a disembodied account, even though perhaps literally an accurate one.

Our ability to understand meaning therefore depends in a strong sense on the speculative nature of language, in that the meaning of what is said rests crucially on what is not said but nevertheless implied. What is unsaid gives a point or a direction to what has been said, in that it allows the possibilities of meaning in what has been said, to become apparent. Things said and things unsaid are thus the unity that makes meaning happen. Gadamer sees poetry as providing the most highly developed form of speculative language, but it is not exceptional for in real, everyday speech the same thing applies :-

> To say what one means, ... to make oneself understood - means to hold what is said together with an infinity of what is not said in one unified meaning and to ensure that it is understood in this way. Someone who speaks in this way may well use only the most ordinary and common words and still be able to express what is unsaid and is to be said. (Gadamer 1989:469)

For Gadamer then, social reality is to be seen in a way that is both thoroughly linguistic and non-static.

This powerfully open-ended view of language and reality carried within it many features that Habermas was to find laudable, but it was also the source of much of his critical concern. One cannot easily hold to such a view and believe that large numbers of people live in a state of ideological deception.

Notes
1. Another author who repeatedly draws out the implications of the internal connectedness of language and action is Charles Taylor. See especially the essays 'Interpretation And The Sciences Of Man',

'Language And Human Nature', and 'Theories Of Meaning', in volumes one and two of Taylor (1985).

2. Heidegger uses the term - apophantic - in *Being and Time*, though though Gadamer does not use it as such, in *Truth and Method*. Nevertheless he does clearly imply it in his opposition to all instrumental views of language, and in the way he refers to the emergence of the 'thing at issue' in a text. Smith (1979:315-321) has provided an excellent discussion of it in relation to Gadamer and Heidegger.

3. I am thinking primarily of those sociologies that derive from Saussurean linguistics, but the ethnomethodological habit of focusing on the mechanics of meaning production, detached from its wider, lived significance, is another example.

4. In fact Gadamer notes that the conscious awareness of language as such, was not present in the earliest Greek philosophy. There it was so much the medium of reality that it could not be conceived of as an object of discussion (1989:403-404).

5. I am conscious that my account does only small justice to the complexity of Gadamer's argument at this point, (let alone Plato), and can only recommend that the reader goes to the source for a fuller picture of what is at stake. The same also applies subsequently to the work of Humboldt.

6. Gadamer's essay 'Man and Language' in *Philosophical Hermeneutics* (1976), provides an amplification of many of the points made in *Truth and Method* (1989), Part 3, Section 3A, p438ff.

7. See some of the works of the French theorist Jean Baudrillard, for example, 'The Reality Gulf' in *The Guardian* newspaper of 11 January 1991, and the extensive critique in Norris (1992)

6 Introductory issues: Popper, Adorno and the concept of totality

Introduction to the texts involved

The essence of the debate is to be found in four main essays, two of them are critiques of Gadamer's hermeneutics by Habermas, the other two are responses and counter critiques by Gadamer. In order of original chronological succession, though not English publication, they are

(a) Habermas's *'On the Logic of the Social Sciences'* 1967, (English translation in Habermas 1988),

(b) Gadamer's 'Rhetoric, Hermeneutics, and the Critique of Ideology: Metacritical Comments on Truth and Method 1967, (English translation in Mueller-Vollmer ed. 1985)',

(c) Habermas's 'The Hermeneutic Claim to Universality' 1970, (English translation in Bleicher 1980) and

(d) Gadamer's 'Reply To My Critics' 1971, (English translation in Ormiston & Schrift 1990)(1).

For the most part I shall be referring to the English translations of these four key essays, but there are a number of other texts written by Habermas and Gadamer which amplify and extend the issues raised in the debate. Adorno et al's (1976) collection *The Positivist Dispute in German Sociology*, contains essays from the Popper-Adorno debate dating from the early 1960's, including two by Habermas in which he uses 'Gadamerian ideas' albeit critically, in broad support of Adorno. Habermas's book *Knowledge and Human Interests* (1972) can be seen as an attempt to place hermeneutics in an important, but subordinate position, within a revised Critical Theory. A summary of his case at this point can be found in the appendix to this book, and in a slightly different form in the earlier essay 'Knowledge and Interests' (Habermas 1966). A later and somewhat similar discussion of Gadamer is to be found in the essay 'Interpretive Social Science vs. Hermeneuticism' (Haan et al 1983). In this though, hermeneutics is contrasted with what Habermas sees as the more objective knowledge produced by the developmental psychology of Lawrence Kohlberg. Kohlberg's work, he claims, is both interpretively and scientifically adequate. Habermas also provides a critical discussion of Gadamer's concept of understanding in volume one of The Theory of Communicative Action (p133-136). In this he asks whether, built into Gadamer's account of how we understand a text, is too much of an uncritical assumption that we are in agreement with what it says.

From Gadamer's side, the essay 'The Universality of The Hermeneutic Problem' (Gadamer 1976), preceded the debate proper, appearing first in German in 1966, but partly can be seen as that to which Habermas responded in an essay that was part of the debate, 'The Hermeneutic Claim To Universality', (b) above. In it Gadamer argues for the universal significance of hermeneutics based on the importance it attaches to language. Because language is universal, in the sense that it mediates both us and the world, all knowledge, not just the human or social sciences, necessarily contains an interpretive dimension. In an essay entitled 'Hermeneutics and Social Science', Gadamer (1975) reaffirms the significance of hermeneutics for the social sciences in the light of his debate with Habermas, particularly as regards the central importance of the moral dimension. He has on several occasions refuted Habermas's accusation, that with its emphasis on the importance of tradition, his work is politically conservative. This is a theme in his introduction to 'The Problem Of Historical Consciousness' (Rabinow & Sullivan eds. 1979), as well as in Supplement 2: 'To What Extent Does Language Preform Thought' and the 'Afterword' in the 1989 revised second edition of Truth And Method.

Preliminary issues: The Popper-Adorno controversy

Although Gadamer's *Wahrheit und Methode* was first published in 1960 Habermas's response to it did not appear until 1967, as part of a long journal article which explored his then current concern to establish the proper logic of the social sciences. The task he set himself was to review relevant literature as it pertained to the way positivistic assumptions distorted sociological analysis. At that time the methodology of the social sciences was still very much dominated by the possibility of being part of a wider 'unified science', based on the model of the natural sciences (2).

The main thrust of *The Logic Of The Social Sciences* can be seen as a development of themes that surfaced a few years earlier in the context of the 'positivist dispute' between Popper and Adorno, where Habermas in support of Adorno set out to show the necessity of grounding the social sciences in a dialectical view of the social-historical totality (Adorno et al 1976) (3). Moreover, I believe that what rather surprisingly comes to light in this positivist dispute, is how much common ground is shared by hermeneutics and Critical Theory, and that this is apparent not only when Habermas joins the dispute, but is there in Adorno's ideas too.

The so called Positivist Dispute In German Sociology is something of a misnomer as none of the protagonists were sociologists, and all disclaimed any connection with positivism. In fact to make the dispute more curious still, both parties were in agreement that positivism should be rejected, what they both found radically disagreeable was the reasons the other party had for that rejection. Popper was a philosopher with a strong background in science, perhaps most well known at the time for two books: *The Open Society And Its Enemies* and *The Poverty Of Historicism*, in which he opposed the positivistic misuse of history, particularly the way, as he saw it, Marx had falsely claimed scientific status for his account of the direction of the historical process. A once only process, like history, could never be subject to the rigours of scientific testing, and to claim such was at best an error, at worst, dangerous. It provided spurious validation for the actions of those who claimed to possess such knowledge, and was thus implicitly totalitarian.

By contrast Adorno was a philosopher with a strong background in classical music, and though perhaps the least Marxist of the Frankfurt School thinkers, shared their view that the 'open societies' of the West had brought off a huge illusion. What appeared to be the openness of things in the West, in fact concealed their invert, namely insidiously high levels of social control. The principles of objectification, calculation, and prediction, which were the stuff of scientific thought, pervaded Western reason generally, with the result that a kind of telos of domination was now built into the very fabric of our thought and action. Through the instrumental application of these concepts we had learnt to conquer nature, ourselves, and each other, and now passively inhabited a 'wholly administered world'. His views were naturally quite at odds with Poppers' over the role science had played in human progress. Where Adorno saw science as virtually equivalent to domination, Popper regarded scientific method as an open process of critique and refutation, providing almost the prototype for a democratic society. All they apparently shared in common was a distaste for the 'scientism' in Marx.

In style too they differed, Popper's initial contribution to the dispute was written in a brisk propositional way, offering some twenty seven theses on the nature of (social) science. Such an approach invited a head-on challenge, perhaps thesis by thesis, but Adorno responded in his own unique and densely convoluted style, sometimes concurring with Popper only to use this apparent agreement as a springboard to dialectically elaborate his own ideas. What seemed strange was that two such distinctive, robust, and generally antagonistic authors, should generate so little obvious opposition.

Certainly it took subsequent papers by Habermas (from Adorno's side), and Hans Albert (from Popper's), to really clarify the issues. Nevertheless though the initial debate is somewhat obscure, it is instructive, and it is surprising that only a relatively small amount of commentary has been provoked by it in English, (Frisby 1972, Frisby 1974, Wilson 1977, Ray 1979, How 1980a, Holub 1991) (4).

Popper's argument broadly consisted of a critique of that version of positivism which assumes that science moves inductively from the careful collection of objective data to the gleaning of scientific laws from that data. Such a view is mistaken, he claims, because the scientist's observation of data is never disinterested but always "problem centred". The scientist does not start from a position of pure perception, but from an already existing problem. Indeed an observation, argues Popper, only becomes significant if it contradicts our expectations, if there is a disjunction between our knowledge and the supposed facts. In almost Gadamerian fashion he declares that if it surprises us, if it shows us something is not quite in order with our knowledge our theories and our expectations, only then, when it creates a problem for us, will it become a starting point for scientific work (fifth and sixth thesis).

As well as rejecting the naive positivist idea that knowledge starts from the direct observation of data, Popper also rejects the old positivist myth that objectivity depends upon the scientist's own value-freedom. Scientists neither can, nor do, eliminate subjective presuppositions, they are partisan members of society like the rest of us, and must be highly motivated to be effective as scientists. Furthermore, in saying this Popper calls up the familiar sociological point that objectivity and value-freedom are themselves social values, and it thus would be paradoxical to ask for them to be removed as a condition for (scientific) knowledge (fourteenth thesis). Objectivity in science springs from the critical tradition in which actual scientists work, it is through an ongoing process of mutual criticism and competition between scientists, that objectivity is established. If scientific objectivity is to be enhanced, then what must be cultivated are the cultural conditions, including the political conditions, which allow it to flourish, (twelfth and thirteenth thesis).

In arguing thus, Popper seemed to side-step one of the standard features of the Frankfurt School critique of positivism, which was that modern (social) science reifies empirical facts, as a result the status quo is given an undeserved fixity, and thereby a subtle and undeserved justification. How things are becomes unwittingly transformed into how things ought to be. In removing objectivity from being the neutral observation of pure facts or data, Popper undermines the criticism that science is morally or politically conservative. In fact scientific method as described by him, seems to have some of those negative, critical, and fallibilistic qualities that characterizes the knowledge produced by Critical Theory, or possibly hermeneutics. Popper believes that true scientific method involves, not the production of positive verified theories, but the falsification of hypotheses. The scientist starts from problems he or she perceives in the knowledge we have of the world, and proposes solutions which must be put into a testable or falsifiable form. If the solution is falsified another is proposed and so on, the point being that the process does not culminate in proven laws, but in temporary solutions to problems, which in their turn will be subject to critical scrutiny.

On this basis, and given his oppositon to the use of scientific claims in inappropriate areas, i.e. scientism, one might wonder why Adorno and Habermas still included Popper's ideas within their pejorative account of positivism. The issues are complex and worthy of more attention than I shall give them here. I am really only concerned with those that were drawn up into the Gadamer-Habermas debate.

Popper clearly saw his 'critical rationalism' applying to both the natural and the social sciences, and believed that social science could, and had, produced theories based on falsifiability. By contrast Adorno pointed up the dubious implications of treating the 'object' of sociology, i.e. society, as though it were part of the same order as nature. He denied that he had in mind the traditional distinction between the *geisteswissenschaften* and the natural sciences, although when Habermas defended and amplified his postion in a subsequent paper, the similarities between Critical Theory and Gadamerian hermeneutics, at least, became apparent. What Adorno did have in mind was the dubious way Popper's assumptions about science's progressive methodology, distorted matters when applied in sociology. Social reality he argued, was altogether more messy than science could acknowledge, and it stood in opposition to the "the clean systematic unity of assembled (scientific) statements". Moreover :-

> the cognitive ideal of the consistent, preferably simple, mathematically elegant explanation falls down where reality itself, society, is neither consistent, nor simple, nor neutrally left to the discretion of categorial formulation. (Adorno et al 1975:106)

He is objecting to the way science assumes, in the concepts it uses, that reality is consistent, well ordered, and neutrally available to be classified according to the categories the scientist uses. This leaves the task of the scientist to gradually uncover the way the orderilness of things is organised. Such an attitude may serve the interests of the natural sciences well, (insofar as they are concernd with prediction and control), but when society is the object under investigation it has the effect of concealing reality. If social reality itself is full of contradictions, a methodology that assumes non-contradiction will have the effect of conjuring away the most essential features of that reality. Instead of providing the objective picture of society it claims, scientific method will present a partial picture in which deep lying contradictions are rendered invisible. What is basically wrong with Popper's methodology is that because it is 'problem-centred', it is localized and fails to grasp the significance of the totality.

The concept of totality

In a manner that seems to echo some of Gadamer's themes Adorno highlights the importance of anticipating the meaning of the whole. For Gadamer, trying to understand a text involves projecting or anticipating an overall meaning, and revising it in the light of one's understanding of the particular parts of the text. There can be no adequate understanding of the text unless this hermeneutically-circular process is given its due, because the parts only make sense in terms of the whole, and the whole in terms of the parts. And as we saw previously, Gadamer expands this idea to encompass the understanding of historical tradition generally. In a similar way Adorno points out that "without the anticipation of that structural moment of the whole....no individual observation would find its relative place" (p107).

It could be argued that Adorno and Gadamer put 'the concept of totality' or the 'anticipation of completeness' to very different uses, and therefore to draw a parallel between them is misleading. Certainly Adorno is intent on using the concept of totality in a negative, critical way, to reveal the tensions and the general contradictoriness inherent in industrial-capitalist societies. This is something he feels cannot be done through Popper's approach, where attention must be focused on singular observable problems which blocks an understanding of how they are generated within a contradictory totality. Adorno's (Marxist) political intent is clear. By contrast Gadamer does not make much of 'the anticipation of completeness', or at least he discusses it within wider concerns such as the projective nature of understanding (1989:268,293-94). In this context he is concerned to demonstrate that being open to the meaning of the whole is a kind of regulative principle that prevents arbitrary judgements about particular parts of a text from taking root. Gadamer has also been subject to quasi-political criticism, not just from Habermas, but more recently from deconstructionist critics who believe that the hermeneutic approach to texts is quietistic. It involves, they claim, too great a faith that the text has a consistent unity of meaning, and this leads to a focus that overlooks the tensions, contradictions, reversals, and ruptures, that are all part of a text's meaning (Warnke 1987: 82-91, de Man 1971, Michelfelder & Palmer eds 1989). However to leave them on this basis, with Adorno as the radical and Gadamer as the conservative, is to oversimplify them both and misunderstand what they share in common.

At one level both are arguing that a dialectical relationship exists between part and whole, but it goes further than that. Neither Adorno nor Gadamer are just describing a dialectical methodology that should be applied to a text or to a society, for what they describe includes the user of the methodology too. What both are trying to bring to the fore is an element that eludes positivistic thinking because it is not an object and therefore is non-observable. It is that latent totality or unity towards which all understanding leans. For something to become intelligible it must take its place within a field of meaning even though that field cannot be directly apprehended. Hence when Adorno talks of the societal totality he is using a so called non-identical concept, i.e. one that is not identical with its object, with what makes it up; no more than when Gadamer is talking about historical tradition he is referring merely to what has happened in the past. Historical tradition does not have a substantive, thing-like existence but is that active, ongoing fusion of temporal horizons that we are. The bias in positivistic thought toward accepting only what is objectifiable naturally finds anathema any idea of an invisible, mutable horizon which plays a constitutive role in social reality.

Of course it might still be argued that Adorno's concept of totality is altogether more alert to the contradictions of capitalist society, between its claims and its reality, than is Gadamer's more unified view of the historical tradition. But Gadamer refers to the 'anticipation of completeness', not to an apriori belief that non-contradiction actually exists. Indeed, from Gadamer's point of view it can be argued that the very capacity to recognize contradiction presupposes a field in which unity is conceivable. Surely Adorno's (1975:115) recognition of the mismatch between the claims to equality and freedom made by liberal society, and the actual inequality of power that determines the relations between people, anticipates a possible resolution. It might also be argued that Adorno's claim to dialectically grasp the real nature of the totality by challenging scoiety's pretensions with what actually is the case, has a rather all knowing, absolute, quality about it. Whereas Gadamer would never accept that knowledge of what is the case, is anything other that part of a mutable horizon. His approach is certainly dialectical, but he expresses it much more modestly than Adorno. In a recent essay he reminds us that the speculative nature of thought and language, that hidden unity of the said and the unsaid, "..precedes any subsequent dialectical sharpening of a proposition to the point of contradiction and its supercession in a new proposition", (Michelfelder & Palmer 1989:111).

However, whatever their differences may be, their common ground is of greater significance for this project, in that it provides a powerful affirmation for a non-positivistic view of the social realm. Like Gadamer, Adorno does not provide a method to underpin the logic of the social sciences, but recommends in hermeneutic fashion, that the researcher attends to the object itself.

Although Popper was always critical of positivism, and even felt he had played a decisive part in undermining its credibility, in Frankfurt School terms he remained within its remit. Clearly the idea of a societal totality or a historical tradition that encompassed both subject and object, was not something that could be put into a falsifiable form. It could not be externalized and tested against the facts, as the facts themselves were already structured and made meaningful by that horizon. There was no Archimedean point outside the horizon from which a scientific test could be undertaken. For Popper this meant that the concept of totality was quite meaningless, and he sought to demonstrate it by paraphrasing what he saw as the empty pretentiousness of Adorno's language :-

ADORNO'S DEFINITION	POPPER'S PARAPHRASE
Societal totality does not lead a life over and above that which it unites and of which it, in its turn, is composed.	Society consists of social relationships.
It produces and reproduces itself through its individual moments.	The various social relationships somehow produce society.

(Adorno et al 1975:297)

It is clear from this is that Popper was intent on finding no content in Adorno's case. The language of the paraphrase is flat and deflationary, robbing the original of both its dialectical style and ambition. He had already attacked the concept of totality in The Poverty Of Historicism (p76-97), where he distinguished between two sorts of totality. There was first, a legitimate sort studied by gestalt psychology, which made a thing "appear an organised structure rather than a mere heap". But secondly, there was an illegitimate sort, where it was claimed that one could know "all the properties or aspects of a thing.. (and)..all the relations holding between the constituent parts", Marx and Mannheim were the villains of the piece. The first was legitimate because although it denoted a whole field it could still become the object of scientific study. Even for example in the study of music, one can select and examine objectively the contribution pitch makes to an overall melody. What he rejected was the possibility of knowing all the parts and relations between them that made up the whole of the societal totality. He equated the impossibility of knowing this, with the political impossibility of controlling all societal relationships. In order to know one must control, and as one applied new controls so new relations would emerge, and the social scientist would be caught manically trying to control the proliferation of ever new elements. Those that advocated the use of such a concept were thereby tarred with both methodological and political totalitarianism. Of course in arguing thus Popper indirectly confirmed his allegiance to two tenets of the Frankfurt School account of positivism; a. that science proceeds on the basis of instrumental reason, seeking to control what it necessarily has objectified, and b. that 'knowing' is equated by Popper with scientific 'knowing'.

There had been a Frankfurt School reply to this in Marcuse's (1959) essay 'Karl Popper And The Problem Of Historical Laws'. In this he pointed out that the totality was not an object made up of other objects, all of which had to be scientifically known. Indeed, strictly speaking it was not part of the object domain at all. It referred rather to an arena that encompassed both subject and object, and because there was no position outside it the to and fro of dialectical thought was needed to bring it to understanding. He accepted Popper's point that selecting particular things to analyse was important, but this did not, as Popper claimed, rule out the concept of totality. In fact to understand the totality one had to locate those things that were most basic to it (Marcuse 1972:191-208).

What was apparent in both these exchanges was that directly describing the differences between analytical and dialectical thought, was extremely difficult. The language of one was not compatible with the other, with the result that in using one to critique the other, there was an inevitable reduction and distortion of it. Totality did not, and could not, mean the same to Popper as it did to Adorno. This is clearly displayed in Popper's 'translation', where he aimed to show the triviality of Adorno's ideas but unwittingly referred to the trivial content of his own translation, (How 1981). Adorno, although accused at the time of using avoidance tactics, perhaps wisely did not attempt to uncouple their differences, developing his own account from some of Popper's starting points. It took Habermas's subsequent essay 'Analytical Theory Of Science And Dialectics' in which he tacitly drew on Gadamerian ideas to clarify the issues.

Habermas' hermeneutic defence of Adorno

Adorno's objection to Popper is that 'the problems' which are the starting point of his approach, are isolated from the totality. They are conceived in a quasi-scientific way as problems to be solved technically. They bring to mind the idea of an individual (social) scientist, as it were, coming across a problem one day. Furthermore, these problems are conceived essentially as intellectual problems, to do with breaks in the normally good order of our knowledge. Working at the level of the problem, necessarily means that the constitution of the problem through the contradictory nature of the totality, is lost from view.

This loss of view of the totality is brought about by the double abstraction of the observer and the problem, from it. What is forgotten is the thoroughgoing embeddedness of both the observer and the problem in the wider social-historical totality. Habermas brings out the implications of Adorno's case in a much more discursive way than Adorno himself. He outlines what he sees as the differences between the concept of totality, and the positivistic sociological view of a (total) social system, a la Talcott Parsons (Adorno et al 1976:132-144).

The diffferences he described were fourfold (a) 'the relation of theory to its object', (b) 'the relation of theory to experience', (c) 'the relation of theory to history' and (d) 'the relation of theory to practice'. What is interesting in the light of his subsequent critique of hermeneutics, is that under these headings he incorporated broadly Gadamerian ideas into his critique of the positivist view of totality.

The relation of theory to object, he argued, in social science should not be one of externality. That is, social sciences must avoid imposing from the outside the kind of formal, scientific concepts that permit only the production of testable law-like hypotheses, as this distorts the nature of social reality. To be adequate to their task of gaining purchase on social reality, the social sciences should proceed dialectically, with concepts that measure up meaningfully to the social object. Such concepts are necessarily encountered only in a "natural hermeneutics of the social life-world", (1976:134). Indeed Habermas warns against any "empiricist immediacy" that tries to break out of the hermeneutic circle. Similarly with both the relationship of theory to experience, and of theory to history, he adapts the Gadamerian insight that we belong to them in a way that precedes our judgements, in support of his own dialectical theory. He then uses these insights to challenge the spurious universality claimed by the concepts of systems theory.

With regard to the relationship of theory to experience he points out that 'analytical-empirical' (natural scientific) modes of procedure are highly constraining in terms of what kind of experience they find acceptable. They will only tolerate :-

> controlled observation of physical behaviour, which is set up in an isolated field under reproducible conditions by subjects interchangeable at will.. (Adorno et al 1976:135)

Any experience we have that falls outside these parameters cannot become the basis on which scientific statements can rest. But if the *social* scientist is to adequately marry up the concepts he uses with the object being investigated, he must draw on kinds of experience that fall outside this highly restricted framework. To make any sense of a social phenomenon we have to look to "the fund of pre-scientifically accumulated experience" as the fundamental benchmark. Indeed, so important does Habermas regard this prior experience of society in establishing an adequate understanding, that he claims even a dialectical theory cannot ultimately contradict it without becoming incoherent (5).

Similarly with the relation of theory to history, he brings hermeneutical elements to bear against Popper's view that there can be no objective laws of history. Habermas does not claim that with the criteria Popper uses, his argument is wrong; to the contrary, there can indeed be no *scientific* laws of history. But the criteria Popper employs are those of natural science, which necessarily restricts what can be accepted as valid knowledge. Popper's claim ultimately, is that to establish a scientific law we need to test hypotheses under controlled, limiting conditions. Historians do not have access to such conditions because the meaning of the phenomena they study are by definition unique. The conditions that led to the French revolution are precisely the conditions which constituted that revolution and no other. Habermas's claim about dialectical laws however, is not that there are historical or anthropological constants by which we could predict the future. Rather, he claims in a somewhat Gadamerian (and frankly elusive) fashion, that history is a once-only process, the laws of which refer to the fundamental relations that determine the meaning of a social life-world or an epoch These laws are dialectical, and he quotes Adorno to the effect that they are made up of "the relationship of the general to the particular in its historical concretion". He also points out that their basic categories are drawn primarily from acting individuals themselves, though Critical Theory will reveal the dependence of these understandings on the wider historical totality. Oddly enough at this point he claims that Critical Theory goes beyond hermeneutics, which measures things solely in terms of the way the actors take them to be. I say, oddly, because the main thrust of Gadamer's hermeneutics is to challenge the naivety of any kind of any version of 'autonomous consciousness'. Although Habermas seems allow to for the fact that this does not refer to all kinds of hermeneutics, he does carry the error over into his subsequent critique of Gadamer.

With regard to the relation between theory, (or science as he now calls it), and practice, Habermas introduces a complication. Instead of simply contrasting the Critical Theory view with a science/systems-theory view, and showing up the limitations of the latter, he builds in a partial acceptance of it. He argues that a rigorous empirical-scientific analysis that seeks a causal explanation of historical events, will only work retrospectively. That is, when you know the 'outcome' you can presumably trace out the causal chain that led up to it. This is a peculiar claim as his previous account suggests that human events resist the objectification necessary for causal explanation, whereas this claim suggests that the only thing wrong with causal analysis is that there are too many variables in a current situation to allow for adequate prediction of the future. This seems to be confirmed when he builds in a limited use for causal analysis, as a scientific auxilliary to rational administration. What he has in mind, I think, is that within a given, limited framework, where the parameters are fixed, for example a cost-benefit analysis of where best to build a hospital, scientific procedures are valid. However, he does point out that social systems stand within historical life-contexts, and these are outside the remit of scientific statements. Any intervention based on technical knowledge inevitably remains within the dimension of 'what is' (Sein), which is set apart from 'what ought to be' (Sollen), the point being that technical knowledge cannot inform us about what is central to the 'object' of the social sciences, namely social life-practice (praxis). Although at this point he does not draw attention to hermeneutics as the appropriate tool for grasping this idea, he does later acknowledge its capacity to uncover the immanent relationship between interpretive understanding and social action :-

> I see Gadamer's real accomplishment as his demonstration that hermeneutic understanding is necessarily related, on the transcendental level, to the articulation of an action-orienting self-understanding. (Habermas 1988:162)

In the remainder of this essay Habermas concerns himself with role of values as they appear in Popper's work. This though does not bear on his debate with Gadamer, so I will not dwell on it much here, except to note that he explicitly cites Gadamer and the hermeneutic circle at one point (Adorno et. al. 1976:112). He does this to show how values are inscribed into the very fabric of all social life, including the process of scientific testing. Popper acknowledges that science, like other activities, is based upon values, but Habermas seeks to show in line with Adorno, that the very idea of a 'value' as something one might or might not hold, is a reification of its more fundamental embeddedness in a life-context. We don't have a free choice about holding particular values, every discussion of them already presupposes a prior orientation toward them. Habermas uses Popper's analogy between the establishment of 'basic observational statements' in science, and the establishment of judgements in law, to make his point. In making a connection between the two, Habermas claims Popper has unwittingly acknowledged the importance of the hermeneutic circle even for science. One cannot apply the law unless one already knows the kinds of fact to which they should apply; but on the other hand establishing the relevant facts presupposes that one knows what the laws refer to. A similar situation exists in science Habermas believes, hence he states:-

> The inevitable circle in the application of rules is evidence of the embedding of the research process in a context which itself can no longer be explicated in an analytical-empirical manner but only hermeneutically. The postulates of strict cognition naturally conceal a non-explicated pre-understanding which, in fact, they presuppose;.. (Adorno et. al. 1976:152-3)

Scientific research is a social institution made up of scientists who communicate with one another. Science may, as Popper claims, be based specifically on the value of falsification which appears to mark it off from other spheres, but it necessarily contains presuppositions rooted in a hermeneutic dimension. Science proceeds on the basis of a taken-for-granted core of normative understanding which has been established by the scientific community. It is therefore a consensus established inter-subjectively, and not the result of controlled observation. Indeed science, like any other social activity, cannot proceed unless certain 'basic statements' are accepted automatically. One cannot render every 'basic statement' problematic without slipping into an infinite regression, the result of which would be that communication would break down. In much the same way as this, there is in everyday life a necessary reliance on a pre-structured core of understanding as the ground for all our interpretations (6).

It is clear that even before his debate with Gadamer, whether he acknowledged it or not, Habermas shared much common ground with him. This was not really apparent in his first critique, for though he claimed aspects of

Gadamer's work to be valuable, his ambition was only to appropriate those parts that suited his needs, and reject to those that did not. This trawling approach to ideas, I believe lead to a kind of lopsidedness in his judgement as to just how comprehensive Gadamer's case was, and ironically to just how deeply immersed he was in it. More is the pity, as Sica (1988:86)) has pointed out, that some commentators have taken Habermas's first word to be the best and last word on the matter.

Notes

1. *'Zur Logik der Sozialwissenschaften'* appeared in German in 1967, there are two English translations. The first is a partial one, 'A Review Of Gadamer's Truth And Method', in Dallmayr & McCarthy (1977). The second, Habermas (1988), is the full translation.

2. It could be argued that the challenge mounted against the naivety of trying to mimic the natural sciences has been fairly successful. One can point to some important reconceptualizations of subject matter since the mid-1960s, not only in sociology, but psychology, human geography, and history writing too. However it is less clear whether the full implications of this challenge has been taken on board.

3. The Popper-Adorno debate originated at a conference held by the German Sociological Association in 1961. Some confusion can arise here as the two papers that commenced the debate were entitled: 'The Logic Of The Social Sciences' (Popper), and 'On The Logic Of The Social Sciences' (Adorno). The latter of course is also the title of Habermas's extended work which opened his debate with Gadamer.

4. While this particular debate does not seem to have provoked extensive discussion in the English speaking world, the issues themselves have been alive since the late nineteenth century - see Glyn Adey's Introduction to Adorno et al 1975. In the mid-sixties attention also veered towards Thomas Kuhn's account of the history of science and the implications it had for Popper's view of scientific knowledge.

5. Habermas continues to give credence to this hermeneutic aspect in his more recent writing, see Habermas (1984:108), and a more extensive account of this idea by Kenneth Baynes in his essay 'Rational Reconstruction and Social Criticism: Habermas's Model Of Interpretive Social Science' in Kelly. M. ed. (1989-90:122-145)

6. In sociology the most famous experiment to demonstrate this is to be found in Harold Garfinkel's *Studies In Ethnomethodology* ([1967] 1984:cht2), where he advised some of his students to insist, in an everyday conversation, that the other person clarify exactly what they meant. Hence, the casual remark 'How are you?', was to be met by 'How am I in regard to what? My Health, my finance, my school work, my peace of mind..' Needless to say, the importance of the core of taken-for-grantedness in communication, was vividly revealed

7 Round one: Habermas' first critique (a) on the virtues of hermeneutics

The basic theme of *On The Logic Of The Social Sciences*.

Habermas's first challenge to Gadamer is to be found in the final sections of *On The Logic Of The Social Sciences*. It is part of an extended critique of the way positivist assumptions have come to imbue the social sciences. The result of this is that our understanding of the social world has become distorted. Habermas explores this theme in a variety of ways, unpicking amongst other things, the misleading nature of the 'stimulus-response' model of social behaviour. He also extends his previous critique of sociological systems theory, showing in more detail how its objectivistic language can gain no purchase on the symbolically structured nature of social reality. Gadamer's work along with that of others, is used for this purpose.

His discussion of Gadamer is made up of two halves, the first is a positive affirmation of hermeneutics which I deal with in this chapter. The second, draws these findings into negative critique of hermeneutics, which I deal with in the next chapter. His overall aim is to incorporate those aspects of hermeneutics he finds satisfactory with a much moderated version of (sociological) systems theory. This will be the basis of a renewed Critical Theory.

While much of *On The Logic Of The Social Sciences* is critical of systems theory and the behaviourist assumptions that go with it, he nevertheless reserves for it a special place. While it remains ignorant of the symbolically structured nature of the social world, it does have the capacity to explain the way different patterns of social action are normatively bound, and functionally linked together behind the backs of the actors, at the level of the system. The caveat for systems theory which was present in a small way in the dispute with Popper, is amplified here and used partly against hermeneutics. It has of course become a central tenet of his subsequent work.

The weakness of systems theory is that in failing to understand the symbolic nature of the social, it represses the needs of human subjects, who in turn develop interpretations of things that overload, and may overshoot the limits of the system. At the end of the book he looks toward the logic of Freudian psycho-analysis as the model on which to base a new Critical Theory, one that will enable him to meld society's 'hermeneutic' and 'systems' elements together under one roof.

It must be added that it is not Freudianism as such he is interested in, but only its epistemological form. He finds several parallels that can be drawn between psycho-analysis and Critical Theory. First, in the same way that the Freudian analyst must incorporate the narrative life-account of the patient with a structural theory of the personality, so the Critical Theorist must link the symbolic nature of the life-world with the structure of the wider social system.

Secondly, in psycho-analysis patients are subject to compulsive behaviours which have a 'quasi-causal' force, in that their origins are hidden in the repressions of a particular person's life-history. So also Critical Theory recognizes that in society, the mass of people may be held in thrall by the repressive demands of a system that has distorted and partially colonized their life-world. What Habermas likes about the Freudian account of human causality is that it sits between a positivist and a hermeneutic explanation of social action. It clearly recognizes the significance of the intentionality of action, rightly seeing human motivation as being situated within a symbolically structured context. Thus, rather than being understood as something which is the automatic effect of an external cause, social action has to be understood hermeneutically. But at the same time it retains some of the force of the more positivist view of causality, in that motivations for action are often unconscious, and therefore concealed from the people involved. In this sense a model of social action bears a resemblance to the cause-effect model used by science in the study of nature. Thus because motives can 'bear the cloak of being causes', Habermas's believes Critical Theory must link the virtues of a hermeneutics of the life-world, with those of systems theory for an adequate explanation.

Thirdly, in the same way that psycho-analysis aims to restore the narrative coherence of someone's life-history, so Critical Theory sees its task in the wider terms of restoring the coherence of history as the wider project of human self-formation. In both cases the aim of the theory is to re-establish the self-directedness of the human project. The status of proof in both theories is therefore of a different kind to that found in more positivist theories It does not depend upon scientific method as such, but upon the parties involved accepting the validity of the relevant interpretations.

On the virtues of the hermeneutic approach to language

Although Habermas is ultimately concerned to balance and bring together the virtues of both the hermeneutic and the empirical-analytic (i.e. the scientific) approaches, he is intent for the most part to peg back the illicit claims of the latter view. Unlike Adorno in the dispute with Popper, he has at his disposal a number of anti-positivist authors within the sociological canon, such as Alfred Shutz, Aaron Cicourel, and Harold Garfinkel, who can be employed to this end. Phenomenolgical sociology, with its challenge to the obviousness of observable data, has successfully broken through the reductionist boundaries of various social science postivisms, such as functionalism and behaviourism. However, in Habermas's view it remains marred by the attempt to explain the social life-world in terms of a pre-social, individualised, transcendental ego. Even in its most 'social' form of Garfinkel's ethnomethodology, where the emphasis is upon the situated practices of members, it reaches a limit in always locating the origin of things in the consciousness of individuals.

More adequate than this is 'The Linguistic Approach', by which he is referring to the work of the later Wittgenstein and Peter Winch. In this perspective the specificity of the social comes into its own. Meaning is not derived from extra-social structures, nor from a pre-social individual, but is constituted intersubjectively. Here the social is correctly seen as involving subjects learning social rules which are internally bound up with language use. However, Habermas still finds two residual elements of positivism even in this approach, which counts against its viability.

First, Wittgenstein sees the ordinary language of the language-game in a misleading way. He tends to see it in too scientific a fashion, as if it were an unambiguous and perfectly ordered calculus, made up of language-rules that are to be mastered in the process of socialization. This mastery consists in being able to apply a rule repeatedly in an identical way, as if it were a scientific rule. Whereas in reality ordinary language is imperfect, and often ambiguous, indeed it is these distinctly non-scientific qualities which are at the heart of communicative dialogue. If ordinary language was underpinned by a set of clear cut rules it would doubtless produce a seamless web of intersubjective meanings, and this would certainly ensure that a common identity prevailed in society. But such a state of perfect communication would be no state of communication at all. Real communication involves more than just the integration of subjects into a set of rules, it requires a kind of ego-effort on their part to bring dialogue into being. If we followed Wittgenstein's account of language-games it would actually threaten the ego-identity of the members of that society in that no effort, but only conformity would be required of them. Information might have to be exchanged but communication would be unnecessary. Total integration into such a regimented scheme would break the delicate balance an ego must experience between identity and non-identity with society, a balance necessary to sustain itself.

Secondly, if Wittgenstein and Winch are working on this basis then it follows that the social scientist who wishes to understand an alien culture must seek total immersion in it. He or she would then be able to perfectly reconstruct the unified language-games of the alien actors concerned. This of course is highly problematic, as Winch himself subtly demonstrated in his critique of Evans-Pritchard's account of the Azande oracle. What is wrong with this approch, believes Habermas, is the way these authors see language-games as internally coherent sealed units, requiring the social scientist to efface the conditions of his or her own society, in order to immerse themselves properly in rules of the other. The residue of positivism here lies in the assumption that social scientists can detach themselves from their presuppositions and take up a purely observational attitude towards other language-games. He likens Winch's outlook to that of Dilthey :-

> Winch seems to be contemplating a linguistic version of Dilthey.
> From his free-floating position the linguistic analyst can slip into
> the grammar of any language-game without himself being bound
> by the dogmatism of his own language-game, which would be
> obligatory for linguistic analysis as such. (Habermas 1988:136)

Such a view is self-contradictory, in that at one point the linguistic approach emphasises the way the analyst's own language is entirely bound up with the practices of his or her own society, and thus how it constitutes the 'world'. At another, the analyst is able to slip the moorings and somehow learn the totally new package of rules that make up another. The superiority of Gadamer's view of language is that it has no truck with the illusions of such cultural self-effacement. Understanding an alien culture is a projective and corrective process, one that is likely to bring to light the key status of the hermeneutic circle.

I have discussed Winch earlier, and so will do no more than reiterate here that I find Habermas's judgement on him to entail a considerable foreshortening of his case, which I regard as close to Gadamer's. There is evidence both in his *The Idea Of A Social Science*, and in the essay 'Understanding A Primitive Society' which clearly signals that Winch is aware that the learning of socio-linguistic rules involves application in the Gadamerian sense, and not merely the mechanical replication of a principle. Similarly, he often refers to the fact that understanding an alien culture entails a disruption and an extension of our self-understanding rather than self-effacement. This foreshortening effect may be endemic to Habermas's work generally. Sica (1988:86-90) is quite bitter at the way Habermas aggressively assimilates Gadamer's ideas to his own, and thus does a great disservice to the full importance of Gadamer's achievement (1). He points out that Habermas appears to quote liberally from Truth And Method, but actually, with a few minor exceptions, comments on only eighteen pages of the Second Part. By contrast Hekman (1986:129ff) regards Habermas's critique as an exceedingly subtle one, in that it avoids the common mistake of dismissing Gadamer as a relativist. In a sense though, both are right. There is an irony in Hekman's claim that they share a common opposition to instrumental reason, in that Habermas does trawl Gadamer's ideas for material that can be assimilated to his own. He does use them instrumentally for a purpose Gadamer never intended. If hermeneutics is centrally concerned with the way our linguistic tradition preforms our understanding, it will scarcely serve a critique of ideology that seeks to dissemble tradition. On the other hand Habermas's use of Gadamer to highlight the weaknesses of other anti-positivist approaches is extrordinarily powerful. He certainly distorts, in the sense of changes, Gadamer's ideas, but in so doing amplifies and directs their power, in ways that highlight the complexity and reach of their application. Indeed, one could even support Habermas with Gadamer's adage that where one understands, one understands differently.

Whatever the exact rights and wrongs of the case, I think it may be more to the point that Habermas understood Gadamer's work rather too well for his own good, in that once he had taken hermeneutics on board he had great difficulty in making off with the ideas he wanted, and leaving the rest behind.

Certainly Habermas sees Gadamer's hermeneutics as the most thoroughly adequate approach to the interpretation of meaning, something which should be central for the social sciences. It is in its account of language and the 'reflexivity' that goes with its use, that it shows its superiority.

Habermas' use of the hermeneutic view of language

The discovery by Wittgenstein of the significance of meaning as something produced by an enclosed linguistic totality, has left those social sciences that wish to proceed non-positivistically with a problem, namely, relativism. If the world is perceived as being fragmented into separate linguistic totalities, each with its own internally valid world-view, then the possibility of translating between them, let alone evaluating their validity, becomes problematic. One way of overcoming the plurality of separate language-games, and thus holding onto the unity of our analytic (scientific) reason, is to go down the path of

Chomsky's structural linguistics. This gives us a theoretical language that is sufficiently distant from ordinary language to overcome its parochial qualities. However, Habermas has an ambition both to limit the claims of analytic (scientific) reason, while extending the range of the concept of reason. He argues that we do not have to move outside the realm of ordinary language to do this, because Gadamer has shown us that :-

> ..every ordinary-language grammar opens up the possibility of also transcending the language it establishes, the possibility, that is, of translating into other languages and from other languages. (Habermas 1988:142)

Ordinary language has the power of transcending itself, in the sense of being able to reach beyond its own point of view. It is not tied rigidly to the local protocols of one language, for its task is to embrace what is alien. This ongoing capacity only really becomes visible when an explicit effort of translation is required. Paradoxically, this capacity can make itself plain when we are faced with the apparent untranslatability of familiar expressions. For to be aware that something is literally untranslatable into another language is, in a sense, to be beyond the confines of ones own language. To know that one will have to render an expression "in other words", means that ordinary language has the flexibility to recognize and accomodate what is alien. The boundary of ones own everyday language therefore may be a limit, but it is a porous limit. In fact in learning your first language you also learn how to learn languages in general, so that in learning a second language you do not discard the first, but learn it through the first. The first language you learn is not a restriction on knowledge, but is the springboard to further knowledge.

This tendency to self-transcendence through language is also where reason resides. It has always been difficult to define exactly what Frankfurt School authors mean by Reason, although they use the term fairly frequently. They use it to refer to something more extensive than instrumental reason, and it usually implies a human capacity not to be determined by physical or material circumstances. In other words it implies a certain human capacity for transcendence. This kind of notion was highly unfashionable at the time of the debate, and has remained so in the face of postmodernist ideas. However Habermas has stuck doggedly to it, and here extrapolates Gadamer's ideas to make his point :-

> Languages themselves contain the potential for a rationality that, expressing itself in the particularity of a specific grammar, reflects the limits of that grammar and at the same time negates them in their specificity. Reason, which is always bound up with

> language, is also always beyond its languages. Only by destroying the particularities of languages, which are the only way in which it is embodied, does reason live in language. It can purge itself of the residue of one particularity, of course, only through transition to another. (Habermas 1988:144)

It should of course be noted that Habermas uses the language of 'reason', where Gadamer tends to use the language of 'being'. This difference is not cut and dried, Gadamer (1970) has written on 'reason', but it does signal a difference in orientation about a similar idea. Habermas does not, for example, refer to Gadamer's account of the speculative structure of language, in which the power of what is unsaid is as much a part of any statement, as what is said. The implication of this is that whatever transcendental power may reside in language, it has to be conceived modestly, for in all our sayings and doings, and our apparent claims to exceed current limitations, we already belong to what is unsaid. To be fair, Habermas does put a caveat into his claim, in the last sentence quoted above, where he states that exceeding the particularities of one language, does not mean we can simply rise above things. Rather, the transcendence of reason lies in the transition from one language to another. Nevertheless, if one compares the quotation from Habermas (on Gadamer), with Gadamer's own view of reason, we find a more limited claim being made. It is what reason cannot claim to do that inflects Gadamer's definition :-

> We do not speak in the name of reason. Whoever does speak in the name of reason contradicts himself. For what is reasonable is to know the limits of ones own understanding and just through this fact to be capable of better understanding wherever it may come from. (Gadamer 1970:15)

In *Truth And Method* (p469), Gadamer specifically holds in check the dialectical account of language with the emphasis he places on the unity of the unsaid with the said. The unsaid can never be fully brought out into the open, but it underpins all that can be said. Thus claims about the dialectical power of language to overstep its boundaries, must always be tempered by an awareness of how much our understanding rests on what is unsaid. In Habermas's hands Gadamer's idea of translation becomes a model for social communication, and this is a move of some significance. It is not that Habermas is wholly wrong in extending Gadamer's ideas in this way, but in making communication the prime 'function' of language, as though it were designed for that purpose, he subtly slides away from the intention behind Gadamer's description. For Gadamer, language is not primarily something we as subjects, do things with, be it communication or translation. Our native language may give us the power to reason, but it does not enable us to transcend its particularities, we cannot destroy the residue of those particularities, as Habermas claims. In all actual understanding our language is always presupposed, it is always with us and can never be purged by us.

Nevertheless for Habermas the real strength of Gadamer's account of language is the dialectical view he has of its boundaries. Gadamer's account, he claims, unlike Wittgenstein's, enables us to see that ordinary language is both outwardly and inwardly porous. It is outwardly porous in its power to translate even something fundamentally alien. It is inwardly porous in that the linguistic rules we learn, which govern our own forms of life, also provide us with the means for interpreting those rules, the means whereby we can evaluate the validity of our existing way of looking at things. When coming to understand an alien culture properly, we do not merely assimilate its ideas, in the sense of reducing its alien concepts to the point where they are identical with our own. Our own native language gives us the power to reflect back upon the conditions of our own understanding and transform it in the process of dialogue with what is alien.

This account of an inward-outward dialectic exceeds Wittgenstein's view, in that he saw the rules of linguistic communication entailing knowledge about how to apply them mechanically, but not about how to (re)interpret them. As Habermas points out, our forms of life are not rigidly reproduced :-

> ..the language-games of the young do not simply reproduce the practice of the old. With the first basic linguistic rules the child learns not only the conditions of possible consensus but also the conditions of possible interpretation of the rules, which enable him to overcome and thereby also to express a distance. (Habermas 1988:148)

It opens up not just the importance of the horizontal relationship between different contemporary cultures, but also the significance of vertical, or historical relationships within ones own native culture. That is, it reveals the significance of tradition. Habermas emphasises that our historical tradition is not something that the sociologist might batten on to an account of contemporary society, it is intrinsic to it. The past lives in the present because "the process of socialization through which the individual learns his language is the smallest unit in the process of tradition".

One of the characteristics of interpretive sociology is the central role it gives to language, and how subjects constitute their world in using it. However, one of the standard criticisms of interpretive sociology is that it is ahistorical. It dwells on the episodic, and lacks any sense of the wider historical context in which particular kinds of social negotiation take place. Alvin

Gouldner (1971) based his diatribe against interpretive sociology in general, and Erving Goffman in particular, on just such a view. Goffman's social actors are accompished 'self-presenters', they are adept at the manipulation of appearances in a world that has little time for matters of substance. This enclosed world of impression-management is taken by Goffman to be definitive of the social world generally. Yet as Gouldner explains it really refers to the way Americans have adapted to the requirements of contemporary capitalism. Goffman's 'dramaturgical approach' to social life merely reflects a situation where the 'self' becomes a commodity like any other, desirous of making a good impression. Hence without an historical context the interpretive sociologist takes the specific, local features of interaction, to be the whole of the story. This defect arises because interactionism places the subject, and the verbal negotiations he or she undertakes, at the centre of things and limits the social to what those people mean by that situation (2). Particular historical formations of power e.g. class, are pushed to the margins in favour of investigating the actors own account of things.

In accepting Gadamer's account of language, Habermas is able to show that even interpretive sociology, which holds language to be the medium of the social, is not limited to the actors own account of their present situation. It is in fact tied internally to their tradition, with all that that implies about history as the fusion of horizons.

Summary of what Habermas finds valuable in the hermeneutic view of language

It may be useful at this point to summarise the main features of Habermas's rather diffuse argument. It is built around the virtues of Gadamer's view of language which he counterposes to the less adequate view he attributes to Wittgenstein and Winch. The Wittgensteinian case has the virtue of recognizing the constitutive role language plays in reality, but is marred by its assumption that language-games are sealed 'monadic' units that are virtually incapable of translation. This assumption derives from Wittgenstein retaining an unconscious committment to the logic of scientific method. He tends, according to Habermas, to see learning linguistic rules as being like learning the formal rules of a scientific discipline; and folowing linguistic rules as knowing how to apply a scientific formula in an identical way. It must be said however, that this is a fairly familiar criticism of Wittgenstein, and one might have wished for Habermas to demonstrate his case rather than just claim it. Indeed as Hekman (1986) points out, this kind of criticism often passes muster on the basis of Wittgenstein's own silence on the matter of translation. It is not therefore, proof that translation between language-games is impossible, and if Winch can be considered a developer of Wittgenstein's ideas, then my account of him suggests that the potential for translation is present in this tradition too (3). If this is the case, then the same potential would also exist for recognizing the intrinsic nature of an historical dimension to our linguistic worlds, and therefore stand against the notion that the 'Linguistic Approach' is automatically ahistorical.

Nevertheless, Habermas does rightly sense that the hermeneutic tradition, with its longstanding concern for 'translation' and 'history', has the conceptual insights necessary to establish foundations for the social sciences. The strength of Gadamer's ideas on language can be summarised under two headings :-

(a) *Language is porous and dialectical, it oversteps boundaries.*

Ordinary language constitutes our world but does so in such a way that allows us to transcend the boundaries of that world. When we learn our native language it does not prevent us from knowing the world from the point of view of another language, it makes such knowledge possible. The recognition of this boundary overstepping capacity hinges on Gadamer's dialectical approach to language. The implication of this dialectical approach extends beyond our capacity to understand alien cultures. The capacity to translate the alien into the familiar reverberates back onto the familiar, altering it in the process. This is what Habermas means by language being both outwardly and inwardly porous, and it opens up another dimension, historical tradition.

(b) *Language enables us to reinterpret the world and have a history*

It follows from (a) that when we learn our native language we are not only learning the rules of how to go on in our own society, but also acquiring the ability to interpret those rules differently. Hence revising our linguistic understanding is not something that only happens when we engage with an alien culture, it also routinely happens within our own. When children are socialized into our society they learn not only what the established meaning-consensus is, but also what it is to interpret the rules differently. Gaining ones own language also gives one the power to express a distance from it. This enables us to have an historical tradition.

In any evaluation of the debate this last point is crucial, as Habermas is acknowledgeing that via his description of language, Gadamer has established the existence of a critical distance between people's understanding and their tradition Traditions are seen to be inherently challangable and malleable. The point is crucial because at a later stage Habermas reverses this recognition, and argues that hermeneutics presents a case that renders tradition all powerful. At this point though he finds in the hermeneutic view of language something vital for his enterprise. It exceeds the Wittgesteinian approach in seeing that socialization is not a process of mere conditioning, and that built in to the constitutive role of language is a critical space for the (re)interpretation of things. Indeed Habermas amplifies the importance of this when he ties Gadamer's interpretively-open view of language in with the human subject's development of an ego-identity. In order for the human ego to develop satisfactorily it must be able to recognize itself through a language that permits it to be both a part of, and apart from the world. Gadamer's account of language clearly articulates the importance of this dialectical insight for the social sciences. Habermas then moves on to evaluate the relevance of Gadamer's account of the fusion of horizons for the practising historian.

On the importance of the 'fusion of horizons' for history writing

Habermas extends his agreement with Gadamer's reflexive account of language, to include the way it provides a model for the historical nature of our existence, as expressed in the idea of the fusion of horizons. He then examines how this process always already embraces the historian and thus impacts upon the task of writing history.

When we want to understand our historical tradition the hermeneutically circular model of translation applies as much as if we wanted to understand an alien culture. When we seek to understand a (historical) text we cannot avoid anticipating the meaning of the whole, but by the same token we also revise this anticipation in the process of explicating the individual parts. he horizon in which our understanding is embedded provides the ground for this projective process and it cannot be extinguished in favour of a methodology that seems to permit direct access to an historical situation. In fact Habermas quotes Gadamer to the effect that we need to already have a horizon in order to place ourselves in an historical situation. In other words to recognize something as historical means to recognize its 'otherness', or the way it is different from the present. The important point is that this is not a matter that is contingent on finding a methodology that will enable us to overcome the gap between present and past, sameness and difference. It is a condition of our temporal existence.

We cannot then dispense with our belongingness to tradition, indeed the failing of the phenomenological, linguistic, and historicist approaches is that each in their own way forgets this belongingness. Habermas uses the term 'communicative experience' rather than 'belongingness' but the meaning is clear These approaches he claims :-

> ..fall prey to objectivism for they claim a purely theoretical attitude for the phenomenological observer and the linguistic

analyst when in fact both of them are bound up with their object domain through communicative experience and thus can no longer lay claim to the role of uninvolved observer." (Habermas 1988:153)

The observational attitude of science, is quite inadequate in hermeneutics for we have no access to the 'object' domain which is tradition, except through participation. In fact any approach which seeks to break this fundamental relationship in the name of increasing its objectivity will actually achieve the opposite. Objectivity in hermeneutics, and by implication the social sciences too, is of a different kind to that found in the natural sciences. Where natural science involves the separation of subject and object to enable pure observation to take place, hermeneutics insists that subject and object are interrelated. This subject-object relationship moreover, is itself but an element in the wider process of the fusion of horizons that is our tradition. Thus objectivity, (if this is the right word), depends upon the ability to recognize the embeddedness of our understanding in our tradition, while at the same time being open to new interpretations. Habermas amplifies at this point the way Gadamer's work reveals the spurious objectivism of methodologies that claim to have bypassed this fundamental belongingness in the name of objectivity. Those that ignore or try to bypass this communicative bond actually move away from, rather than closer to the things they are trying to investigate. On these hermeneutic grounds Habermas declares that :-

> Objectivity can be assured only by reflective participation, that is, through the control provided by the initial situation, the sounding board from which hermeneutic understanding cannot be detached. On the level of communication, the possible objectivity of experience is endangered precisely to the extent to which the interpreter is induced by the illusion of objectivity to conceal his indissoluble bond with the initial hermeneutic situation. Gadamer's excellent critique of the objectivistic self-understanding of the Geisteswissenschaften applies to historicism and to the false consciousness of its phenomenological and linguistic successors as well." (Habermas 1988:153-154)

I have quoted Habermas at some length because it is clear that he attaches considerable importance to the Gadamerian idea of belonging to tradition. This indissoluble bond, as he calls it, seems as axiomatic for his view of the social sciences as it is for Gadamer's view of hermeneutics. Yet he gradually tries to slip the moorings from it, so as to establish a position for Critical Theory that has some autonomy from tradition. How successful he is in doing this is the essence of his debate with Gadamer.

Nevertheless at this point he develops the idea in terms of its implications for the writing of history. He re-states Gadamer's argument that the meaning of an historical text is not given and fixed by the original author, or the context in which the text first appeared. A text's meaning is, as it were, a movable feast. What a text means is the outcome of the accumulated meanings it has acquired in its various historical interpretations. There is no pure original meaning to a text, every understanding of it involves the projection of the prejudices of a particular historical horizon, whether the historian is aware of it or not. These prejudices are played against the 'object' and the mediation between the two produce a sedimented accumulation of meaning. This is always in principle, incomplete, in that new horizons will retrospectively open up new aspects of meaning in the historical text.

On Danto's Ideal Chronicler, or 'the stance of the last historian'

Habermas then exemplifies the importance of this insight for history writing by reference to the work of Arthur Danto (1968). Danto, he argues, confirms Gadamer's insight by showing how historical statements are always located within a narrative. Narratives present the reader with stories which have a beginning and an end, and which are held together by a plot. Historical events are always reconstructed within this framework so that they can be located in relation to other events that followed them. In fact historical events are like narrative events in that they require the use of categories which were not available to the participants at the time. Thus, an historical event needs to be placed in relation to subsequent events, in order for it to make sense as history. Historical statements such as :-

> "The Thirty Years War began in 1618" presupposes at least the occurence of events relevant to the history of that war up to the Peace Of Westphalia, events that no observer could have described at the time of the outbreak of the war. (1988:156)

As a result 'The Thirty Years War' is not something fixed, but depending on the narrative in which it is placed it can mean not only a military event lasting thirty years but "the political collapse of the German Empire, the postponement of capitalist development, the end of the Counter-Reformation, the theme of the Wallenstein drama," and so forth. Each narrative places the War in relation to subsequent events in order to explain it. In other words the meaning of historical events is determined by the ongoing fusion of historical horizons.

We can compare this to the supra-historical statements that are proper to empirical-scientific theories, and so highlight important differences between them. The language of science is neutral with respect to the historical time of the events being observed. It matters nought for science when something occurred in a historical sense, in fact its location in historical time must be completely bracketed off for the observation to be valid. Again Habermas is alongside Gadamer in recognizing that history and tradition are fundamental to the human sciences. He points out that if one wanted to merge the language and protocols of the human and the natural sciences, one would run into insurmountable difficulties. If one wanted to represent a predicted scientific event, such as a solar eclipse, as an historical one, it would have to be inserted into the narrative frameworks of the lives of all those for whom it had significance. In so doing it would become historically specific and cease to be science. In a similar fashion the historian who wishes to proceed like a scientist, would have to have access to what Danto called, The Ideal Chronicler. The Ideal Chronicler would be a machine that disinterestedly records all historical events at all moments, and would be able to make them available to the historian. This fictional machine however, even though it was a 'perfect eyewitness' in terms of being absolutely accurate in recording events as they happened, would be of little use to the real historian, unless it had access to the lifeworld of at least one 'living eyewitness'. This is because statements about history have to be embedded in narrative accounts which have an intentional character. Historical events are not mere data that can be observed and recorded, for in order to be historical they must anticipate events beyond the time of the observation. The Thirty Years War began in 1618, but only became the Thirty Years War after it finished, and then by being placed within one of the narrative stories we tell about ourselves. Historical descriptions of events thus always exceed the empirical observational possibilities of the time.

This is not to say that the historian can ignore the intentions of the people at the time, but must mesh the anticipations that were built into their actions with horizons that came afterwards. Indeed, actors only become aware of the fact that they are participating in a coherent historical narrative after the fact. Thus Habermas confirms Gadamer's view that people's intentions should be conceived, not in a psychological, but a hermeneutic way. The unintended consequences, and indirect results of horizons, are to be grasped as intentional possibilities that existed within that horizon, even though they were unforeseen at the time. As subsequent historical horizons emerge so new aspects of the event emerge, its relation to other events in other stories reshape it and reveal it in a different light.

What is to be concluded from this, according to Danto, is that a complete and definitive account of an historical event could only be written at the end of history. Only the 'last historian' could know how all the intervening events, narratives, and horizons, were interwoven in re-defining it. As it is impossible for any historian to take up such a position without a speculative philosophy of history, i.e. without presupposing knowledge of its outcome, history writing must remain essentially incomplete. There will always be, declares Danto, an element of sheer arbitrariness in the writing of history.

Up to this point Habermas is in agreement with both Gadamer and Danto, but he wishes to put their insight to a purpose more in tune with his own project. He argues against Danto, (though still with Gadamer), that the fact that historians are unable to write complete histories should not be seen as a deficiency. It is only a deficiency if one is mistakenly trying to apply criteria that are proper to the natural sciences. Clearly, if one is looking for a total description of an historical event, in order to produce instrumentally exploitable knowledge, perhaps for predicting the future, then history writing will always fail. But if the character of historical phemomena is different from that of natural phenomena, in that it informs our life-practice rather than enabling us to predict things, then this puts a very different complexion on matters. It means what Danto sees as the deficiency of historical knowledge, Habermas sees as the transcendental condition for its possibility. He amplifies Gadamer's case that understanding history is a hermeneutic activity, and this involves projecting our present prejudices onto the fragments of the past to produce a provisional totality of meaning. Without our present historical prejudices we would be unable to project a provisional closure of meaning onto the past. We would be unable to identify events as belonging together within a narrative frame that has a particular historical significance. In fact it is only because we are placed within a particular horizon, and project meaning from it, that historical events can inform our life-practice. In fact he sees Gadamer's real accomplishment to have demonstrated that the hermeneutic nature of understanding is transcendentally related to our self-understanding, and thus to our social life-practice. As we understand more about history we understand more about ourselves so understand more about history.

However Habermas introduces an emphasis which again draws his ideas unsuspectingly away from Gadamer's, though he uses them to make his point. While the idea of the last historian is a fiction if thought of as an ideal scientific observer who stands at the end of history, practising historians actually take up this position, but from within their contemporary horizons. Every historian actually takes up the stance of the last historian in trying to write as complete and definitive a history as possible. What Danto claims to be impossible, and therefore illegitimate i.e. that historians should work with a philosophy of history in mind, Habermas declares to be part of what historians should do. Certainly, he rejects those that might claim to know the outcome of history, but argues (using Gadamer), that historians must reconstruct the past on the basis of present prejudices, which contain anticipations of the future. These are legitimate, he claims, because they are subject to the revisions of the hermeneutic circle. He thus seems to assume the validity of Gadamer's ontological account of historical existence. This is surprising as he always actually avoids using the language of 'being', and finds ontologically based analyses not to his taste as they are invariably conservative. Nevertheless he is willing to have his hopes for Critical Theory's philosophy of history underwritten by Gadamer. What the historian can know, he declares :-

> ..cannot be grasped independently of the framework of his own life-praxis. In this context, what is in the future only exists within the horizon of expectations. And these expectations form the fragments of previous tradition into a hypothetical totality of preunderstood universal history. In the light of this history every relevant event can in principle be as completely described as is possible for the practically effective self-understanding of a social life-world. Every historian implicitly operates as Danto would like to forbid the philosopher of history to operate. He anticipates from a practical perspective end states in terms of which the multiplicity of events is easily organised into action-orienting histories." (Habermas 1988:160-61)

A hermeneutic reservation

Although Habermas is clearly embracing Gadamerian ideas here, I find the meaning of this passage problematic. There is an emphasis incorporated into it which actually runs counter to Gadamer's ideas. When he states that our expectations weld the fragments of tradition into a hypothetically universal history, he is claiming something Gadamer specifically denies. For Gadamer there can be no anticipation of universal history, be it of a hypothetical or any other kind. In fact Gadamer opposes the idea of history per se, always weaving it in with the concept of tradition. Hence when Habermas refers to 'expectations', these are quite different to what Gadamer means by 'prejudices' or 'prejudgements'. The latter, for Gadamer, always refer to the way we are embedded within our tradition, and thus scarcely the material from which universal history could be formed. Certainly our prejudices do contain 'expectations' that some degree of meaning-unity can be found in history, but for Gadamer they are tentative, provisional unities, and do not have that universalising thrust Habermas attributes to them. The ease with which Habermas claims the contemporary historian can write as if he were the 'last historian', describing events as completely as possible from the point of view of his life-world, is anathema to Gadamer. For Gadamer knowledge can never be complete, it always depends on certain kinds of question being asked, which means that other questions, and the knowledge they might produce, must be left in the dark. The truly knowledgable person is the one that recognizes the limitations of his own knowledge. By contrast, Habermas is implicitly working on a linear model of history that assumes progress involves a move from a state of mythology or deception, to one of enlightenment or knowledge. Gadamer made plain this was *not* his model :-

> One has to ask oneself whether the dynamic law of human life can be conceived adequately in terms of progress, a continual advance from the unknown into the known, and whether the course of human culture is actually a linear progression from mythology to enlightenment. One should entertain a completely different notion: whether the movement of human existence does not issue in a relentless inner tension between illumination and concealment...One has to ask whether progress, as it is at home in the special field of scientific research, is at all consonant with the condition of human existence in general. Is the notion of an ever-mounting and self-perfecting enlightenment finally ambiguous ? (Gadamer 1981:104-5)

What is important about the way Habermas describes his agreement with Gadamer, is that it is accented in such a way as to make his subsequent criticisms more plausible. This is not to suggest any cynicism on his part, only to note that their fundamental projects diverge, and that his commentary entails a transformation of key hermeneutic ideas, which will subtly make certain parts of them more or less serviceable to Critical Theory.

Life-practical knowledge is real knowledge

Habermas still has not quite finished with what he finds valuable in hermeneutics. The final matter he describes is the nature of praxis. His intention here seems to be to reaffirm the distinctive features of the social world as compared to the natural world. He rehearses some of Gadamer's ideas but pulls them into sharp focus to maintain the critical anti-positivist edge of his own project.

He reminds the reader that Gadamer found an immanant connection between understanding, application, and interpretation. One does not first understand something and then apply it in a subsequent interpretation. Rather, using the examples of theology and jurisprudence, he recalls that Gadamer illustrated how the act of understanding something, always at the same time involved an application of it to the present situation, and in this it was also an interpretation. This insight is important to Habermas because it hauls the idea of understanding meaning away from being just the grasping of an external, objective fact, and moves it towards including evaluations based on our own present self-understanding. And like his Frankfurt School predecessors he has always rejected as spurious the separation of fact and value, something characteristic of positivist modes of thought. Indeed, the rightness of placing the evaluative dimension at the heart of the human sciences is confirmed a second time in the way Gadamer links hermeneutic understanding to Aristotle' account of practical knowledge.

To do this Habermas sharply contrasts the differences that determine practical, technical, and scientific knowledge. It is the validity of practical knowledge, with its specific kind of legitimacy, that most concerns him. Aristotle's account of practical knowledge is, as Gadamer has shown, co-extensive with hermeneutics, and gives the human sciences access to their 'object', namely social reality. He follows Gadamer in pointing out that unlike other forms of knowledge, life-practical knowledge is reflexive in form and therefore entails self-knowledge. Unlike technical knowledge which remains external to us, practical knowledge is internalized by us and "has the power to determine drives and shape passions". We may forget technical rules if we stop practising them, but practical rules become part of our personality structure. They have general, law-like qualities, but these are general in a different way to the rules that underpin technology or science. With scientific rules, the law-like qualities take the form of the particular case being determined by, and subsumed under the general law. But with practical (or social) knowledge, the particular case is involved in an ongoing process of mutual determination with the general rule.

I will not recount the full case that Habermas brings, as it follows what I have already covered in describing Gadamer's work. Suffice to say that Habermas clearly finds important insights in hermeneutics, which he wants to graft onto Critical Theory. Indeed, I suspect that what he finds remarkable about Gadamer's work, is the way it appears to have so thoroughly and successfully articulated some of the themes that Critical Theory would want to claim for its own. Moreover, it has done this in the terms of a very different intellectual framework, one which has quite different implications to some of the libertarian hopes of Critical Theory. Hence, in order to justify this amalgamation, he will gradually withdraw his full approval from hermeneutics. However before moving on to this it will be useful to clarify how these hermeneutic insights are going to serve the interests of Critical Theory.

On how hermeneutic insights can serve Critical Theory

(a) *Critical Theory gains a meta-norm: the telos of language to reach agreement through dialogue.*

Habermas believes hermeneutics, more than any other approach, has been able to dispel the objectivism endemic in positivist human sciences. It has been able to show that the 'objects' in the social world are constituted in language, and not independently of it. However, unlike some language based approaches, hermeneutics does not see linguistic world-views as determining social life in a prescriptive way. Its dialogic account of language involves an awareness that horizons of understanding are not fixed, but change in the very process of coming to a common understanding. Indeed the hermeneutic insight that the purpose or telos of language is to arrive at a genuine agreement has become the crucial meta-norm for virtually all Habermas's subsequent work (4).

His aim has been to ground Critical Theory's emancipatory hopes in a theory of language where the possibility of consensus is built into our condition as language users. He develops this insight sociologically through the concept of 'communicative action', which is the species-wide capacity we have for intersubjective agreement over norms and values. The possibility of such an agreement originates in Gadamer's account of our common understanding in language.

Habermas believes that the possibility of establishing a *genuine* consensus has been shown by Gadamer's dialogic account of language. When we properly understand an alien culture, or an historical text, we do not merely appropriate it, reproducing the norms and values of our own contemporary society. The dialogic nature of language permits us to experience some distance from those norms and values, and thus to challenge and reinterpret them and arrive at a new consensus about things. Indeed this dialectic between proximity and distance made possible through language is also at the heart of our social health, for an individual's 'ego-identity' depends on them knowing themselves both as a part of and apart from a social community.

However while Gadamer has shown us the possibility for genuine consensus exists, Habermas will spend the second, more critical part of his discussion challenging what he sees as the naivety of Gadamer's belief that consensus is an actuality not just a potentiality.

Genuine consensus, Habermas will maintain, presupposes what he will call 'the ideal speech situation'. This is the meta-norm that he claims is tacitly present in all language communication. It is based on the idea that for a consensus to be genuine, all parties must have an equal, 'dialogical' chance to contribute to it. However, though these moves are often marvellously audacious, whether they can be seen as a justified extension of Gadamer's ideas is quite another matter.

(b) *Understanding their tradition could 'move' people*

Habermas also seems to want to draw a political implication out of hermeneutics. Because it has shown an 'internal connection' exists between tradition and our current self-understanding, Critical Theory might develop accounts of tradition that could become a source of action for particular social groups.

> By its structure, hermeneutic understanding aims at gaining from traditions a possible action-oriented self-understanding for social groups and clarifying it. It makes possible a form of consensus on which communicative action depends. (Habermas 1988:164)

He is much less clear cut in drawing out this implication from hermeneutics as he also sees Gadamer's emphasis on tradition as an essentially conservative one.

Nevertheless he clearly finds this hermeneutic insight to be of importance. Hermeneutics has shown how the dimension of history enters into all understanding. Moreover the process of socialization, whereby we learn the norms and values of our society, is not a process of mere inculcation in which a seamless web of agreement is passed on from one generation to the next. It is a linguistic process based on dialogue and interpretation through which succeeding generations necessarily re-interpret their social identity. This opens up the intrinsic significance of historical tradition for the human sciences, as well as for Critical Theory.

Our social identity, is not to be understood in an individual, psychological way, but in terms of being embedded in horizons of meaning that are thoroughly historical. In the same way that the dialectical model of translation describes the language side of understanding, so the idea of the fusion of horizons, in a parallel way, describes the historical dimension of our understanding. Thus not only do we belong to language, we also belong to our historical tradition, both are constitutive of our lives.

The importance of Gadamer's insight is that we have what Habermas calls, 'an indissoluble communicative bond' with our tradition, and this is something that cannot be eliminated by objective methodologies that claim to transcend history. He follows Gadamer in pointing out that we can only know history through the horizon of our own life-practice. There is thus an immanent connection between understanding history and our self-understanding. This contrasts with more orthodox positivist theories which take up an objectivistic attitude, treating human subjects as objects bearing only causal relations to other objects. In other words hermeneutics offers the potential for drawing up accounts of tradition that could be a source of action for social groups, and thereby possibly social emancipation. If it could be successfully harnessed it would fulfill the longstanding ambition of Critical Theory, to be able to 'move' people in a non-instrumental way.

More hermeneutic reservations

It should be noted though, that however laudable these ambitions are, they are not Gadamer's ambitions. As I have already suggested, the elements of hermeneutics Habermas wants to incorporate into his own project have involved him in a subtle, but unacknowledged re-shaping of those ideas. Certainly one effect is to make them into material better suited to the emancipatory aspirations of Critical Theory. In Habermas's hands the dialectical power of language to overstep boundaries is the vital insight, it means that the possibility of challenging the status quo is intrinsic to language use. But this emphasis shrugs off another Gadamerian insight about language, that 'the unsaid' of our tradition provides a force that helps to form and limit what can be said by us. In short, critique based on Gadamer's view of the potentiality of language, would never be as total as Habermas would wish it to be. We can never be the sovereign authors of our own ideas, even the ones where we are being most critical of the status quo.

Similarly Gadamer's account of language as having consensus as its goal is slightly misleading. There is an element of this in his account, but it is shaped rather differently from the way Habermas sees it. Habermas is working on the basis of a consensus theory of truth, where truth is achieved through intersubjective agreement. For Gadamer the truth of something is not just a matter of subjects coming to an agreement about it, but also involves attention to the something (Sache) itself. The nature of the 'object' matters, it must be allowed to command our attention, to unfold and reveal itself through language. The difference between them is subtle but significant, and perfectly expressed by Hoy when he says "whereas a consensus theory of truth suggests that agreeing about something makes it true, Gadamer's sense is more that we agree to something because it is true. So truth is not the result of agreement but agreement the result of truth" (1994:89).

Likewise, in Habermas's hands the projective, anticipatory nature of historical understanding, becomes an underpinning for the writing of a hypothetically universal history. But for Gadamer the 'stance of the last historian', even as a regulative principle by which historians might write such a history, is a contradiction in terms (5). To posit the possibility of an historian at the end of history, is to project an unhistorical principle onto history. Such a principle, for Gadamer would not enhance, but undermine the recognition of just how historical we are. For him the prejudgements of our historical horizon should serve as the basis for a deeper understanding of the temporal nature of our existence, of the tradition that we are, and they should provide encouragement to immerse ourselves more thoroughly in it. They certainly should not be the grounds for fleeing towards an imaginary state of perfect enlightenment, beyond the finiteness of any historical horizon (6).

In a similar vein, if it is Habermas's hope that a new social praxis might emerge from hermeneutics, one that might be thought relevant to the interests of a particular social group, this seems somewhat at odds with Gadamer's ideas. Certainly, Gadamer claims that all understanding entails the application of an idea to our current life-praxis, but this 'application' is not something that is consciously or deliberately applied according to someone's will. It is rather, an implicit moment in all understanding. So if the idea is for Critical Theory to utilize this insight for its own explicit purposes, it would become an instrumental concept, and run counter to its role in hermeneutics. History appropriates us not we it.

Notes

1. Margaret Canovan (1983) makes the same kind of point with regard to the way Habermas (1977) uses Hannah Arendt's ideas, and notes the irony of him being an advocate of undistorted communication. Canovan (1977) also provides a good, sympathetic introduction to Arendt's work.

2. Critics often use this as an opportunity to point out that historical contexts are also structured by factors such as class, which powerfully influence the outcome of social negotiations, and are ignored or seriously played down in the interpretive perspective. The social world thus described has a spurious openness to it, seemingly free from the effects of an uneven distribution of power. As well as Gouldner (1971), see Fay (1975) for this kind of critique of interpretive sociology.

3. John Heaton (1993), for example, provides a very different account of Wittgenstein's view of language.

4. See Hoy's discussion of the way Habermas has altered the trajectory of Gadamer's account of language to meet the 'universalist' ambitions of Critical Theory in Hoy & McCarthy (1994:177-200).

5. It is not only Habermas who wants to abstract regulative principles such as the 'the stance of the last historian', and 'the ideal speech situation' from Gadamer's work. Karl-Otto Apel, who was a contributor to the

hermeneutics-Critical Theory debate, identifies 'the ideal communicative community' as a transcendental norm which could function as a critique of those language-games that don't follow the norm, (Apel 1980:chts 2, 4, & 5; Apel in Baynes, Bohman, & McCarthy eds. 1987). For helpful commentary see Hoy (1978:107-117), Bubner 1981:70-92). Gadamer responded to Apel's comments in his 'Replik' (1971)

6. To be fair, Habermas has remained cautious in the claims he makes over the degree to which regulative principles are 'transcendental', preferring to emphasise their hypothetical character. He has not developed the idea of 'the last historian', but instead the notion of 'the ideal speech situation' merging its implications into his 'discourse ethics' (Habermas 1990:43-116). By contrast Apel has pursued a more clear cut transcendental argument to ratify the validity of the 'ideal communicative community'. See Apel in Benhabib & Dallmayr 1990, as well as discussions by these authors in the Introduction and Afterword.

8 Round one: Habermas' first critique (b) on the vices of hermeneutics

The tide turns: down with prejudice and the authority of tradition

Having delicately redrawn the context of Gadamer's ideas so as to provide ground for the emancipatory hopes of Critical Theory, Habermas is now ready to reveal their limitations in meeting these hopes. The heart of his objections lie in what he sees as the specious authority Gadamer accords to tradition. The various points he makes all hinge on the need to challenge the dubious implications of the way Gadamer implies the necessity of submission to tradition. To do this Habermas must find ways of showing how tradition may be breached, and the social scientist, at least partially, step outside its confines. Tradition, for Habermas, is not that untrammelled 'dialogue that we are', but an historical process riven with forces of domination that distort dialogue. Because these forces impose themselves on tradition in a extra-dialogic way, then the sociologist needs some conceptual means to extricate him or herself from tradition, in order to bring them to light. Hermeneutics, as it stands, fails to do this, whereas science offers some autonomy.

Science can breach tradition

Gadamer's account of the pre-structured nature of understanding has, according to Habermas, rightly undermined the false claims inherent in objectivistic methods. But this does not mean that the social sciences are absolved from the need to establish adequate methods. Gadamer, in Truth and Method has produced the impression that what faces the human sciences is the choice, truth or method, as though those who pursued adequate (scientific) method debar themselves from wider issues of truth. In fact, in order to be able to reflect at a suitable level on these issues, we must undertake a "controlled distancing" from the object of concern, so as to "raise understanding from a prescientific practice to the status of a reflective process" (1988:166-67).

What Gadamer has done, Habermas claims, is to absolutize the hermeneutic experience as one that transcends scientific method, and therefore has no need to concern itself with such things. In doing this he has unwittingly sided with those positivists who would devalue the humanities and social sciences in calling them unscientific. If we are to consider the hermeneutic critique of objectivistic method satisfactory as it stands, one would expect it to have some consequences for the natural sciences. Habermas implies that it does not because it refuses to engage with the issue of method, and if Gadamer's aim was to show the role of historical influence in all understanding, it has thereby failed. Gadamer stays at the same level of analysis as Heidegger's ontological philosophy which bypasses method (1); his power to criticize positivism is thereby blunted. Habermas's own position with regard to science has always been a complex one. He has never been as obviously antagonistic towards it as some of the older generation of Critical Theorists, and in terms of intellectual biography, is certainly familiar with, and sympathetic to, social scientific authors such as Parsons, Piaget, and Kohlberg (see Dews ed. 1986:149ff). What I think he admires in their work is the appropriateness of the systematic methods they use to deal with systematic aspects of social reality.

One of the things he believes Gadamer underestimates, is the profound impact that science and the assumptions that accompany it, have had in breaking up the continuity of tradition. The effects of this have been twofold. First, it has meant that however misguided historicism is as a methodological approach to history, its 'objectivating attitude' has had the effect of throwing us into a different, less accepting, relation with tradition. We can now see it much better for what it is.

Secondly, the language-game of empirical science is not an arbitrary one, but is deeply anchored in the human need to exploit material circumstances for the sake of survival (2). Moreover, the generic success of science as a source of technical progress, means that many of its assumptions have been invisibly incorporated into the organisation of daily life. The language of science and technology has been institutionalised in such a way that it binds thought and action to the technical imperatives of the economy, the polity, or more broadly, the social system. The only way the sociologist can gain some explanatory purchase on how these systems work, is to adopt the quasi-causal language of the empirical-analytic sciences, where the force of technical reason is the explanatory tool. Sociology can find this in Parsons's structural-functionalist accounts. His systems theory can provide a general framework that goes beyond tradition in explaining people's actions in terms of forces that structure the context of possible action :-

> A functionalist approach has the advantage of systematically grasping objective-intentional contexts. The objective context, in terms of which social action can be understood without sacrificing intentionality, is not woven solely of the threads of transmitted meaning and tradition articulated in language. The dimensions of labour and domination in it cannot be suppressed in favour of subjectively intended symbolic content. A functionalist framework can also do justice to non-normative conditions. Cultural tradition here loses the semblance of absolutism that a hermeneutics become automonous had falsely claimed for it. (Habermas 1988:186-7)

Tradition, then, is to be placed within a wider totality, and can be understood in terms of how it functions as part of a system, even though those functions are not visible "in it and as such". Systems theory can therefore service Critical Theory in uncovering the ideological functions of tradition.

Of course Habermas does not intend to simply rehabilitate functionalism as a replacement for hermeneutics in the sociological canon. He has in mind a 'hermeneutically-enlightened functionalism'. Parsons was too preoccupied with establishing a general methodology, one suitable for an empirical science of society, to recognize how important the understanding of meaning is in gaining access to social facts. He saw the 'end-state' of the social system only in descriptive terms. That is, for Parsons the states of equilibrium to which systems tend, have no validity other than to balance the elements of that system through normative controls. By contrast, if Critical Theory wishes to adopt an empirical-analytic understanding of the system, it will have to concern itself with the validity of communicative experience, and thus the validity of the end-state of the system. It will have to be able, in principle, to link the categories it uses to the self-understanding of the actors concerned. Under these circumstances the functional relations between elements will lose their instrumental quality, and mere equilibrium will be replaced by 'self-formation', as the system's anticipated end-state.

Some people have seen Habermas's aim here, as no more than a version of the old chestnut of trying to find a methodology that will link system and individual. Certainly he expresses his ideas in the epistemological terms of how adequate various methodologies are, but there is also a powerful emancipatory thrust beyond these traditional concerns. His aim in drawing on the full weight of Gadamer's hermeneutics, and then mediating it through Parsons's systems theory, is nothing less than to enable the completion of human self-formation. No small ambition, and one never countenanced by the likes of interpretive or functionalist sociology.

Reflection can breach tradition

If the issue of the role of science in the social sciences appears to be a methodological one, it has another, arguably more important moral one to play. Gadamer, Habermas believes, has brought hermeneutic research, and tradition, to a single point. That is, when the hermeneut undertakes research, he or she can do no more than reinforce an already existing tradition. The conservative political implications of this are plain. Hermeneutics, in its willingness to assert the ultimate validity of tradition, is blind to the way it is also the site for social domination. In emphasising the omnipotence of tradition Gadamer consistently plays down the power that reflection has to challenge tradition. Habermas by contrast states that :-

> Against this stands the insight that the reflective appropriation of tradition breaks the quasi-natural substance of tradition and alters the position of subjects within it......when reflection understands the genesis of the tradition from which it proceeds and to which it returns, the dogmatism of life-praxis is shaken.(1988: 168)

In other words, the force of tradition that would claim us, and make us over into what it would wish us to be, does not go unchallenged when reflection is given its due. It is through the power of reflection that we can trace back the origins of our understanding of things in tradition, and take up a different, less dogmatic attitude towards them. Reflection enables us to place ourselves in a different relation to things that we had previously understood in an automatic way.

Gadamer, Habermas claims, so loses sight of the importance of this, that he drives his valid insight into the role of prejudice (or prejudgement) in all understanding, into a rehabilitation of prejudice as such. Habermas asks whether the inevitability of prejudices should function as tacit proof of their validity ? The unspoken answer is of course, that it should not.

Habermas likens Gadamer's conservatism to that of the eighteenth century English philosopher Edmund Burke (3), in that both believe that authority is not necessarily authoritarian. He cites what he calls "that harsh sentence" of Gadamer's "that authority has nothing to do with obedience, but rather with knowledge". Gadamer's point, it may be recalled, highlighted the idea that accepting the authority of others (tradition) is not necessarily a blind, or irrational act. It may spring from a recognition that one's own view is limited and that of the other is greater, and should therefore take precedence. Habermas senses in this claim a naive and possibly dangerous extension of the significance of prejudices into being something to which we *should* submit. Not surprisingly he bridles at such an idea, pointing out the political implications of this undialectical view of enlightenment. Gadamer's account is undialectical in that he allows no scope for the power of reflection to break up the knowledge that has been inculcated by tradition. The dialectical to-ing and fro-ing between the grounding prejudices of our tradition, and our reflective power to challenge their authority, is lost in Gadamer's work. For Gadamer, tradition always wins, nullifying or rendering absurd our emancipatory aspirations. Implicit in this, Habermas believes, is a dangerous German political attitude that would claim superiority for its own tradition over and above that of other Western countries. What he presumably has in mind is the role played by tradition in twentieth century German nationalism, Nazism in particular.

It is not exactly clear whether Habermas believes that Gadamer has just downplayed the emancipatory potential that should come with reflection, or whether his description of the power of tradition is altogether mistaken. There are times when he seems to be claiming that tradition is wholly the product of domination, involving no dialogue at all; a view that itself would seem to be undialectical.

However, ostensibly what hermeneutics lacks is a proper awareness of the way the substantiality of tradition is broken up when reflected upon. Gadamer has described, without acknowledging its authoritarian implications, an educational process in which the educator legitimates the prejudices of his or her tradition through a mixture of sanctions and gratifications. The receiver's identification with the educator as a role-model, enables norms to be internalized, prejudices to be sedimented, and thus tradition to go on. This less than rational force which underpins the process is invisible in Gadamer's hermeneutics. Habermas agrees that our prejudices are the preconditions of possible knowledge, and hermeneutics seems also to have the capacity to make transparent the normative framework within which they work. But a prejudice whose structure is rendered transparent should no longer be able to function as a prejudice. Yet this, according to Habermas, is precisely what Gadamer's account implies. Because Gadamer sees knowledge, and the authority of tradition, as coextensive with each other, anything that might challenge the legitimacy of tradition must be regarded as a form of non-knowledge. The prejudices that were inculcated by the educator can only be confirmed in the reflection of the mature adult, because knowledge, on Gadamer's account, always stays within the limits of tradition. The problem, as Habermas sees it, is that hermeneutics comes up against the limits of tradition, as it were, from the inside, and therefore can take up no really critical attitude towards it. For hermeneutics, tradition is always ultimately right.

The basis of Habermas's critique is partly methodological in that he believes that science can help us breach the force of tradition, but there is an insistent moral point being made too. Besides science, Gadamer's underestimation of the power of reflection is also, in effect, a denial of the wider Enlightenment hope for human self-determination, a denial of the intellectual movement that grew up in Western Europe in the eighteenth century which, though it took various forms, broadly recommmended that human beings, through the application of reason to all aspects of life, could free themselves from the repressive and superstitious nature of tradition. Habermas wishes to link this Enlightenment aspiration with left-wing hopes for political emancipation. Even to the present day, in his opposition to postmodernism, he finds a dubious conservatism in those who would undermine the Enlightenment's 'discovery' of reflection. Failure to acknowledge the importance of reflection leads to the confirmation of traditional relationships of domination and subordination. For Reason to be fully itself we must, through reflection, be able to discern the difference between things which have been illegitimately forced upon us, and those that we rightly accept.

> Substantiality disintegrates in reflection, because the latter not only confirms but breaks dogmatic forces. Authority and knowledge do not converge. Certainly, knowledge is rooted in actual tradition; it remains bound to contingent conditions....But as reflection recalls that path of authority through which the grammars of language games were learned dogmatically as rules of worldview and action, authority can be stripped of that in it that was mere domination and dissolved into the less coercive force of insight and rational decision." (Habermas 1988:170)

The tide turns again: down with language and idealist illusions

Habermas then turns his critique from the misplaced ubiquity Gadamer attributes to tradition, to the medium that allowed this illusion to arise, namely language. He has emphatically supported Gadamer's account of language up to now, repeatedly showing what he sees as its superiority to the phenomenological and Wittgensteinian outlooks. He further recognizes that as social action is constituted only in ordinary language communication, it is a good idea to conceive of language as a key social 'meta-institution' on which other social institutions depend. However, while for this reason Gadamer's account of language is vital for the social sciences, the full weight of the empirical social world has not been appreciated by him. There are forces that impose themselves on language, as it were, from the outside, such that one cannot rely on language to be the unfettered medium of being. Language must be thought of not only as the medium of communication, but also of power and domination. It not only brings things to light, but keeps things out of sight too. Hermeneutics, he believes, stays at the level of truth as it is expressed by a society, which means that those truths which that society finds unpalatable will be repressed. In absolutizing language, i.e. making it the sole meta- institution, Gadamer overlooks its status as an ideological force that naturalizes relationships of systematic social inequality, in short, it functions to legitimise class domination :

> ..clearly this meta-institution of language as tradition is dependent in turn on social processes that cannot be reduced to normative relationships. Language is also the medium of domination and social power. It serves to legitimate relationships of organised force. Insofar as legitimations do not articulate the power relationships whose institutionalisation they make possible, insofar as that relationship is merely manifested in the legitimations, language is also ideological. In that case it is not so much a question of deception in language as of deception with language as such." (1988:172)

This last point is important for what Habermas is saying is that language may be systematically distorted, so that from the outset certain social outcomes will favour certain social groups. That is to say, the rationality of everyday life, expressed in linguistically mediated norms, will necessarily ensure the superiority of some groups and the subordination of others. In sociology, Dale Spender(1980) has drawn attention to what she sees as the patriachal norms that are built into the English language in its everyday use. The effect of this is to structure experience in such a way as to validate 'masculinity' as the norm against which the 'feminine' is seen as either aberrant or inferior. This process structures not only men's experience, validating their place in the world, but it also structures women's experience, legitimising their relative inferiority as it pertains to social position and power. Women come to experience their subordinate position as natural. If some actual women wish to attain positions of power they necessarily must reject feminine norms and adopt masculine ones to do so. Hermeneutics, Habermas believes, would fail to recognize this kind of systematic distortion which underpins gender inequalities, because it involves "a deception with language as such". The patriarchal assumptions of language are non-normative in Habermas's terms, because although they are present to language, they do not come into it in a thematized way. They certainly structure social relations through language, but do so invisibly, and thus subvert the dialogic qualities claimed by hermeneutics as intrinsic to language. Gadamer assumes a dialogic symmetry exists where a systematic assymetry may be the norm.

The distinction Habermas draws between a deception in language and one that happens with language as such, is an important one for sociology as it now underpins most contemporary accounts of the workings of ideology. These take for granted that there is something systematically deceptive about the way forms of social control are brought off on a daily basis. The implicit claim is that because we are not dealing with local misunderstandings, or deceptions that happen in a system of communication, but with the deceptiveness of the system itself, only a theory of the system can gain access to its workings. I will deal with Gadamer's response to this challenge later, and only note here that its implications for the concept of ideology are considerable.

However, it is not power alone that shapes language to particular ends, Habermas also claims that systems of labour (i.e.work in the Marxist sense) impose themselves upon language from the outside. As with power, Habermas does not deny that the effects of work organisation happen in language, but they enter unannounced :-

> A change in the mode of production entails a restructuring of the linguistic worldview....Certainly, revolutions in the reproduction of material life are in turn linguistically mediated, but a new practice is not set in motion by a new interpretation. Rather, old patterns of interpretation are also attacked and overthrown "from below" by new practices.(4) (Habermas 1988:173)

In the modern world, science and technology are important productive forces, not only because of their capacity to enhance material production, but also because they feedback a flow of information that addresses the sphere of instrumental action. Habermas believes that this regular flow of information necessarily has an indirect, but real impact, upon our linguistic worldviews. Science and technology now exert the same kind of influence on linguistic world-views that used to be exercised by changes in modes of production. They are not arbitrary language-games in the sense that they could disappear sometime in the future, but rather are "anthropologically deeply anchored". They are the modern way we exploit nature for our own material benefit, and are based on instrumental interpretations of the world that could not be done away with(5). That is to say, the logical structure of purposive- rational action has an intrinsic role to play in the material self- preservation of the human species, whatever the particular historical conditions in which it is located. The system of propositions that make up the modern empirical sciences may relate in the end to "ordinary language as the ultimate metalanguage", but the relation, Habermas believes, is one of impact from the outside. It makes certain kinds of manipulative action toward nature possible and in the process refracts back onto society's wider organisation, altering our linguistic self- understanding. In effect Habermas is bringing Marx to bear against Gadamer, arguing that our relation to the material world cannot be reduced to intersubjective ideas and practices that happen in the medium of language. Hence if interpretive sociology follows Gadamer in seeing language as the essence of tradition, it will fall for a naive idealism, one that believes "linguistically articulated consciousness determines the material being of life-practice". Rather :-

> ..the objective context of social action is not reducible to the dimension of intersubjectively intended and symbolically transmitted meaning. The linguistic infrastructure of society is a moment in a complex that, however symbolically mediated, is also constituted by the constraints of reality: by the constraint of external nature, which enters into the procedures of technological exploitation, and by the constraint of inner nature, which is reflected in the repressions of social relationships of power. (1988:173-4)

Instead, what sociology needs, Habermas claims, is a system of reference, or framework, that will meet two criteria. It must be able to acknowledge the hermeneutic importance of the linguistic and symbolic nature of social action, and not reduce it to a stimulus-response relationship. But at the same time it must not fall prey to hermeneutics' linguistic idealism, it must be able to recognize the force with which the processes of labour and domination impose themselves upon society behind the back of language. In short, sociology must find a theory that is both hermeneutically and causally adequate to explaining its subject matter. The model that meets this dual requirement, he suggests, is Freud's psychoanalysis. The psychoanalyst uses a unique method that combines hermeneutics and functionalism for the purpose of diagnosing distortions in the life of an individual. When the process is successful it breaks up the power unconscious forces have in determining people's lives and hands back to them the power of true 'self-formation'. Habermas has the same practical ambition for a Critical Theory, which instead of working at the level of individual life-history, will work at the level of historically orientated society.

Diagnosing hidden causes requires more than hermeneutics

Habermas finally moves to challenge the claims of a would be hermeneutic sociology by expanding on the theme of social causality. Although he has spent much of the book undermining positivist conceptions of causality in terms of their inapplicability to the social world, he nevertheless sees the absence of causal explanations as the decisive weakness of hermeneutic sociology. His aim is to outline an alternative view that embraces some of the force with which cause and effect are related in nature, but one that doesn't naively ignore the symbolic constitution of social reality.

He acknowledges that there has been no explicit development of a sociology based on either Gadamer's hermeneutics or Winch's linguistic style of analysis, although the work that has come out of the tradition of symbolic interactionism bears close resemblance to them in its concern with linguistic interpretation. He has in mind Cooley, Thomas, George Herbert Mead, and particularly Anselm Strauss, who has purged the behaviouristic elements from his own linguistic analysis. Strauss's sociology, as Habermas describes it, deals with the process of change from the angle of linguistic frameworks of meaning. His starting point is the way new situations and problematic events generate new vocabularies of meaning in people. These vocabularies have to be confirmed in daily interaction, but from them a new self-identity can develop. The reality of alienation, for example, may be experienced in terms of a loss in credibility of one's world-view. The linguistic reference system by which one lives may lose its cogency, and in order to restore it and one's own identity too, a new common linguistic terminology must be developed. Certainly, Habermas believes, these processes of change are well analyzed as changes in language - but the change itself remains unfathomable from the standpoint of interpretive sociology.

Strauss, he claims, sees the ego as a "linguistically creative spontaneity" somewhat akin to the vitalistic account given in Sartre's existential philosophy. Society is seen as an "unresisting medium for new language projects and playful revisions of world-views". There is an assumption that the subject moves freely about creating frameworks of meaning as the need arises, for Habermas such a view of course merely echoes the weaknesses of Gadamer's linguistic idealism. The weakness is that social action is always and only explained in terms of motives that are identical with the actor's own linguistically mediated situation.

> The limitations of a linguistically oriented sociology are the limitations of its concept of motivation. It explains social action in terms of motives that are identical with the actors own interpretation of situations, and thus identical with the linguistically orientated meaning in terms of which the actor

orients himself. The subjective approach, whether it is grounded in phenomenolgy, linguistics, or hermeneutics, thus rules out a distinction between observed segments of behaviour and the actor's interpretation. (1988:177)

It is therefore insufficient for the sociologist to rely on motives as surrogate causes for social action. The sociologist must move beyond the hermeneutic starting situation and embrace causality for a fully adequate explanation of social action.

However, this is not all there is to Habermas's case. It must be remembered that he constantly tacks back and forth between two theoretical poles, and here, no sooner has he limited the significance of 'motives' in order to emphasise the importance of 'causes', than he tacks back again to save 'motives' from being eliminated by 'causes' at the hands of A.J.Ayer.

Ayer's positivist argument attacks the distinction between motives and causes on the grounds that the former can be reduced to the latter and treated as observable data like any other. Behaviour can be described in terms of some given physical state of affairs, or as part of some system, with the result that 'motives' can be identified as causes without reference to any transmitted human tradition of meaning. That is to say people's motives can be explained as surrogate causes within a wider system of cause and effect relations. However Habermas believes that this approach breaks down at two points. First, he does not see how systems that include our motives can be described at all without reference to our social tradition of meaning, i.e. our motives inevitably refer to the meanings accumulated by our culture in its history. Secondly, although Ayer recognizes that 'physical' and 'social' descriptions are different, and a process of decoding is required to move from one to the other, he fails to see just how problematic this may be. The controlled observation that science undertakes is not done neutrally, but from the point of view of technical control. Moreover, this interest in technical control is indifferent to questions of meaning, and yet what the 'data' means to the actors concerned constitutes the nature of that 'data'. What the 'same data' means can vary highly from one situation to another(6).

Clearly Habermas does not want to simply batten a traditional positivist notion of causality on to Critical Theory, but how best then to hold on to the poles of both meaning and cause ? He does not believe that the positivist version of causality is the only way to conceptualise the force with which work and domination impinge on the social world, Freud's model of the human personality provides him with the solution. His interest in Freud is not with the details of the theory but in the rationale of the ideas, or what they open up epistemologically speaking, for the social sciences.

Of course Habermas is well aware that in the social sciences the possible analogy between motives and causes is a minefield of problems. Indeed in his previous discussion of the contribution of Aristotle's thought to hermeneutics, he clearly accepted the importance of the differences between the technical laws of nature and the normative rules of social life. Yet he wants to hold to the idea that there is an important resemblance too. Freud's concept of unconscious forces structuring our conscious actions carries both elements. Explanations of behaviour using the concept of the unconscious are intentional explanations in that they are bound up with the meaning of our lives and the significance we attribute to things. The motives people have for their actions may not be conscious, but they are purposive in charcter, and part of a symbolically organised network of meaning which can only be understood hermeneutically. It is their unconscious quality that disguises their real nature and makes them function as if they were causes :-

> Unconscious motives, like conscious ones, take the form of interpreted needs; thus they are given in symbolic contexts and can be understood hermeneutically. Dream analysis proceeds hermeneutically, as does the interpretation of hysterical symptoms or compulsive behaviour. On the other hand these motives are not given to the acting subject; they are excluded from consciousness through repression....On the one hand, unconsciously motivated actions are objectively meaningful; they can be interpreted. On the other hand, these motives have the status of causes, because they prevail outside the subjects' awareness. (1988:180)

However the process of uncovering unconscious 'causes' is not the straightforward hermeneutic exercise that it might seem. Though Habermas has just tacked away from Ayer's account of causality to avoid its naturalism, he next veers back in the opposite direction, ths time away from Alastair MacIntyre's account of motivation to avoid its lack of awareness of the force with which hidden motives can function like causes. In MacIntyre's hands, he claims, Freud's concept of unconscious motivation is no different from the ordinary sense of motivation. For MacIntyre, psychoanalysis is just a therapeutic form of linguistic- hermeneutic analysis, albeit of unconscious motives. It is still only mere interpretation. So keen is MacIntyre to purge Freud's work of its positivist connotations, and promote motives at the expense of causes that he is unable to see the significance the categorial framework that Freud developed.

Habermas is trying to hold the line between science and hermeneutics and Freud's framework provides a model that contains features of both, but fends off the weaknesses of both. How effective he is in opening up what is in effect a new middle ground is important, because he will later use it to establish the relevance of what he calls the 'reconstructive sciences', i.e. Kohlberg's moral development psychology and his own universal pragmatics. They, like psychoanalysis, sit between science and hermeneutics, and have objective critical qualities. He describes Freud's framework as permitting :-

> ..the reconstruction of particular life-histories in accordance with a generally binding model. It is to this model that psychoanalysis owes its appearance of being a general theory. In actuality it is a systematically generalized history. (1988:182)

Psychoanalysis then, resembles science because it has a general framework within which particular life-histories can be explained. But this general framework is actually a "systematically generalized history" drawn from individual cases. It is not easy to say exactly what Habermas intends in specifying a difference between the general in psychoanalysis and the general in science. Clearly, he sees psychoanalysis as having a general framework under which particular cases are subsumed - much like science. However some difference is intended and this seems to revolve around the relations between the parts of the personality which have to be seen, contra-science, in a non-instrumental way. Nevertheless he finds clear advantages in psychoanalysis having a general that functions like the general in science. It is based on the regular patterns and stages of mental development that individuals go through from birth to maturity. This, Habermas believes, forms a kind of 'objective narrative' that enables the analyst to say that some behaviours are normal and some deviant. The advantage of this is that it abolishes the relativism implicit in MacIntyre's 'mere hermeneutics of motives'. With Freud's work we can explain problems and conflicts, and indicate what a correct solution would look like; whereas a hermeneutics of motives would only leave us with the insoluble problem of choosing between competing interpretations.

Habermas presses the claims for a quasi-scientific psychoanalysis still further by emphasising the human personality as a functional system made up of inter-dependent parts. The system may originally have been understood in hermeneutic fashion, but now must be understood, at least partly, in a different way from the way we understand texts. Where the interpreter of a text is always involved in the circular process of correcting prejudgements against what the text says, Freud has established a once and for all framework for analyzing the human personality :-

> One can perhaps see this framework as the result of repeated clinical experiences, which have themselves been accumulated in

> accordance with the more elastic procedure of hermeneutic anticipations that are confirmed in a circular fashion. Once established, the interpretive framework no longer permits such correction. In compensation, it offers the advantages of a functionalistic framework." (1988:183)

Thus the individual's biographical details become the interdependent variables which make up a system which has some causal force. Of course Habermas is careful not to extend the analogy too far. He retains an awareness of the significance of what hermeneutics has discovered. The functionalist system of the personality has to be interpreted properly, in terms of meaning which is produced, rather than given as an object to the analyst. The process, he believes, should be likened to drama rather than to the automatic behaviour of a purely objectivised system. The relationship between the parts and the whole of the personality, in the drama model is mediated through the power of reflection rather than taking the mechanical form of a purely objectivised system. The system is both subject and object - 'a formative process in which we are both actor and critic at once'.

Freud's framework is therefore a "general interpretive model" rather than a straightforward "general theory". The psychoanalyst takes his framework to be a general background narrative which can be used to fill in the interrupted processes of self-formation from which the individual is suffering. The analyst will be able to piece together the fragments of a life from the patient and reconstruct it in its fullness as a narrative. He will be able to anticipate the significance of certain experiences, something which is outside the capacity of the patient, but can suggest interpretations of their life-history that can only be confirmed when the patient recognizes them as their own. It is only then that the unconscious causal force of the motive can be seen to be broken. This seems once more to place Habermas in the hermeneutic camp. Confirmation of the truth of the interpretation cannot be operationalised through scientific method, its truth can only be recognized in the communicative situation, as Gadamer would suggest. On the other hand Habermas remains distrustful of hermeneutic procedures alone, for if the analyst's interpretation is not accepted by the patient, this may be because the power of the causal forces still prevail over the patient. He seems to be saying that this is a dilemma which has to be accepted.

Overall he finds that the model of psychoanalysis brings home the limitations of a linguistic-hermeneutic sociology, and in this directs us to the importance of law-like relationships. It highlights the fact that there are classes of 'invisible' social phenomena, of "need- interpretations", which are not socially sanctioned, but which nevertheless structure the lives of mature adults. The 'tradition' that Gadamer describes, according to Habermas, has no space where these phenomena can appear, they are censored and disguised and misunderstood within the framework of everyday interpretation. They are established behind the backs of acting subjects but still orient the meaning of their social action. They may be symbolic in character, and in this be entirely in line with Gadamer's description of our 'linguistic being', but because they are concealed they have the causal power to determine matters. To understand how this power works requires a functionalist approach that can penetrate the systematic effects of hidden causes on tradition. It can reveal how these forces shape tradition even though they are external to it.

However, while he finds clear limitations to a sociology based on hermeneutics, he simultaneously warns against a functionalism that sacrifices the intentional nature of the social in the process of explaining it. He has Talcott Parsons' work in mind. Parsons understands the telos of a social system in a purely descriptive way, in effect any way that 'equilibrium' can be achieved. This ignores the constitutive importance of the actors own self-understanding, and the categories they use in orienting their action. If these approaches are to be properly knitted together then we should forget about the desired end-state of the system being a neutral 'equilibrium'. This is a goal based solely on a system's instrumental capacity to regulate itself. A Critical Theory that has emancipatory hopes must replace this with one that anticipates the goal that is human self-formation. Psychoanalysis provides a model of theory that manages to do this at an individual level, something which Critical Theory should aspire to do at a societal level.

Notes

1. Paul Ricoeur has explicitly taken up the mantle of carrying the ontological analyses of Heidegger back to the level of methodology.

2. The notion here only referred to, that forms of knowledge have 'interests' built into them is developed in a thoroughgoing way in *Knowledge And Human Interests* (1971). The argument is that different forms of knowledge are guided by quasi-transcendental interests which orientate the meaning of what they can produce. Hence the empirical-analytic sciences are guided by an interest that produces knowledge suitable for instrumental exploitation. The hermeneutic disciplines are geared toward reaching common agreement over social and moral matters. There is a third interest in emancipation, which characterizes critical disciplines, such as pschoanalysis and 'ideology-critique' or Critical Theory). It was Habermas's claim at the time that these were anthropologically deep seated, i.e. they were in effect part of the human condition.

3. The analogy is not merely polemical either, Gadamer (1989:273) acknowledges Burke as one who also challenged the Enlightenment

antipathy to prejudices, recommending that we look much more carefully at the latent wisdom within them.

4. It is interesting to note that some ten years later, in the essay 'Historical Materialism And The Development Of Normative Structures' (Habermas1979:cht3), he claims almost the reverse. Namely, that it is reinterpretations in the sphere of ideas that leads to changes in systems of production. In this later essay he is concerned to show that changes in worldviews, contra-Marx, exhibit a developmental rationale of their own and are (a) triggered by the need to resolve moral problems internal to worldviews, and (b) that this enables changes to happen at the level of society's productive forces. As he puts it :-

> ..there are good reasons meanwhile for assuming that learning processes also take place in the dimension of moral insight, practical knowledge, communicative action and the consensual regulation of action conflicts - learning processes that are deposited in more mature forms of social integration, in new productive relations, and that in turn first make possible the introduction of new productive forces. (Habermas 1979: 97-98)

5. He developed a similar kind of criticism in relation to Marcuse in the essay 'Technology And Science As Ideology' which appeared in *Towards A Rational Society* (1972). He shared Marcuse's antipathy to technical reason, but denied that it could be superceded by our developing a more fraternal relation with nature. His opposition to technical reason was that it had become universalized as the only form of reason. It would of necessity continue, though hopefully stripped of its universal pretensions. See McCarthy (1978:389:note15).

6. For example Ken Plummer (1976) comes up with the vivid phrase "nothing is sexual but naming makes it so". He is concerned to show the wide variety of different situations that can be described as sexual. These situations are sexual by virtue of the way they are defined by the actors concerned not by virtue of their biological features

9 Round two: Gadamer's first reply (a) on the real scope of hermeneutics

On the real scope of hermeneutics

Gadamer's almost immediate reply to Habermas' first critique came in the form of the essay, 'Rhetoric, Hermeneutics, And The Critique Of Ideology'. The two translations of this, in Gadamer (1976) and Mueller-Vollmer (1986), do not make easy reading for the Anglophone. It is quite difficult to discern from them the real adequacy of his response, his argument at first sight seems awkward and tangential to the issues Habermas raised. I shall quote from both of them according to which seems to provide the clearest account of Gadamer's response (1).

Unlike Habermas, Gadamer has no grand theoretical goal against which to measure the validity of particular elements. Nor is it his style to offer any kind of polemical response, instead he writes in an enquiring, exploratory manner, gradually searching out the claims Habermas makes, not to dismiss them, but to ask further questions about them - questions that challenge the whole project of Critical Theory. Indeed in the first instance he does not directly address Habermas' critique at all, but restates in the broadest terms what he sees as the essence of his own hermeneutics.

The task of philosophical hermeneutics is to show how an interpretive dimension exists in all our understandings of the world:-

..from interpersonal communication to social manipulation, from the experience of the individual as a member of society to his experience of that society itself, from the tradition comprised of religion and law, art and philosophy, to the liberating, reflective energy of the revolutionary consciousness. (Gadamer 1986:274)

Though Habermas is not mentioned by name at the outset, there is an implication that he has tried to close down in an entirely misleading way, the full reach of hermeneutics. Hermeneutics in fact embraces those phenomena, such as social control, and revolutionary challenges to that control which Habermas placed beyond tradition and thus beyond the capacity of hermeneutics to comprehend.

Gadamer refuses this closure spreading his net wide in order to reaffirm the full scope of the ideas he developed in *Truth and Method*, pointing out that his own choice of starting points, in the experience of art and history, should not be seen as limitations to the hermeneutic project. They were not meant to indicate that hermeneutics was good at analysing these and not other things. In fact they culminated in an account of the essentially linguistic character of our entire relation to the world. The phenomenon of 'linguisticality' does not exclude but embraces all things, though they will unfold differently in different dimensions. This is the basis, Gadamer claims, for the universality of hermeneutics.

He then links together three intellectual areas; rhetoric, hermeneutics, and sociology, through the common connection they have particularly with 'linguisticality', and also 'praxis' (2). The purpose of this, I think, is two-fold. First, to show that what characterises rhetoric and hermeneutics may also be characteristic of sociology. Secondly, that when Habermas champions scientific objectivity over hermeneutics, and in spite of all the qualifications he makes to his case, he quite mistakenly restricts hermeneutics to the study of 'the mind'. This assumption then artificially places 'the mind' in opposition to the 'real world' which must become an object for scientific method. Of course such a division is symptomatic of the same positivist outlook that Habermas is seeking to challenge. It should be added that Gadamer does not present his case in this explicit way but invites his readers gradually towards this conclusion.

Rhetoric, hermeneutics, and sociology

Although the disciplines of rhetoric, hermeneutics, and sociology, are distant from each other both historically and intellectually, they are all intimately tied in with language. The skill of rhetoric, for example, which developed in ancient Greece, is positively tied in with language in that it was concerned with the active art of persuasion through language. It was Plato who challenged the shallow but flashy skills of the Sophists in order to establish the proper foundation of rhetoric. By contrast hermeneutics' relation to language is a negative one, being (originally) concerned with the explication of things already written down. Unlike rhetoric, hermeneutics' concerns were detached from the immediacy of speech, in the sense that the audience for a text was removed from the writer's own direct concerns. Indeed it arose in a quite different set of circumstances in the modern world, where our relationship to tradition had become problematic. Its task was to re-animate what had become strange and distant by building a bridge between past and present. But in spite of these differences the act of making sense of a text, Gadamer claims, has the same autonomous quality that the orator brings to bear in making a speech. Gadamer does not expand on just what he means in saying this, but I take him to mean that in understanding a text the reader, like the orator making a speech, is an active participant in the production of meaning. In both cases the shaping, suasive character of language is of the essence. This same quality, he implies, is necessarily relevant to sociology because 'linguisticality' is also "deeply woven into the sociality of human existence", as Habermas himself demonstrated. The significance of it however does not lead in Habermas' direction.

'Rhetoric' and the truth of the plausible

Hermeneutics champions a claim to truth that is confirmed by rhetoric and is different in kind from the claims made by science. Where science demands proof to establish certainty, rhetoric, hermeneutics, and by implication sociology, must necessarily be wedded to the idea of truth as plausibility.

> And where else, indeed, should theoretical reflection on the art of understanding turn than to rhetoric, which from the earliest days of the tradition has been the sole champion of a claim to truth which vindicates the plausible, theeikos (verisimilar), and that which is illuminating to common sense against science's claim to proof and certainty? (Gadamer 1986b:278-9)

Gadamer is arguing that Habermas has set hermeneutics in opposition to science, as something that needs lifting out of its pre-scientific naivety, but in so doing he fails to properly recognise the validity of a whole other species of rationality. This, even though he seems so thoroughly to have agreed with his views on the way language constitutes rationality.

Gadamer's use of the art of rhetoric is provocative because it challenges our contemporary understanding of it as 'mere rhetoric', that is as a deception done with language, certainly as something superfluous to the truth. But Gadamer claims rhetoric has its own rationality which is akin to that of hermeneutics, and is the rationality which underpins everyday life. It entails the art of persuasion, where what is being claimed asks for recognition through its evidentness to common sense; it shows itself valid without scientifically proving itself. Such knowledge is necessarily malleable but not thereby insubstantial, it exists in the realm of the possible and the probable, which is also of course the social. Gadamer in fact draws attention to the relation between rhetoric and hermeneutics not only in this essay but elsewhere too (Gadamer 1981:119-23,1986a:17, 1989:19-21,88-89,485,567) (3). However his purpose here is quite specific. He is suspicious that Habermas has hopes that language can be purified of ideology, and that this involves a misunderstanding of the basically rhetorical nature of language. Language's suasive power should not be seen as creating a deformed communication which might be straightened out by a critique of ideology, it is the universal form that human communication must take insofar as language shapes, indeed constitutes 'the world'. There is an added irony in that Habermas himself writes in a galloping, oratorical style, the better to convince others of the validity of his case. And certainly any tradition that includes Adorno, Marcuse, and Horkheimer, cannot be thought innocent of using rhetoric (4).

Gadamer's main claim however at this point is that the role of rhetoric has not been diminished one iota by the development of science. In fact science itself depends on rhetoric :-

> nor is.....this vast realm of illuminating convictions and prevailing opinions (rhetoric) in the least diminished, gradually or otherwise, by the progress of science, however great that may be; on the contrary, it expands to take in every new advance in scientific knowledge, in order to claim it for itself and bring it in to conformity with its own nature. The ubiquitousness of rhetoric is truly unlimited; for only through rhetoric does science become a social factor in our lives. (1986b:279)

Gadamer means that science is a force in our lives because it enters and is taken up into the everyday world through language. In the process it necessarily gains its practical significance through the rhetorical field that is everyday life. The language of everyday life for Gadamer has priority over scientific language in a logical as well as a chronological sense, and this marks a difference between him and Habermas, albeit one that only becomes clear in their second exchange. In the second exchange Habermas still accepts that the lifeworld has many of the qualities described by Gadamer, but chooses to sharpen up the differences between these and the qualities that characterise scientific languages. He does this in order to highlight once more the limits of hermeneutic thinking. It also I think signals a subtle but importance difference between them over whether language is fundamentally rhetorical or logical, which I shall raise in the discussion that follows.

However at this point Gadamer cites Henri Gouhier's work on Descartes, which has shown that even such an advocate of "method and certainty" as Descartes, used the tools of rhetoric with consummate skill. In saying this Gadamer almost seems to echo some of the ideas of the earlier Frankfurt School authors who recognised that science's claim to neutrality was itself rhetorical in nature.

Praxis and sociology

Gadamer presses the interdependence of rhetoric, hermeneutics, and sociology a bit further, shifting briefly from his discussion of 'linguisticality' to a discussion of 'praxis'. In this he is again drawing attention to a feature of his work that Habermas previously endorsed. He points out that all three disciplines have an important relationship to, and are ultimately determined by, praxis. As a result any scientific status they might wish to claim will necessarily be equivocal. Success in these areas, particularly rhetoric, and hermeneutic understanding, does not depend on following theoretical rules but on acquiring skill through praxis. The ability to persuade others, or to understand the meaning of a text, or indeed to make sense of the social world, does not depend on adhering to a given method, but on the experience gained in life-practice (praxis). At best theory will be able to explain why the skill of one gifted individual surpasses that of others - but only after the event, after the quality and meaning of the skill has been established in praxis. The relationship between theory and praxis in these areas is therefore the opposite of that which holds in science. In these areas theory has a secondary position, it is an afterthought, an abstraction derived from what has already been established by praxis.

Gadamer does not expand on the account of Aristotle's view of praxis and its relation to theory (science), but by implication Habermas, who wants to establish an historically oriented theory of society, with the practical aim of furthering the self-formation of the species, has got the relationship back to front. He sees social-historical praxis (tradition) as something distorted and in need of rectification by a (Critical) theory. In this, even though he acknowledges the need for reciprocity between theory and praxis, he is closer to the modern positivist idea of science as something that bequeaths the truth, and demands that practice follow in its wake (5). Gadamer by contrast, I think sees praxis and the wisdom that accumulates in it as the fundamental datum of our social existence, and something quite different in kind to theoretical knowledge. Praxis has its own dialogic volition and provides the backdrop to theory which is a particular kind of social praxis that has developed in the West.

In this opening part of his first reply to Habermas Gadamer is reminding the reader that hermeneutics has a certain kind of universality based on the 'linguistical' quality of all things. This stands in counterpoint to the claims of scientific reason, which Habermas invokes as reason of a higher order. At the same time he wants to show more substantively that his analysis of hermeneutics does not only refer to written texts, but by virtue of 'linguisticality' also to the social and political realms. It was, of course, the unrecognised force with which political domination imposes itself upon tradition that was at the heart of Habermas' criticisms of hermeneutics. Thus when Gadamer shows there are links between rhetoric, hermeneutics, and sociology, he is trying to open up the limitations Habermas has imposed on it - for the social and the political are surely realms where rhetoric, the art of plausible persuasion, not science, actually holds sway.

Hermeneutics and critical sociology

It is in both rhetoric and hermeneutics that language shows its limitlessness in being able to embrace everything - not just our cultural heritage, "but everything pure and simple"(p279). This statement is reminiscent of the way Gadamer described language in the final sections of Truth And Method: "Being that can be understood is language" (P474), which of course echoes Heidegger's claim that language is the 'house of Being'. In fact though he cites Plato's idea that only through the mirror of speech do we become fully aware of things in their undiminished truth. He also points to Plato's equally profound insight that all cognition is re-cognition, the idea of a "first cognition" is as impossible as a first word (6). Gadamer is reminding us is that all our understanding takes place within a language in which we are always already embroiled. Language is not just a particular social-historical artefact, it is that medium through which we have a 'world', and thus nothing that is intelligible remains outside it. Habermas it will be recalled, acknowledged that language was a key social meta-institution, but one amongst others which imposed themselves on it from the outside.

Gadamer also again points out that it is a mistake to assume that hermeneutics is not universal because it originally dealt with texts that had been misinterpreted or were incomprehensible. In fact bringing texts into comprehensibility is only a special case of what happens in the world at large, where what is strange to our expectations is brought to understanding through language, and a new familiarity engendered. These two elements, (the strange and the familiar), flow together through the medium of language and form our tradition. In saying this Gadamer is highlighting the fact that things which are incomprehensible or have been misinterpreted, i.e. those elements that

Habermas might call ideological, are in fact the very stuff of hermeneutical activity. The implication is that Habermas' ideology-critique is in fact a special case of hermeneutics, and not the other way round as Habermas claimed (7). Gadamer frequently reiterates the point that the critique of ideology as an activity, is hermeneutical through and through. He does this to highlight the doubtfulness of Habermas establishing a distance for Critical Theory from social praxis through the use of science, while claiming to want to influence it.

Gadamer notes that when Habermas adopted hermeneutics it was for the purpose of making it serve the methodology of the social sciences. This move was of considerable moment because it severed hermeneutics from its original project. In essence Habermas' social science seeks an emancipation from tradition, but this contrasts with hermeneutics which has sought to recover the best from the past, not its elimination.

Of course as Gadamer acknowledges the essence of modern science, is "methodical alienation", and it is present throughout the humanities (8). By "methodical alienation" he means the controlled distance from the object of investigation that those working in the humanities and social sciences achieve by using (scientific) method. Nor did he intend to simply demean method by suggesting it was irrelevant. There was no simple opposition in his account between truth and method, such that method need be rejected to achieve truth, as Habermas claimed. Rather, the humanities were chosen because they are based on experiences that ultimately lie beyond science, even where those experiences are part of a tradition that has been profoundly affected by science.

Gadamer has in mind of course the experience of art, and of one's own cultural tradition. The hermeneutical experience is operative in these and other experiences too, but it is not the outcome of "methodical alienation". That is, you do not arrive at this experience of art by adopting methods that will produce it for you. Quite the reverse. The hermeneutical experience precedes "methodical alienation" and allows the appropriate questions to emerge and be asked of the subject matter. It is only then that the possibility of using methods comes to the fore. Yet Habermas is suggesting, Gadamer believes, that sociology needs to lift itself out the hermeneutical experience, in order to stop it being a pre-scientific activity and become a fully conscious one.

More than once Gadamer draws ironically on this juxtaposition between science and consciousness in Habermas' writings, as its assumptions represent a peculiar amalgam for one developing the Frankfurt School tradition of thought. For his predecessors, and to some extent for Habermas too, positivist procedures were a source of obfuscation, not least because they reified rather than clarified consciousness. So to find them now being used as a catalyst for emancipation has a distinctly contradictory air about it.

Certainly, Gadamer acknowledges that science has developed by replacing the ad hoc inventiveness of individual effort with controlled methods that can be learnt. It may also be the case that social sciences which are aware of the hermeneutical dimension are able to develop from them "methodical contrivances" that benefit them. However in parenthesis he asks whether the discovery of so-called "real structures" of society entails no more than the use of the "sedimented truisms" of our linguistic tradition i.e. the taken for granted assumptions of everyday life. And that the social scientist is often not interested in understanding what these things mean, but only in forgetting the hermeneutical dimension as soon as possible, the quicker to arrive at a structural account. In other words, if Habermas' aim is to make hermeneutics serve the methodology of the social sciences then the hermeneutical experience will lose its socially constitutive role and shrink to become no more than a pool of hunches. The real significance of the experience will be lost in being tested for validity only as empirical hypotheses. In these circumstances one must ask whether methodical alienation simply leads to alienated understanding ? Which was, of course just what Habermas set out to overcome.

However, even if this does happen, Gadamer still believes that hermeneutical reflection will not be contained by the diminished role social science allots to it. It will continue to reflect on the alienated basis of social science methodology regardless of any positivist denigration. He does not say why this will happen, but I assume that given the ontological basis of the hermeneutical experience it cannot be completely extinguished even by the cultural pre-eminence of scientific method.

Notes

1. The translation by Jerry Dibble in Mueller-Vollmer (1986) is usually taken to be the more comprehensive, but the translation by G.B.Hess and R.E.Palmer entitled 'On The Scope And Function Of Hermeneutical Reflection' in Gadamer (1976) reads more clearly and purposefully in English. The latter translation originally appeared in *Continuum* VolVIII, 1970.

2. Gadamer's choice of rhetoric that shares things in common with hermeneutics is of more than casual significance. He links rhetoric or the art of speaking well with 'the beautiful', i.e. both, in the way that all things that are meaningful, have the quality of 'shining out' or 'speaking to us' in ways at odds with deductive modes of thought.

3. Klaus Duckhorn (1980) in a very informative review claims that the tradition of rhetoric is more significant in *Truth And Method* than is usually thought. For example he identifies the key concepts in Part 1, i.e. *Bildung* (edification), *sensus communis* (common sense), *judgement,* and *taste,* as having their origin in the rhetoric tradition.

4. In the Afterword of the 1989 revised edition of *Truth And Method* Gadamer confirms this :-

    When I considered the conflict between hermeneutics and ideology together with the powerful role played by rhetoric, this was no literary accident but instead a well considered sketch of a thematic whole. Marx, Mao, and Marcuse - whose names are inscribed on many walls these days - certainly do not have "unconstrained dialogue" to thank for their popularity. (1989:567)

5. One commentator, Rudiger Bubner (1975), finds the theory/practice relationship to be the nub of the debate.

6. It is interesting to note that Gadamer uses Plato in support of his case on this point rather than Heidegger. Heidegger's challenge was to the whole Western tradition of metaphysical thinking, *including* science. Habermas criticises Gadamer for what he regards as his opposition to science but may in fact be wide of the mark in not considering fully the differences between Gadamer and Heidegger. Gadamer's discussions of Plato generally suggest that he has a more sympathetic attitude towards the philosophical tradition and is less anti-science than Heidegger.

7. I am referring to the general tenor of Habermas' case in *On The Logic Of The Social Sciences* where he tries to draw a line beyond which hermeneutics cannot reach but Critical Theory can. This culminates in the statement that "hermeneutic experience, encountering this dependence of symbolic context on actual relationships, becomes a critique of ideology" (p172).

8. I have put - scientific - in brackets to indicate that Gadamer is referring to a broad attitude of mind rather than the use of scientific method as such. He is referring to something that imbues not only the social sciences but the humanities generally. As Mueller-Vollmer notes Gadamer uses the English term 'the humanities' at this point. Richard Palmer (1969) was one of the first to recognise the presence of this even in the study of literature.

10 Round two: Gadamer's first reply (b) language is more than it seems

You can't have one without the other: 'linguisticality' and 'historically effected consciousness'

As Gadamer's account of language is so central to the overall argument in *Truth And Method,* as well as being crucial to Habermas' case, it is no surprise that he spends some time and effort clarifying what he means by 'linguisticality'.

He asks questions about the particular and peculiar way Habermas employs 'linguisticality' in relation to 'historically effected consciousness'. The argument is rather difficult to grasp, but essentially Gadamer is trying to tease out a contradiction he sees between Habermas' claim that 'linguisticality' opens up history for us, and a contra-claim he makes that the concept of 'historically effected consciousness', closes history down, or at least makes hermeneutical study of it a waste of time.

Habermas identified the "linguistic approach" as the distinctive contribution hermeneutics had made to sociology, in that it recognised human sociality as fundamentally linguistic in nature (4). Gadamer acknowledges this, and notes that his approach to language was also identified as more adequate that Wittgenstein's or Winch's, because it opened up the significance of our involvement in history. However Habermas seems only to want to take those bits of the 'history' argument that suit his case.

It may be recalled that Habermas criticised the language-games approach because it was based on the idea that to understand something socially or historically alien, we had to efface our own linguistic prejudices for the sake of objectivity. By contrast, Gadamer's description of the dialogic nature of language enabled us to see that (language) boundaries are porous in both directions, and that our prejudices are actually required for understanding to take place. Moreover, these prejudices also make up our 'effected historical consciousness', i.e. (roughly speaking) our awareness of being constituted by history.

As a result of Gadamer's account, Habermas had argued that we could now grasp the importance of the historical dimension and conceptualise it without falling prey to a naive objectivism. However, Gadamer believes that while Habermas accepted part of the case, (that inherent prejudices accompany all thought and action), he did so for reasons that are at odds with other aspects of hermeneutical reflection, notably the role of 'effected historical consciousness'.

Gadamer notes that Habermas asked what hermeneutical reflection on 'effected historical consciousness' is able to accomplish in its own right ? It may challenge a full blown philosophy of history, but can it do anything else ? If historians are the products of historical tradition in being tied to the prejudices of their horizon, what use is this knowledge to them ? Habermas' answer was that it is of no use, and of no consequence to practising historians. He countered this lack with the importance of projecting a 'universal history'. That is, the idea that every historian inevitably writes as if from the point of view of 'the last historian'. Every historian necessarily writes in such a way as to anticipate the final, complete meaning of historical events. As this is the case, (at least Habermas asserted it was so), then it is misleading to claim that every historical account is only provisional and subject to revision.

Gadamer does not however respond in quite the way you might expect. He does not point out that Habermas has overlooked the systematic connections between 'linguisticality' and 'historically effected consciousness', such that the prejudices of our linguistic horizon open up our history, but by definition can never open up 'universal history'. Instead, he directly answers the question about what real hermeneutical reflection *can* do and warns of the dubious implications present in Habermas' alternative :-

> My thesis is - and I think it is the necessary consequence of recognising the operativeness of history in our conditionedness and finitude - that the thing which hermeneutics teaches us is to see through the dogmatism of asserting an opposition and separation between the ongoing, natural "tradition" and the reflective appropriation of it. For behind this assertion stands a dogmatic objectivism that distorts the very concept of

> hermeneutical reflection itself. In this objectivism the understander is seen - even in the so-called sciences of understanding like history - not in relationship to the hermeneutical situation and the constant operativeness of history in his own consciousness, but in such a way as to imply that his own understanding does not enter into the event (Gadamer 1976:28)

Here is Gadamer's clearest statement yet about how his project differs from Habermas' own, and it highlights a fundamental divergence in orientation between the two thinkers. Gadamer's most basic attitude orients him towards seeing the connectedness between things, finding complicity even between oppositions. By contrast Habermas attitude actively heightens dualism, for example setting off reason in direct opposition to tradition.

In this quotation Gadamer is claiming that there can be no simple opposition, let alone final separation between the fact that we inhabit tradition, and the fact that we can reflect upon this habitation. The act of reflecting on tradition happens as an event of tradition, and this act cannot sever its relation to tradition but actually furthers tradition itself. He suspects is that Habermas, with his claims about the power that reflection has to dissemble tradition, is concealing a "dogmatic objectivism". That is, the way Habermas talks about tradition, as something from which we can gain distance through using (scientific) method, is a reduplication of the positivism he is trying to overcome. It entails the objectivist assumption that we can take up an Archimedean point outside tradition which will enable us to make tradition into an object for analysis. It is dogmatic because it forgets the operativeness of history working in the critical theorist or historian, and claims a quite spurious authority for views based on that forgetfulness.

Gadamer argues the point further. He claims that the historian who is critical of tradition, will in fact be all the more thoroughly aware of how much conditioned he is by tradition. In other words, to be critical of tradition the historian must become more, not less thoroughly immersed in it. Such historians, so far from dissolving their tradition, actually become 'national historians' in contributing to its ongoing formation (5). It is only a naive and unreflective kind of historicism that would claim to have finished with tradition and be able to start something entirely new.

What he tried to show in *Truth And Method*, Gadamer declares, was that linguisticality operates in all our understanding, and that a process of linguistical mediation constitutes our historical tradition. This means in effect that we can no more step outside our tradition than we can step outside language. By implication, Habermas' talk of 'the last historian' as someone who has tacitly projected themselves beyond their hermeneutic horizon, is as empty in its forgetfulness as the idea of there being a world wholly independent of language.

It is through language we encounter domination; it is through language we challenge it.

Against the breadth of this account of linguisticality, Habermas set up a rather shrunken version of the hermeneutic approach in the form of a kind of "linguistic idealism". It was based on the idea that our linguistic tradition is no more than mere "cultural tradition", an area where only norms and values reside. As such it necessarily appears as a restricted part of the totality, one capable only of furthering the process of cultural transmission. When it comes to the realms of work and domination it is helpless, and to be effective would have to transform itself into a critique of ideology. Gadamer finds this reduction of his views entirely misleading, and to be the product of Habermas' particular wish to harness hermeneutics to the interests of his critical sociology. But again he points out that rhetoric and hermeneutics have parallel ambitions to the critique of ideology and all three are fundamentally tied in with linguisticality. Rhetoric (as theory) aimed to cut through the "bewitchment of consciousness through the power of speech" by establishing a distinction between things that are warranted and those that are unwarranted. Hermeneutics' aim was to re-establish intersubjective agreement, in particular by overcoming an epistemology based on objectivism. Similarly, there is an emancipatory interest at work in (critical) sociology, which tries to bring the unjustified compulsions of the social world to consciousness. These compulsions tend to legitimise themselves in and through language, and the task Habermas sets the critique of ideology is to expose these "deceptions with language". But where does this exposure take place if not in language itself? As with rhetoric and hermeneutics, so with (critical) sociology, language is at the heart of things; one cannot shunt it to one side for the temporary convenience of ideology critique.

Gadamer makes the point forcefully, through a series of questions, that language as he described it, embraces *just* those things that Habermas claims are outside it :-

> Who says that these concrete, so called real factors are outside the realm of hermeneutics ? From the hermeneutical standpoint, rightly understood, it is absolutely absurd to regard the concrete factors of work and politics as outside the scope of hermeneutics. What about the vital issue of prejudices with which hermeneutical reflection deals ? Where do they come from ?

Merely out of "cultural tradition" ? Surely they do, in part, but what is tradition formed from ? (Gadamer 1976:31)

The answer to the final question and thus to those that precede it, is that tradition as he described it, is formed precisely from elements such as labour and political domination, and that these are bound up with our prejudices: but as factors in our tradition they also happen in and through language, not outside it.

Gadamer believes Habermas' claim that hermeneutics 'bangs helplessly against the walls of tradition from the inside' could only be true if Habermas could oppose it with an 'outside'. Only if there were things that did not enter the world we interpret but somehow changed it, and only if there was simultaneously some position from which we could observe these changes completely and in an entirely detached way, would there be some truth in his argument. Of course the world is made up both of things that are intelligible and *unintelligible* to us, but no such position as this exists, especially not in Habermas' 'philosophy of history with a practical intent'. Gadamer insists that his account does not reify or absolutise cultural tradition as something which overbearingly determines us, but amounts only to the claim that hermeneutics wants to understand everything that will *allow* itself to be understood. This is what he meant by the statement "Being which *can* be understood is language" (emphasis added). Through our linguistic tradition we will come to understand things in a particular light, but in so doing other aspects of things will be put in the shade, the light of understanding can never be total.

The ontological character of language: Gadamer's flight from dualism

In two or three difficult paragraphs (Gadamer 1976:31-32, and in Mueller-Vollmer 284-5) Gadamer reiterates what the ontological character of language amounts to, and in the process refutes what he sees as Habermas' reductionist view of tradition.

First, it does not mean that through language we acquire knowledge of an already 'known' tradition, i.e. we do not appropriate dead meanings that are fixed because they are handed down to us from the past. Habermas tends to reduce the central role of linguistic tradition to being something that merely legitimises the dead hand of the past on the present, whereas in *Truth And Method*, it will be remembered, Gadamer comprehensively described just the opposite case, viz., one based on the projective nature of understanding, the fusion of horizons, and the finite, mutable nature of tradition.

Secondly, and in a similar way, contra-Habermas, the so called cultural meanings found in language are no mere supplements set in a secondary relation to supposedly more real economic and political factors. On the contrary, everything that is, is encountered in language, because the 'world' has its being in language. Language, Gadamer declares is like a mirror, in that everything that can be, is reflected in it. Even those things that are not encountered by us in everyday life, can be encountered in language. In effect we are our language in a way that exceeds the particular things we believe to be true including what we know about ourselves. Gadamer, I think means by this, that because of the speculative structure of language any particular claim we make will invariably be exceeded by the swell of meaning that follows it. Overall he is trying to break through the objectivist assumptions that he thinks underpin Habermas' view, where language is brought round the front for inspection as one social institution amongst others. He wants to make clear that his view of language is a more embracing and reflexive one.

Indeed, to this end no sooner has he adopted the metaphor of language as a mirror, than he drops it. The idea of language as a mirror, he feels, still carries with it a vestige of objectivism in that it suggests language is something we stand apart from and gaze into, a kind of window on the world. As such, it may well embrace material, as well as cultural factors, but it still does not do justice to the full import of his ontological account.

There are two intertwined reasons for this. It wrongly suggests that reality exists separately from language, and the task of language is therefore to reflect accurately what is going on in reality. It also ignores our perpetual immersion in language (and thereby reality), the fact that we are always already engaged with it as players in a game. He puts it this way :-

> When all is said and done, language is no mirror at all, nor is that which we catch sight of in it a reflection of our own and of all existence. Rather it is the continual definition and redefinition of our lives, in the concrete dependencies of work and dominance as well as in all other dependencies which make up our world. Language is not the ultimate anonymous subject, discovered at last, in which all social-historical processes and actions are grounded, and which presents itself and the totalities of its activities, its objectifications, to the gaze of the detached observer; rather, it is the game in which we are all participants. None less so than any other. Each of us is "it", and it is always our turn." (Gadamer in Mueller-Vollmer 1986:284)

There are three points in this that seem to speak against Habermas' case. First, Gadamer is marking off his account of language from any that suggest it reflects reality. Habermas, though he ostensibly sees language as constitutive of reality, nevertheless claims that in being ideological it distorts reality. This implies that reality exists separately from language, and ideology is an incorrect reflection of it. If he wishes to embrace hermeneutic ideas about language he cannot meld them with a concept of ideology that rests on this kind of assumption.

Secondly, when Gadamer says "language is not the ultimate anonymous subject in which all social-historical processes and actions are grounded", he is also marking off the hermeneutic approach from others that may simply put language centre stage. It will be recalled that Habermas saw hermeneutics as a more adequate version of the "linguistic approach" in sociology. Gadamer, I think, accepts the compliment, but not the implication: that being - hermeneutics enthrones language as the source of meaning, and like other, similar approaches is guilty of linguistic idealism. To be sure, language is of crucial importance to Gadamer, but he does not subsume reality under it, any more than he posits reality as separate from it. The two exist in mutual reciprocity. The criticisms Habermas levels against linguistic idealism, i.e. its naivety in believing that language is the unencumbered source of meaning, might apply to some varieties of interpretive sociology, but not, I think, to Gadamer's hermeneutics.

Thirdly, he is emphasising the participatory nature of language. It is always our turn in the game of language, we are always "it", whether we are actually using language or not. It embraces us and involves us in meaning beyond our subjective control. As such it cannot be conceived of in a proprietorial fashion, as Habermas implied, as though it belonged to a particular social group or class. Habermas saw it as serving the interests of dominant groups, in the sense that it could legitimise the apparent rightness of their ascendancy. Of course Gadamer is not denying that some players are more likely to win the game than others, but he is insisting on the real game-like qualities of language. This means that language cannot be conceived of as a one way process of domination, it cannot be used as the vehicle for the mere deception and control of one group by another. In fact he momentarily, and cunningly, allies himself with Habermas, to argue that language is at its most game-like when we uncover things and recognise them in a new and truer light.

> That is true whenever we understand something, especially so when we see through prejudices or unmask pretences which disguise the truth. Yes, there most of all we "understand." When at last we have got to the bottom of something which seemed to us strange and unintelligible, when we have managed to accommodate it within our linguistically ordered world, then everything falls into place, just as it does with a difficult chess problem where only the solution renders the necessity of the absurd set-up intelligible, down to the very last piece on the board. (Gadamer in Mueller-Vollmer 1986:284)

In briefly allying himself with ideology-critique in this way he draws attention to a contradiction in Habermas' work, viz., that language is viewed by him both as a system of total deception, ("a deception with language as such"), and as a vehicle for liberation (via reflection). The point being that you can't have it both ways. Language, cannot be one thing and the opposite at the same time. Gadamer's account of it allows for the possibility of both happening in language, but they exist in a muted form, together, because of the playful nature of language itself. Where Gadamer's ontological account avoids any simple dualism between language as 'deception' and as 'liberation', Habermas' account rests on this opposition. Habermas' theory needs language as 'liberation' in order to be able to rescue people who are being deceived by 'language as such'.

Reason and authority again: still flying from dualism

The contradiction that can be found in Habermas' account of language, surfaces again in the relation between reason and authority. Gadamer points out, that though we understand acutely when we see through some subterfuge, or unmask ideology, this is not the only way we understand things. Habermas tends to assume that we only understand when exercising reflection and critique, the rest of the time we are subject to the illusions of ideology. But Gadamer asks why we should not suppose that we also understand when we find our prejudices borne out by life. Habermas, he believes, is intent on seeing the real power of reflection only in a hermeneutics that "shakes the dogmatism of life-praxis". In doing this he is operating with a prejudice that is as dogmatic as any he would unmask, for reflection may well not dissolve prior convictions, but confirm them. This of course might lead to the endorsement of authority, something that Habermas finds unacceptable because he implicitly defines authority as nought but dogmatic power.

It is the way Habermas sets up an abstract antithesis between Enlightenment reason and the authority of tradition, to which Gadamer objects. Habermas seems to assume that the authority bound up in tradition is the very antithesis of reason. Hence, after the Enlightenment, to reason, has come to require of us the suspension of tradition, the blanking off of the norms, values, and common sentiments, that are the very backbone of our historical lives.

Here as elsewhere, Gadamer sets about moving his case between the oppositions that Habermas has erected to ensnare him. He insists that his account does not fix tradition as something that we inevitably obey, and it is therefore quite misleading to oppose it with a version of reason that denies tradition. The relationship between authority and tradition, Gadamer believes, is not to be seen as one of antithesis, but as one of ambivalence, something to be explored, not casually accepted. Indeed there is a considerable danger in accepting the relationship as antithetical, because it gives to reason a bogus independence. It allows those who claim it for their own, to misunderstand just how dependent they remain on their tradition, and in this lets them fall into the delusions of idealism.

Of course Gadamer does not deny that there are innumerable instances where authority is dogmatic, "from the system of education through the chain of command in army and government, to the power structures of political and evangelistic movements". But this does not explain why obedience to authority goes on in a structured way. If authority commanded obedience only through force alone, surely disorder and disruption would be the norm ? It is however, not the norm, and what he regards as crucial in this, is the significance of the fact that we acknowledge authority. This is quite a difficult notion to accept if one comes from a sociological background, where authority is invariably viewed with suspicion. But what he is getting at is that there is a distinction to be made between the way the powerless are forced to accept something, and an authentic acceptance, or acknowledgement of authority. He does not make the distinction sharp, and implies that there is no apriori way of distinguishing one from the other. In fact even where authority appears to be dogmatic, it may still contain a core of legitimacy, in that it has been "dogmatically accepted". By this he means that we concede to others an authority based on what we perceive as their superiority in matters of judgement, knowledge, or some other quality.

Authority ultimately prevails because it is based on this "free" acknowledgement (6), and he suggests that one can see the truth of this in situations where authority is in decline. He further raises the interesting idea, that a decline in authority may not be the result of emancipatory critique, but emancipatory critique may be the result of a decline in authority ! This, of course, reverses the usual assumption that emancipation springs from challenges to authority by those who have reflected on their oppression, and want to change their situation (7). However in characteristic fashion he does not express himself in simple opposition to the usual assumption, but asks the reader to think through the relation, even suggesting that the two processes are virtually indistinguishable :-

> Whether one can really say that loss of authority comes about through emancipatory critique and reflection, or ought to say, instead, that the loss of authority manifests itself in critique and reflection is a question that may be let drop and which perhaps involve a distinction without a difference after all. The point at issue is simply whether reflection always dissolves substantial relationships or can equally well result in their conscious acceptance and adoption.(Gadamer in Mueller-Vollmer 1986:285-6)

Clearly Gadamer does not accept the idea that reflection must always be critical, in the sense that it necessarily entails the rejection of what one has learnt, or acquired through tradition. One may, on gaining some maturity simply adhere to the ideas of that tradition - but equally one may not. Tradition, Gadamer says, is no proof of validity, but by the same token one cannot prove the validity of everything that one reflects on. The finiteness of ones existence, and the particularity of reflection, makes such a grandiose idea impossible.

The impression that Habermas has given is that it is easy to distinguish between authority and mere domination, that the latter can be stripped away from the former, and its power dissolved through "insight and rational decision". This seems to Gadamer to hugely overrate the power of reflection, and to beg crucial questions about what constitutes "rational decision" - is it something to be decided with the help of Habermas' critical social science ?

As Gadamer sees it, Habermas has amplified the power of reflection to almost idealist proportions, and in this, despite claims to the contrary, has slipped into traditional, (scientistic), subject-object ways of thinking. That is, ways of thinking where a radical split is assumed to exist between thinking subjects, and the world of objects about which they seek knowledge. Contained in this assumption is a kind of dogmatic belief that reflection on these objects can be 'pure', though it is an idea, Gadamer believes, to which the work of Husserl and Heidegger should have put paid. The capacity to see the world and its contents as 'objects' springs from language, but what we reflect on and thematise as an object in language, is only a part of that "effective reflection" which unfolds as our linguistic tradition. Gadamer means that there is a distinction to be made between those things we reflect on and construe as objects when we use our language, and the way language uses us. He is referring to the way our Western languages have allowed everything to be made into an object for us, and thus established the ground for modern science, and the civilisation that accompanies it. What he is also pointing out is that this process has entailed a lack of reflection on our part, a kind of forgetfulness over how we are related to the world through language and tradition. We tend to assume a proprietorial attitude towards all things, including our own lives, because we now so automatically objectify things. It is the naivety of this unreflective attitude he finds present ironically in the ambition Habermas has for reflection, i.e. of liberating us from the wider context of tradition.

How much is psychoanalysis a partnership ? On the hermeneutic limits of Critical Theory

In the final section of his first reply Gadamer once more brings to the fore his concern to explain the true range of the hermeneutic experience. The claims he makes about it are in fact quite modest, but he is insistent that they be understood properly, and that their implications are not closed down by those, like Habermas, who wish to accept them only to turn them to other purposes.

Hermeneutical reflection, like ideology critique, and other forms of reflection, aims to clarify the understanding we have of ourselves and of the world around us. Certainly, when we reflect on our current preconceptions we are able to bring before us things that would otherwise go on behind our backs. But equally clearly, he argues, not everything can be brought forward in this way. Our 'effected historical consciousness' i.e. what emerges through our embeddedness in tradition, should not lead us into any arrogant assumptions about the potential power and autonomy of our consciousness. It is indeed the case that reflecting on our preconceptions will help us to avoid being naively enslaved by them, in that we can freely judge how warranted or not they are. But "freely" here, Gadamer insists, means always that in any critical encounter with our preconceptions, new ones will be formed out of the old.

In academic fields including Gadamer's own, the effect of hermeneutical reflection has been quite plain, it has shaken up fixed presuppositions and opened up a certain progress by making new questions possible (8). In the social sciences too, Gadamer declares that Habermas has presented the significance of hermeneutical reflection in a particularly astute way. However, this is not all that hermeneutical reflection has done, it has also shown us just how far the alienation produced by scientific method has gone in structuring everyday consciousness.

The social effects of applying method in the natural sciences is, Gadamer believes, of little consequence, (method is obviously also a prerequisite for doing science). The true scientist simply knows the range and limits of his realm of knowledge and wisely does not make claims that go beyond it (9). The social sciences though, are in a peculiar position, because their progress as disciplines has been tied in with the application of scientific method to society, and this plainly has had implications. In an insidious way they are complicit with :-

> ...a world which thus finds itself exposed to scientific disposition in planning, management, organisation, development - in short, in a multitude of offices which determine from the outside, so to speak, the life of every individual and every group within society. The social engineer, who looks after the operation of the social

machine, thus seems sundered from the society, of which he is nevertheless a member. (Gadamer in Mueller-Vollmer 1986:290)

Clearly, this is also the kind of thing that Habermas is objecting to, yet Gadamer senses the same dubious element of social engineering being attempted in the psychoanalytic model that Habermas wants to adopt. Gadamer fears that because Habermas sees no real distinction between psychoanalysis and Critical theory he unwittingly treats society as if it were mentally ill and in need of treatment. His ambition seems to be to bring society's unconscious, ideological compulsions, into the full light of reflective awareness, thereby removing the compulsive element from them. While this seems laudable it does tend to assume that there can be a perfect alignment between motives and actions at the level of the individual and at the level of society. If this were the case the distorting influence of the unconscious, or of ideology would be removed entirely. Gadamer believes that a state of perfect self-understanding, either individually via psychoanalysis or collectively via ideology-critique, is a rationalist fiction. We are never in a sovereign position vis-a-vis ourselves either individually or collectively in that we can never stand outside the finite, situated condition, in which we always find ourselves.

This is not to say that Gadamer is blind to the idea that people's conscious understanding of themselves is only part of their story, clearly much else is going on besides. In fact Gadamer's claim is quite the opposite, he insists that consciousness is *not* the source of meaning. Hermeneutics makes its claim to be of universal importance because it insists that meaning can be experienced even when it is not intended i.e., we can find meaning in social action even when that meaning is not ostensibly claimed by the actors or the society concerned. Indeed much of the second part of Truth and Method was devoted to showing how the meaning of a text always exceeds the author's intention. Thus Gadamer does not deny the significance of meaning that is hidden from consciousness, and believes that hermeneutics has a fundamental part to play in psychoanalysis, though it is a rather larger and more awkward part than Habermas would admit.

He accepts Habermas' idea that psychoanalysis should be seen in hermeneutic fashion, as the attempt to recreate the interrupted narrative of an individual's life-history. It can be restored through the to and fro of dialogue, and thus allowed to unfold more fruitfully, and with much greater awareness by the individual. However in spite of this, there remains a problem that Habermas fails to address. For Gadamer, in Freud's ideas there is still a distant, but real connection with a natural scientific view of social relations. Although Habermas recognises that the truth of any particular analysis depends on it being found adequate by the individual patient, and it thereby meets the hermeneutic demand for dialogue; the claim to knowledge made by psychoanalysis itself does not depend on these grounds alone. If it claims to be knowledge in the wider sense then it ought to be open to further hermeneutical reflection - but this is not what Habermas seems to have in mind for a Critical Theory which uses it as a model.

Gadamer is saying is that psychoanalytic theory, as theory, also ought to be open to further hermeneutical reflection, but because it sees its knowledge in quasi-scientific terms it does not make this move. Moreover, in transferring this to a sociological level Habermas exposes some dubious aspects of his own ambitions. For what, Gadamer (1986:290) asks :-

> ..is the relationship between the knowledge of the psychoanalyst and his professional position within the social reality, of which he is, after all, a member ?

It is one thing to get behind the repressive social taboos that distort individual understanding, it is another thing to claim the right to diagnose the ills of the society of which you are a member. To be a member of a society means being involved in a network of linguistic-communicative relations which Gadamer described using the idea of a game. What kind of partner in the game, he asks, is one like the Critical Theorist, who always "sees through" his partner ? A spoilsport of course, someone to be avoided !

Gadamer believes that Habermas has failed to recognise a boundary between psychoanalytic reflection and reflection in general. The reflective power the psychoanalyst has to emancipate an individual is a particular capacity, one that may be understood in terms of the wider social context within which it is placed, a context which in effect shapes and limits it. However, this wider context, which Habermas claims Critical Theory should address, is one where analyst and patient along with everyone else, *including* the Critical Theorist, come to understand themselves. Gadamer means that the Critical Theorist cannot lay claim to knowledge of the social totality in the way the psychoanalyst claims to understand the individual. This is because the Critical Theorist, like everyone else is constituted in the game-like to and fro of the social totality. In this arena Critical Theorists must accept that they are players like others, and can claim no special, or final status for their knowledge.

Gadamer of course does not use the language of 'totality', though the point he is making bears some resemblance to the one Adorno made in the essay 'Sociology and Psychology' (1967) (10). However, Gadamer's way is to remind us rather more gently than Adorno, that hermeneutics does not lead the sociologist away from the totality but towards the realisation of our common embeddedness in it. He puts it like this :-

> ..hermeneutic reflection teaches us that social community, with all its tensions and disruptions, leads us back time and again to a

social understanding, by virtue of which it continues to exist. (Gadamer in Mueller-Vollmer 1986:291)

The moral tone of his final remarks are clear; because Habermas has not brought out these differences and does not indicate that there is any boundary between psychoanalysis and Critical Theory, the analogy he hoped to establish must be considered problematic. Where, asks Gadamer, does the patient-relationship end and a more reciprocal social partnership begin? Is Critical Theory entitled to search behind all our social practices and into every aspect of our self-understanding in pursuit of its revolutionary aims? Clearly Gadamer does not think so, and feels that to do so would undermine our very social identity. He admonishes Habermas for tacitly justifying an image of society as an "anarchistic utopia", where all our connectedness with, and obedience to, the authority of tradition is dissolved in critique. In effect he sees Critical Theory as the subtle but dangerous harbinger of an Orwellian 'Brave New World'.

Notes

1. It is interesting to note that Gadamer uses Plato in support of his case at this point, rather than Heidegger. Heidegger's challenge was to the whole of the Western tradition of metaphysical thinking, including science. Habermas criticises Gadamer for what he regards as his opposition to science, but may in fact be wide of the mark in not considering fully the differences between Gadamer and Heidegger. Gadamer's discussions of Plato generally, suggest he has a more sympathetic attitude towards the philosophical tradition and could be thought less anti-science than Heidegger. See Kelly (1987).

2. I am referring to the general tenor of Habermas' case in *On The Logic Of The Social Sciences* where he tries to draw a line beyond which hermeneutics cannot reach but Critical Theory can. This culminates in the statement that "hermeneutic experience, encountering this dependence of symbolic context on actual relationships, becomes a critique of ideology" (p172).

3. I have put - scientific - in brackets to indicate that Gadamer is referring to a broad attitude of mind rather than the specific use of scientific method as such. He is referring to something which imbues not only the social sciences but also the humanities generally. As Mueller-Vollmer notes, Gadamer uses the English term "the humanities" at this point. Richard Palmer (1969) was one of the first to recognise the presence of this attitude even in the study of literature.

4. Gadamer I think pointedly puts inverted commas around the term - "linguistic approach" - he clearly finds it rather contrived and constraining, and not at all in line with his ontological account of linguisticality. The term seems to suggest that the linguistic approach will inevitably be one amongst others, and thus unconsciously confirms the rightness of Habermas' criticisms about the limits of hermeneutics before they are properly considered.

5. He compares two nineteenth century German historians, Droysen and Ranke. The former saw through the "eunuch like objectivity" of contemporary history writing and became highly influential for middle class culture. The latter was much less influential because he wrote apolitical, 'epical' histories that tried to rise above tradition, but in fact merely reflected life in an authoritarian state.

6. This distinction is akin one developed by Hannah Arendt (1970:44), though she argues that authentic power, (rather than authority) is distinguishable from coercion. Power, (like authority for Gadamer), rests on a common acceptance of things :-

    Power corresponds to the human ability not just to act but to act in concert. Power is never the property of an individual; it belongs to a group and remains in existence only so long as the group keeps together. When we say someone is 'in power', we actually refer to his being empowered by a number of people to act in their name

7. In a comparable way Peter Munz in his book *Reflections On The Theory Of The Revolution In France,* argues that revolutions are not the result of people responding to particular injustices, or grievances. This model assumes too 'rational' a view of human behaviour, in that it sees revolutions, like all social action as the effect of people responding to causes. More adequate, he believes is a model that emphasises revolution as an attempt to recreate a tradition of common sentiment, where common sentiment has become so weak that it cannot sustain society. Thus it was not so much critical responses to poverty and injustice that brought the Ancien Regime down, worse had been suffered before without revolution, rather it was the moral vacuousness of the regime, i.e. a decline in its authority, that enabled critique to take root.

8. Gadamer is referring to his own first fields of interest, art and historical philology. Art history, for example has been shaken up by the realisation

that style is not 'autonomous', but is tied in strongly with wider features of life. Similarly in *Truth and Method* he undertook to show how "the fusion of horizons" should be seen as mediating the gap between past and present generated by historicist ways of thinking.

9. Gadamer takes the natural sciences' own positivist self-understanding as accurate, leaving the humanities and the social sciences to be hermeneutically reflective about the open-ended nature of their claims to truth. He demotes natural science knowledge to being 'subjective', in that it is the product of the willed application of method. The hermeneutical sciences, by contrast are 'objective' in that their truths are not ultimately the product of deliberate method, but the outcome of processes beyond subjective control. However, Nicholas Davey (1993), drawing on Lyotard, has pointed out that scientific discoveries also 'happen' to the scientist, and are thus also unpredictable.

10. Adorno (1967) argued that psychology and sociology are often thought to be at opposite ends of a continuum, psychology dealing with the individual, sociology with the social. However this view fails to appreciate the way the individual and the social are determined through their dialectical relation within the *totality*.

11 Round three: Habermas' second critique: Method reaches the parts that hermeneutics can't

On what method reveals and hermeneutics conceals

In his second critique, the essay 'On Hermeneutics' Claim To Universality' (1) Habermas moves his challenge to a slightly different vantage point. He shifts his concern to highlight what he sees as the cognitive limitations of hermeneutics as much as its critical, moral, or political ones, though these are not ignored entirely. He identifies two broad weaknesses in the hermeneutic claim to universality, and though both figured in his first critique they are clarified and given much more substance here.

1. First, there is the possibility, contra-hermeneutics, that there are non-linguistic elements which structure human understanding. These elements are not the product of a language based consensus but are forces that impose themselves 'invisibly' on those consensuses. In the human sciences he believes the cognitive development work of Piaget, Chomsky's linguistics, Marxist ideology-critique, and psychoanalysis, have all been able to describe the workings of these forces.

2. Secondly, in order to understand such phenomena a *theory* has had to be constructed to explain them. Habermas also introduces a new factor here in his

critique, for theoretical knowledge is not exactly the same as the scientific knowledge he previously wanted to incorporate. Instead he introduces the idea of a 'reconstructive science', which is different from an empirical-analytic (natural) science, but nevertheless produces knowledge which exceeds hermeneutic dialogue. The term is used to describe theories based on the reconstruction of the the implicit rules or deep lying structures of various kinds of knowledge or competence. He sees the work of Chomsky and Piaget in this light, the latter having discovered the deep lying structures that underpin the various stages of human cognition.

He develops these arguments in three sections. In section one he adopts the same strategy as before, initially describing what he believes is hermeneutics' particular area of competence, viz ordinary or natural language, and emphasising the qualities that Gadamer's work has revealed about it. In reiterating these virtues he also describes their obverse, vices that make our linguistic tradition a site for the reproduction of ideology. To validate this claim he argues that underpinning the hermeneutic realm are systems of rules that are presupposed by ordinary language but which are not capable of being thematized in it.

In section two he argues the case that hermeneutics has definite limits by describing in a dense and fairly extensive way the nature of psychoanalytic knowledge. He uses the work of Alfred Lorenzer to do this, showing how it can explain aspects of an individual's identity that are beyond hermeneutic comprehension.

Finally, in section three, having established once more to his satisfaction that hermeneutics is trapped within the boundaries of tradition, and in order not to place his own locus of truth (quite) beyond it, he introduces a new 'internal' principle to regulate interpretation: 'the ideal speech situation'. I shall follow the sections of Habermas's paper.

Section 1. Hermeneutics has many virtues, but.....

Habermas begins once more by tackling hermeneutics from the inside. To do this he redescribes some of its important insights circumscribing each one with negative characteristics. This will enable him to hold on to its virtues while placing it alongside other realms of knowledge which will effectively delimit its universalist claims. To start the ball rolling in this direction he introduces a distinction between "hermeneutics" and "philosophical hermeneutics" (2). The former refers to the natural ability we all acquire in coming to learn our native language. It is the source of how we are able to understand the meaningful nature of things, and it is, he thinks, an artistic skill that can be cultivated. He follows Gadamer's earlier line in recognizing the common ground between hermeneutics and rhetoric :-

> The art of interpretation is the counterpart of the art of convincing and persuading in situations where practical question are brought to decision. Indeed the same thing that is true of hermeneutics is true of rhetoric as well; for rhetoric too, rests on a capability which belongs to the communicative competence of every speaker but can be artificially developed into a special skill. (Gadamer in Mueller-Vollmer 1986:294)

By contrast, "philosophical hermeneutics" is somewhat different in that it adopts a critical and reflective attitude towards experiences that are the product of exercising our communicative competence. It is, as it were, one step removed from the ordinary realm of hermeneutic experience, and because of this can be oriented towards a philosophical elucidation of the structures of that realm. In making this distinction Habermas is opening up a space for the idea of reconstructive science that parallels (hermeneutic) philosophy's detached and reflexive position.

Adopting this reflective attitude he goes on to elucidate what he sees as the two main structural capacities that language makes possible in the realm of hermeneutic experience. These are :-

1. the art of understanding and explication, and

2. the skill of convincing and persuading others.

However, as this is to be an exercise in delimiting Gadamer's claims about the universality of the hermeneutic dimension, he provides a 'downside' as well as an 'upside' to both structural capacities.

1. *The art of understanding and explication*

On the 'upside' of 1. Habermas affirms Gadamer's that ordinary or natural language, which is the vehicle for hermeneutic experience, is massively reflexive. It is capable of clarifying the meaning of anything, no matter how inaccessible. It can translate the characteristics of the most alien culture from the most remote period into a form that is meaningful and familiar to us. At the same time as addressing the unfamiliar the familiar is challenged, and the ongoing interplay of these two moments ensures that our hermeneutic experience is both "limitless and fragmentary", i.e. forever open and incomplete. Unlike formal, "constructed" languages, which are closed in terms of their applicability, natural language provides its users with an extraordinarily 'meta-communicative' tool. Roughly speaking Habermas means that "constructed" languages such as mathematics or logic, can only generate the meaning designated by their rules, whereas in natural language we are free to comment on the meaning of things, cross meaning boundaries, even to change the rules of application for a statement.

However, on the 'downside' of 1. he believes that in spite of this apparent freedom, in a sense we are trapped in our natural language because "this freedom of movement is a palpable bondage to linguistic tradition". By which he means that our natural language works within the remit of its own tradition, and as such the meanings we find in it are part of a longstanding context that for the most part has been dogmatically transmitted. To be sure, in the hermeneutic realm the prejudices of tradition can be thematized and modifications made, but these changes, Gadamer argues, will only involve the introduction of new prejudices ! Unlike the languages we have "constructed" we cannot get outside our natural language to see how, as a system, it produces and reproduces meaning; at least we can't if we follow Gadamer. We will need some *theoretical* knowledge produced by a 'reconstructive science'if we are going to break through the objective force of our tradition.

2. *The power of persuasion*

On the 'upside' of 2. he follows Gadamer in recognizing that hermeneutics and rhetoric have shown us the importance of the art of persuasion for the social world. Arriving at a consensus in the social world does not and cannot rest on the kind of "compelling proof" that underpins science, but nor should it be regarded as merely arbitrary. A social consensus is concerned with practical issues that relate to the social standards we use when we judge the norms and values of our society. Thus Habermas accepts that here the importance of "plausibility" comes into its own. While he notes that the decisions we make in this arena are ineradicably the result of persuasion, he also notes a certain tension or ambivalence between 'persuasion' and 'conviction'. What he means is that social decision making always runs the risk of being the product of persuasive force alone, that is where conviction overwhelms the properties of dialogue that are proper to a social consensus. With perhaps some regret he notes that any rationally motivated consensus may have to depend on an amalgam of both the cognitive and expressive uses of language.

Nevertheless the creative nature of natural language does enable its users to respond to the world by defining and redefining it, and this gives people a certain power to innovate, recognize their tradition differently and thereby act differently. However, even though natural language has this innovative power only occassionally is it used to overturn the ingrained framework of tradition.

Indeed, Habermas claims that the creative nature of natural language has served "obfuscation" as much as "enlightenment".

Given that what he has described is supposed to be the 'upside' of language's suasive power it comes as no surprise that that he finds the 'downside' to be the powerlessness of human subjects vis-a-vis their familiar language games. He argues that if we want to modify our language games we must first have participated in them, this means that we have to have internalized the rules, not just in the manner of intellectually learning them, but to the point where they structure our personalities. Moreover, as Wittgenstein demonstrated, there is an immanent connection between natural language and social praxis, such that "language and behaviour interpret each other reciprocally". All of which is to say, because natural language is also the complete way of life in which we are immersed the chances of substantially changing it from the inside are limited.

We can get beyond self reflection through rational reconstruction

Having described what he sees as the inside of the hermeneutic realm, Habermas turns to the task of describing methods that will in his view, reach beyond it. He draws on (structural) linguistics in the first place as a 'method' that is not tied to the hermeneutic dimension. He notes that just as philosophical hermeneutics is different from ordinary hermeneutic consciousness, so linguistics as a form of knowledge is distinct from both. Linguistics, he argues, is concerned with language as a system (langue), and specifically excludes the pragmatic (hermeneutic) dimension of language use (parole). The goal of linguistics is quite different from hermeneutics, it does not reflect on meaning but aims to reconstruct :-

> ..the rule system that underlies the production of all the various grammatically correct and semantically meaningful elements of a natural language, whereas hermeneutics reflects on the principle experiences of a communicatively competent speaker (whose linguistic competence is tacitly presupposed). (Habermas in Mueller-Vollmer 1986:298)

The key words here are 'tacitly presupposed', for what Habermas is trying to bring out is the idea that even though we can express anything in language, we still have to follow the invisible linguistic rules that constrain and govern the production of sense.

He intends to haul the idea of linguistic rules across into the realm of hermeneutic consciousness, or as he now calls it, communicative competence

(3). He will then be able to argue that working behind the backs of social actors are the tacitly presupposed rules of communication. The form that these tacit rules take are summarised by the phrase, 'the ideal speech situation'. This format is to become the normative centre-piece of his theory and be the benchmark for critique. It should enable us to distinguish between a genuine dialogic consensus, where the rules of 'ideal speech' hold sway and one that is the product of distorted communication (4).

However, before bringing this concept into play more ground must be cleared and the distinction between reflection (characteristic of hermeneutics) and rational reconstruction (characteristic of linguistics), sharpened up.

Habermas is using the distinction to mark off the kind of knowledge that is produced by a human subject in the process of reflecting on things in his or her natural language. He accepts that this hermeneutic consciousness is not 'subjective' or 'objective' in the traditional sense, but defines itself in terms of an ongoing communicative horizon. However, he still believes that actors cannot gain access to the rules that underpin their communicative competence through self-reflection alone. What he has in mind here is the idea that social actors have the skill and general know-how to perform complex activities, but they don't thereby know the standards, rules, and principles they are applying - any more than speakers know the grammatical rules they are using to speak sense. Thus beyond hermeneutic consciousness, he claims, is a pre-theoretical realm which is accessible only through rationally reconstructing its deep lying structures and organisational principles.

He cites Piaget's work in support of his case; it suggests that there are developmental structures inherent in our goal-orientated thinking that are independent of language. He acknowledges that the full development of these cognitive processes depends on their being integrated into language, but :-

> ....there are ample indications that language is merely "superimposed" on categories such as space, time, causality, and substance, and on rules which govern the combination of symbols according to the laws of formal logic - both of which have a pre-linguistic foundation." (Habermas in Mueller-Vollmer 1986:200)

If Piaget's case proves to be true then he believes the hermeneutic claim to universality meets an insuperable limit. The limit being the schemata which underpin the stages in human cognitive development, and which are monologic in character in that they exist prior to and independent of any hermeneutic dialogue. Scientific languages are therefore quite right to describe phenomena like these in monologic, subject-object terms.

There is though a certain ambivalence in Haberms's claims for he is also aware that the schemata described by Piaget are in a sense surrounded by the meanings of natural language :-

> ..it is possible to offer a plausible explanation why monologically erected language systems, while they cannot be interpreted without reference to a natural language, can nevertheless be "understood" without involvement in the hermeneutic problematic: for on that presupposition the conditions of understanding were not the same thing as the conditions of colloquial communication. That would only be the case when the content of rigorous theories were translated into the context of speech in the everyday world. (Habermas in Mueller-Vollmer 1986:300-301)

He is claiming here that while an interpretation of Piaget's scheme will implicitly refer to natural language, the scheme itself does not require any dialogue to be "understood", unless it is going to be translated into the context of everyday life. I must confess to some bafflement here as I cannot see how the scheme can be beyond the hermeneutic dimension while in order to interpret it one has to refer to the hermeneutic dimension. Part of the problem may be because the sciences of 'rational reconstruction' on Habermas's account are set halfway between being hermeneutic and natural scientific in character (5). Whatever the case Habermas only uses Piaget to illustrate his argument and does not pursue the implications of it.

If philosophical hermeneutics yields so little, why bother with it ?

Habermas asks this question to clarify, perhaps both for himself and the reader, where the interface between Gadamer's insights and his own work now lies. He finds four reasons for still valuing hermeneutics :-

1. Hermeneutics has demolished the mistaken objectivist claims of the traditional human sciences. Because interpreters are bound to their hermeneutic situation, their objectivity and impartiality in understanding things should entail greater reflection on their tradition, rather than the attempt to abstract themselves from it.

2. Hermeneutics also alerts us to the fact that in the social sciences the field of investigation is symbolically pre-structured. This means that gathering data effectively involves a communicative relation to the field rather than one based on controlled observation. This idea should also be reflected at the level of

theory, where the categories a sociologist uses should be chosen tentatively and on the basis of what the field suggests.

3. Hermeneutics has some impact on the natural sciences too, not in terms of their methods, but in terms of the fact that natural language plays the role of the "ultimate" meta-language in providing the context in which discussion take place. Decisions justifying research strategies, discussions about what counts as scientific progress etc, all take place within the scientific community where everyday colloquial talk is the medium of communication. Hermeneutics can reflect on how the nature of consensuses are reached in this area, revealing the rationale behind them as well as their open-endedness.

4. Hermeneutical consciousness also is important for the interpretation and translation of scientific information into the natural language of the social world. Habermas quotes Gadamer here to the effect that physics, like all sciences that aim to be of practical importance, have to employ rhetoric and are thus subject to interpretation. Moreover, given the speed with which scientific and technical knowledge is produced in industrial societies it is vitally important to set this knowledge in relation to the practical needs of the social world, not merely valorise it instrumentally.

It can be seen that 1. and 2. are largely repetitions of the things he found worthwhile in his first critique, whereas 3. and. 4 are developments actually designed to place formal limits on hermeneutics. Hermeneutics, he is claiming, only bears on science before and after the fact, not on scientific activity as such. Science as such proceeds on the basis of its own monologues, its statements stand apart from everyday life and have to be understood within their own self-referring terms. Moreover, Habermas believes if hermeneutics is to be effective in mediating between science and the social world, it is going to have to come to terms with this fact, withdrawing to some extent from its dialogic stance. Only then will it see the significance of scientific theory for an understanding of purposive-rational behaviour (6).

However his wider aim is not to discuss hermeneutic's failure to deal with scientific language as such, but to examine the case that even in the human sciences, though one is dealing with a symbolically structured reality, there are approaches that do actually bypass natural language (7). He feels that if even the social meanings found in natural language can be explained through a theory based on (scientific) method, he can rightly deny the universalist claims Gadamer makes.

There are two broad avenues that seem to do this. On the one hand there is (Chomsky's) 'generative linguistics' which has pursued the task of reconstructing the universal rules of our linguistic competence. If this were thoroughly successful it could assign a structural description to every element in natural language, subverting hermeneutic understanding with a general theory. On the other hand there is the critique of ideology and psychoanalysis. Both of these fields deal with the objectifications found in natural language, but where the subject is unaware of the intentions being expressed in them. These intentions can only be understood, claims Habermas, as elements of a "systematically distorted communication". They will be properly understood only when the pathological conditions that produced them have been disinterred. How psychoanalysis does this is the matter dealt with in section two.

Section 2. Psychoanalysis reaches those parts hermeneutics can't

In section 2. Habermas describes in a dense and convoluted way the method of "scenic understanding" used by the psychoanalyst Alfred Lorenzer (8). It is as usual packed with insight that is difficult to disinter.

The limits of hermeneutic experience start to become apparent, he argues, when it is faced by unintelligible expressions that cannot be deciphered even by the most artful interpreter. In some cases such as understanding an alien culture we may know what is lacking, for example we may not have an equivalent alphabet or a lexicon, or know how the rules of meaning apply in different contexts. In these circumstances at least we know what we don't know, but beyond this there is systematically distorted communication: "here the unintelligibility results from a faulty organisation of speech itself".

It is not even the case, Habermas claims, that the hermeneutic argument is shaken by openly pathological disturbances in language use, such as in psychotic illness, for here deviance from the norm is plain for all to see (9). Its lack only becomes clear when what goes for normal communication includes elements that are systematically distorted. He acknowledges there is no universal criterion that we can call on to tell us when we are involved in such misleading communication. However, Freud's work does explore this region. Freud uses dreams as a basic model for such phenomena, and extends the idea to include much else besides, not the least of which is the possibility that entire social systems may be built on neurosis and mis-understanding.

Habermas identifies three criteria which he thinks defines "neurotically distorted or specifically unintelligible expressions", and marks them off from normal (hermeneutic) communication.

1. On the level of linguistic symbols systematic distortions show up in the way the application of the rules of public language are broken. Freud has shown us,

for example, that our dreams involve such rule breaking things as condensation, displacement, and reversals of meaning.

2. On the level of behaviour we can identify distortions in the way some of our behaviours are compulsive. We act compulsively when we respond blindly to the 'same' stimulus regardless of the meaning of the wider situation.

3. Finally, a process of systematic distortion is apparent when discrepancies between 1. and 2. become obvious, i.e. when the relation between language and action and the usual gestures and expressions that accompany it, breaks down entirely.

Whatever the precise mix of the distortion it involves a breach in the rules of publicly recognizable communication and a blocking of the relationship between our inner selves and the outer world in which we participate.

Scenic understanding and depth hermeneutics

The development of an inner self at odds with the world of publicly acceptable forms of communication requires psychoanalysis to take the form of a 'depth hermeneutics'. While this term suggest it might be close to Gadamer's work, Habermas is actually drawing on the ideas of Alfred Lorenzer to highlight what it means, and to sharpen up its distinctiveness from Gadamer's project. At the same time he also wishes to maintain a discreet distance from the scientism implicit in Freud's work.

Depth hermeneutics assumes that in the case of neurosis the patient is playing out a role in a deformed language-game, where his or her behaviour is unintelligible and conspicuously at odds with normal expectations. The key to unlocking the deformed language-game is for the analyst to do a kind of scenic comparison. This involves reconstructing alongside the present scene an analogous, original one, from the patient's own childhood. With the analyst acting as mediator in the transference of meaning from one scene to the other, a decoding of the private meanings that have accrued in the neurotic scene can take place. The patient can then hopefully come to terms with his or her neurosis through an authentic act of self reflection.

The original scene is likely to have involved a child in trying to ward off the implications of some intolerable conflict. This would be accompanied by a process of desymbolisation where the child, in order to manage the situation excludes the experience from public communication by splitting off the relevant symbol from its object. The gap that results is filled by the neurotic symptom, and the content of the conflict is removed from the domain of public communication, including the patient. The symbol, however does not lose its force for the patient, but distorts their ability to participate in public communication by forming an aberrant, private language-game. If the analyst can establish an adequate level of congruence between the two scenes a process of resymbolisation can take place in which the symbolic content that was excommunicated can be reintroduced into public forms of communication.

Habermas is once more steering a path midway between Freud's scientific principles and Gadamer's non-causal hermeneutics, and in doing this hopes to outflank both. It is notable that he doesn't use the language of 'instincts' and 'repression' a la Freud, but of 'symbols' and 'language-games' a la hermeneutics. At the same time he is equally claiming that to decipher what is unintelligible requires more than the ordinary hermeneutic competence of a native speaker. It requires in addition the reconstruction of scenes using theoretical hypotheses. To unlock the neurotic scene involves bringing to light those factors outside it which contributed to its construction. As Habermas rather abstractly puts it :-

> The What - the meaningful content of the systematically distorted expression - cannot be "understood" if the Why - the origin of the symptomatic scene in the conditions responsible for the systematic distortion itself - cannot be "explained" at the same time. (Habermas in Mueller-Vollmer 1986:305)

Scenic understanding is based on theoretical knowledge

Habermas outlines two ways in which psychoanalysis (as a 'depth-hermeneutics' (10) is not only hermeneutical but *theoretical* too. In being theoretical of course, he is declaring it to be distinct from being merely hermeneutical.

First, though the doctor-patient relation is clearly a communicative one, in its own way it also meets the conditions for being an *experiment*. Scenic transference, for example, involves the analyst in controlling the re-creation of original scenes, reflectively drawing on the patient's free-associations, and inhibiting his or her own automatic reactions. Thus the psychoanalyst is more an experimenter than an interlocutor.

Secondly, the analyst selects and places particular constructions on the material that emerges in analysis. This is not merely the application of preconceptions, but involves a deliberate interpretation of things based on established *models* of childhood development. Both of these factors suggest to Habermas that Gadamer's dialogic model of hermeneutics is insufficient to meet certain kinds of phenomena.

However he wants to press the case still further by describing the theoretical hypotheses that are presupposed in this kind of activity. He places these hypotheses into three broad groups and then splits them down further into subdivisions.

1. In doing their work psychoanalysts have to presuppose a definition of the structure of undistorted communication, i.e. they must know what normal communication is like. It has, he claims, the following interrelated characteristics :-

(a) The levels of communication, (viz symbolic-language expressions, actions, and gestures), are at one with each other and mutually supplement each other. There may be some contradiction between levels but this is intentional in nature and carries a message of its own. Habermas has in mind, I think, that there may be differences between ways of talking, acting, and gesturing within a culture, but that this is normal and explainable in terms of social class, or regional difference.

(b) In normal communication we conform to publicly valid grammatical rules and are able to recognize the applicability of these in varied but 'appropriate' situations.

(c) In normal communication situations we are able to discriminate between opposites such as subject and object, internal and external, private and public. These kinds of discrimination, as well as that between reality and appearance depends on the normal ability we have in grasping the difference between the linguistic symbol, its meaning, and the thing to which it refers. This ability also underpins (b).

(d) In normal communication language has both an analytical and a reflexive dimension. The analytical dimension enables us to classify things, but the reflexive dimension is more important. It enables us to recognize ourselves simultaneously as unique individuals and as part of an intersubjective community; the 'I' and the 'we' emerge dialectically. The reflexivity of language also enables us to be both a part of and apart from the things we describe in using it.

(e) Normal discourse enables us to talk about the relationship between human subjects and between physical objects in quite different ways. Habermas points out that "causality, space and time" mean different things when used in different discourses. The concept of 'cause', for example, is appropriate when used to describe connections between empirical chains of events, but 'motive' is appropriate when applied to intentional action.

It is difficult to see why Habermas calls these ideas '*theoretical hypotheses*' as they seem to be claims of a distinctly philosophical kind, and certainly not hypotheses testable in a scientific way. They also seem the kind of claim to which Gadamer would not take exception. However, the second group of hypotheses, as we can see are clearly non-Gadamerian.

2. Psychoanalysis, Habermas argues, deals with the relationship between two successive stages in symbol organisation, one of which, the paleosymbolic, lies *outside* language. Paleosymbols are powerful archaic symbols that have their origin in prehistory, and in an altogether more primitive human relationship to the world.

(a) The paleo-level of symbolic organisation exists prior to the normal organisation of symbols in language and resists being assimilated by it. It appears in Freud's work through his analysis of pathological speech and his analysis of dreams. Paleosymbols have a force in our lives but they exert this from beyond our normal discursive practices. Hence they present themselves in an irrational manner :-

> Freud himself notes the absence of logical relationships in his dream analyses. He points in particualar to "representations through the opposite", which have preserved on the linguistic level the genetically earlier characteristic of a unification of logically incompatible - that is antithetical - meanings. (Habermas in Mueller-Vollmer 1986:308)

Habermas notes that because they are external to linguistic communication paleosymbols do not permit the kind of reflexive freedom and 'distance' from specific contexts that is available in normal symbolic interaction. Their effect is therefore to amplify the privacy and emotional charge of their meaning. Another effect of their being outside the realm of intersubjective communication is in preventing human subjects from categorising the world in a stable and objective (i.e. intersubjective) way.

(b) It is the externality of these symbols that Habermas is keen to emphasise for he is arguing that our only access to this level of organisation is through a *theoretical* reconstruction. We cannot decode the meaning of these systematically distorted communications without a model of normality. Lorenzer's linguistic psychoanalysis provides a stage-model of development, and from it we are able to analyse neuroses in terms of regressions from one stage of communication to an earlier one, or of the irruption of earlier forms into later ones. The work of analysis therefore is interpretive at least insofar that it involves retracing the process of repression, which Habermas describes as 'a flight through and from language'. In some circumstances the task is to rescue the Ego in its flight from conflict, and 'resymbolise' into normal communication those 'objects' that have been expelled. In other circumstances the Ego defends itself by denying what is real through 'projection', here the task is to expel the uncontrolled intrusion of paleo-symbols from normal communication. However, in either case success depends on the analyst being able to isolate the different levels of organisation and discern those misplaced elements that have become 'encysted in language like alien bodies' (11).

3. Although the process of mediating between different stages or levels resembles the process of translation described by Gadamer, Habermas insists that it involves more. It involves a *controlled* translation, which is needed because these deformations do not originate in language but have become part of the structure of communication itself. Moreover, the point about controlled translation is that it is based on a "systematic preunderstanding" of language in general, rather than the more local preunderstandings of tradition which is the starting point for hermeneutic translation.

The processes described above can be explained by integrating them with Freud's structural model of the personality; id, ego, and super-ego which he derived from the experience of analysing the personality's defence mechanisms. However Habermas is still intent that psychoanalysis be 'exceeded' as much as hermeneutics, and argues that Freud's method relies on a model of distorted communication which in turn can only be justified in the framework of a theory of communicative competence. This becomes the subject matter of section three.

Section 3. Toward a theory of communicative competence

In section three Habermas sets out his alternative, he outlines some of the basic features, as well as some of the problems that could be solved by a *theory* of communicative competence. He sets these against the weaknesses he perceives in Gadamer's ideas, which are still very much those he described in his first critique.

He asks two questions: (a) whether the hermeneutic claim to universality still holds good in that all theoretical languages ultimately refers to ordinary language as "the last metalanguage"? And, (b) whether the application of knowledge gained from general theories still requires a basic hermeneutical skill? He answers these questions somewhat equivocally by declaring that we would not have to rely on our interpretive skill with ordinary language if we developed a theory of communicative competence. Clearly he does not like relying on what he sees as the vagaries of interpretation, and what he has learnt from psychoanalysis suggests to him that 'systematically distorted communication' should lead us away from a reliance on Gadamer's philosophical hermeneutics.

Consensus may not be dialogic

As before he declares that Gadamer has turned the idea of the context-dependency of all understanding into the inevitability of our having to submit to the context of our tradition. When he (Gadamer) ontologises tradition Habermas believes that he is forced to accept that 'the consensus which precedes all understanding' is a legitimate one, something quite unacceptable to Habermas' political sensibilities. Habermas puts it like this :-

> If I understand correctly, then Gadamer is of the opinion that the hermeneutical clarification of incomprehensible or misunderstood expressions always has to lead us back to a consensus that has already been reliably established through converging tradition. This tradition is objective in relation to us in the sense that we cannot confront it with a principled claim to truth. The pre-judgmental structure of understanding not only prohibits us from questioning that factually established consensus which underlies our misunderstanding and incomprehension, but makes such an undertaking appear senseless". (Habermas in Bleicher 1980:204)

Certainly, he admits the contents of tradition are not beyond criticism in Gadamer's work, but the tradition as such cannot be properly questioned. To do this would involve examining its claims to legitimacy behind the backs of its participants. But to make these demands stick we would have to engage in a dialogue with the participants and thus accept for the time being their background consensus. In these circumstances it would be senselesss to abstractly condemn the consensus as spurious, because the tradition cannot be transcended.

Habermas seems to recognize the dilemma set for him by Gadamer in the first response, in that he no longer clearly talks of challenging tradition from the outside. Nevertheless he still believes that 'depth-hermeneutics' has revealed the possibility that a consensus may be the product of pseudo-communication. He quotes Albrecht Wellmer (1971:47) to the effect that :

> The Enlightenment knew what a philosophical hermeneutics forgets - that the 'dialogue' which we, according to Gadamer, 'are' is also a context of domination and as such precisely no dialogue.....The universal claim of a hermeneutic approach [can only] be maintained if it is realised at the outset that the context of tradition as a locus of possible truth and factual agreement is, at the same time, the locus of untruth and continued force

In the absence of knowing if a consensus has been achieved without the distorting influence of force we should at least be suspicious of its legitimacy. The insight into our prejudices that hermeneutics gives us is not sufficient to assume that the actual context in which it takes place is a true one. In fact if Habermas subscribes to Wellmer's statement that tradition is "precisely no dialogue", then only a critical hermeneutics that has incorporated knowledge of systematically distorted communication will enable us to distinguish insight from delusion. To achieve this, Critical Theory must have its interpretations guided by a regulative principle.

A regulative principle: ideal speech as unconstrained dialogue

The pursuit of a regulative principle to guide interpretation has been one of the key elements driving his subsequent work, and it must be remembered that much of what he has to say here is quite sketchy and receives more substantial treatment in the later writings. Nevertheless, the origin of this pursuit of an alternative form of 'objectivity' for the social sciences is to be found in this rather speculative attempt to exceed Gadamer's hermeneutics.

For Critical Theory to avoid deception, Habermas believes it must be oriented towards the kind of consensus that is produced through the principles of 'rational discourse'. These principles are those necessarily tied in with a form "of communication free from domination". The conditions of free and unconstrained dialogue are what, in principle, will guarantee the emergence of truth as opposed to deception. He therefore sees truth, unconstrained dialogue, and rational discourse, as interdependent elements that will provide a springboard to escape the dependency on tradition that bedevils hermeneutics.

He cites the work of his colleague Karl-Otto Apel as also recognizing the need for a regulative principle, one that will provide a sort of counterfactual format to guide social investigation. For Apel the regulative principle is "universal agreement within the framework of an unlimited community of interpreters" (12). The wording is slightly different from Habermas's but the idea is the same (13), viz, that truth is the product of intersubjective agreement, and the ideal of achieving such agreement in a situation free from domination is what guarantees that Critical Theory will not fall prey to deception.

But the argument goes further. He directs his regulative principle of ideal speech in two directions, albeit only hinting at its potential rather than elaborating it clearly or thoroughly. It is the audacity of these kinds of move that make his work so stimulating. First, he quotes George Herbert Mead to the effect that the reciprocity of communication in human discourse has political implications, in that it directs us to anticipate the validity of democracy. An ideal community would involve us in a sense of mutual (democratic) recognition and this would be normatively orientated towards "an idea of the true life"

Secondly, he hints that the idea of 'ideal speech' is built into the very act of communication itself, suggesting that implicit in all colloquial communication through language is the anticipation of dialogic consensus and truth, i.e. in communicating we invariably seek to convince others of the validity of what we say. However, Habermas recognizes that claims like these require far greater justification than he is prepared to give them here. His immediate task is to highlight what he sees as the uncritical implications of Gadamer's falsely ontological view of natural language (14). In this he reiterates his familiar criticisms.

If you ontologise language you nullify critique

Although he has not developed a general theory of language Habermas believes he has enough evidence to convict hermeneutics' "ontological self-understanding". It is not hermeneutics' per se he wishes to refute but that version which stifles critique because it is based on ontological inevitability.

Habermas believes that the ontological primacy he gives to (linguistic) tradition has led Gadamer to see no real opposition between its authority and reason. What he means is that on Gadamer's account we accept the authority of tradition because we stand within its linguistic purview. Hence our assumptions, basic values, and taken for granted norms, which are the grist for our reasoning mill, all confirm and extend tradition. Tradition does not force its authority on us we reflectively recognize its legitimacy. Of course for Habermas even Gadamer's acknowledgement that many aspects of tradition may involve domination is insufficient to alter the basic weakness of this case. We still need some principled way of distinguishing between the dogmatic knowledge that authority imposes, and knowledge that has been freely accepted.

Moreover, if we are right to believe that reason and authority are at odds with each other then another claim of Gadamer's is suspect. He challenged the moral rightness of Critical Theory adopting the role of society's psychoanalyst, arguing that it is one thing to liberate an individual from the distortions of the unconscious, quite another to claim the right to enlighten society at large. The latter relationship should be seen as a game amongst partners, for the current interpreter, or Critical Theorist, is as tied to the prejudices of tradition as anyone else. However Habermas believes there is evidence to suggest that whole social systems may be pathological in that they are based on the pseudo-communication of ideology. Critical theory must therefore not be limited to individual pathology but develop regulative principles it can use to expose a spurious social consensus. All radical thinking has political implications.

Nevertheless Habermas does acknowledge that even depth-hermeneutical interpretations can only be thought finally successful within the remit of social dialogue :-

> To be sure, critique too, remains bound to the traditional context which it reflects. When it comes to monological self-certainty, which critique merely arrogates to itself, Gadamer's hermeneutical objection is valid. There is no corroboration of depth-hermeneutical interpretation outside of the self-reflection of all parties involved - a self-reflection which is found in and carried out through dialogue." (Habermas in Mueller-Vollmer 1986:317)

Finally, with a gesture of generosity, he declares that it may be more important to restrict the universal pretensions of critique than those of hermeneutics, though the latter must be critically examined.

Notes
1. There are two complete translations of this essay, the one I shall refer to is by Jerry Dibble and is found in Mueller-Vollmer (1986); the other is by Josef Bleicher and is found in Bleicher (1980) as well as Ormiston & Schrift (1990). It bears the slightly different title, 'The Hermeneutic Claim To Universality'. Parts of the essay were translated as 'On Systematically Distorted Communication' in Inquiry 13, 1970, pp205-218.

2. I am not convinced that this is a distinction Gadamer would accept, at least not in this formal way. Certainly if Habermas is suggesting that different knowledge realms are subject to different truth criteria, which is

the case he brings here, Gadamer would argue that truth is the product of dialogue in both hermeneutics and philosophical hermeneutics.

3. As in the first round, when Habermas brings new categories into the picture it has a skewing effect on Gadamer's argument. When he defines hermeneutic experience as communicative competence it brings to mind the interactive ability of two human subjects. Gadamer's hermeneutics are emphatically not centred on the human subject.

4. Habermas' description of the ideal speech situation is far more sophisticated than I suggest here. It is not a blunt instrument to be imposed on actual situations, but one that will function negatively as a counterfactual principle to aid analysis.

5. Thomas McCarthy (1978:276-78) provides a useful account of the differences between the three forms of knowledge.

6. In some ways this could also be seen as reiterating a point made previously, namely that hermeneutics should become more like Critical Theory.

7. There seems to be some confusion here because at 3. above, Habermas recognizes that even in the natural sciences natural language serves as the 'ultimate meta-language', but then changes his mind to claim that certain social sciences bypass natural language

8. See 'Symbols and Stereotypes' by Alfred Lorenzer in Connerton (1976).

9. I don't see why psychotic symptoms present no challenge to hermeneutics, as Habermas clearly uses the psychoanalytic accounts of mental illness generally as an exemplar of how to explain systematically distorted communication. I can only think that he finds dreams and neuroses closer to what is normal, and therefore better at showing how mis-communication may be built into apparently normal communication.

10. Though Habermas is trying to keep a foot in both the hermeneutic and the scientific camps, Holub (1991:71) is surely right when he says that 'depth hermeneutics' is a misnomer because it is not a hermeneutic procedure but an explanatory one based on principles of method.

11. Habermas also recognizes in parenthesis that paleo-symbols are sometimes used deliberately in creatively coining new phrases or in

cracking jokes. In the former, communication is enhanced and extended, in the latter we are lured into a pseudo regression, laughing in relief at having transgressed the boundary of morality knowing full well we have surmounted the earlier stage.

12. See 'The Communication Community As The Transcendental Presupposition For The Social Sciences' in Apel (1980).

13. Their subsequent writings however indicate that some considerable difference has developed between them over the status of these principles. Habermas has let the importance of the ideal speech situation subside somewhat, contenting himself with its hypothetical and fallible quality as a counterfactual principle, rather than reifying it into some instrumental first principle, whereas Apel has become more insistent on the primacy of 'communicative perfection', wigging Habermas for not pressing forward the logic of his own ideas. See Apel's essay 'Normatively Grounding "Critical Theory" through Recourse to the Lifeworld ? A Transcendental-Pragmatic Attempt to Think with Habermas against Habermas' in Honneth et al (1992).

14. There is something doubtful about Habermas' singular rejection of Gadamer's ontological account of language as his own account seems also to rely on the primacy of 'the being of language'. See Kisiel (1978).

12 Round four: Gadamer's second reply on the dangers of ideal speech and the importance of modesty

Introduction

In the essay 'Reply To My Critics' (1971) Gadamer offers a wide ranging response not only to Habermas, but other authors who addressed his work, including Apel, Bubner and Giegel (1). I shall be mainly concerned with his response to Habermas but will highlight other elements as they seem relevant to the truth of the paper. Gadamer frames his overall response within the terms of an interrogation of the nature of *rationality*. He is concerned once more to remind his critics of the full breadth of the hermeneutic enterprise, and the specificity of the claims it makes. In doing this he repels many of their criticisms and asks fundamental questions about their enterprises.

Gadamer introduces his paper with a broad reminder that though hermeneutics is about reaching agreement, it will be difficult to agree about its nature so long as his critics carry with them certain key concepts, unclarified. He believes that three interrelated concepts, viz science, criticism, and reflection, have been at the forefront of their discussions, but have not been understood properly. Because science seems to offer us complete control over nature and can be used to regulate social life, its cultural charisma has led his critics to underestimate the pervasive power it exercises over all aspects of our thinking. Science constantly revises any weaknesses it finds in its own hugely successful project, and tirelessly generates new targets for research. However, because of its obvious success we have become deluded into pursing this sort of progress in other areas of life. The effect has been for us to reproduce a system that structures the world in a way that diminishes practical wisdom. Practical knowledge has no place in a world driven by scientific progress.

These comments are clearly directed against Habermas and Apel who would batten together some version of science, criticism and reflection in order to stimulate social progress. Although they are claiming to share with him a concern for praxis, in fact they are complicit with a scientific culture that denigrates practical knowledge. Thus Habermas' concern with (sociological) systems theory mirrors a system of thought which denies any substantial role for praxis. Moreover, trying to escape from this way of thinking does not involve, as Habermas suggests, rushing in the opposite direction into the arms of *romanticism*. Rather, it involves recognising that discussions about the goals of human society direct us towards a form of knowledge that is not science based; viz praxis, which is based on phronesis or prudent judgement.

Gadamer, I think, believes that Habermas and others have not fully grasped the implications of the distinctions Aristotle made between different forms of knowledge, and which he (Gadamer) built into philosophical hermeneutics. As a result, these distinctions have become blurred in their work and with contradictory consequences.

It may be recalled that Gadamer adopted Aristotle's distinction between phronesis, techne, and episteme. Episteme is the basis of what we know as scientific knowledge and refers to things that are universal, and impose themselves on us of necessity, i.e the laws of nature. It is knowledge that is fixed and can be didactically taught. Phronesis on the other hand is the basis of social praxis and refers to knowledge of a mutable kind where what is universal always exists in a reciprocal relationship with what is particular. This knowledge cannot be taught in the same way for it involves the human subject in bringing his or her own ethical know-how to bear in concrete situations, but knowledge it is, nevertheless. It bears some resemblance to a third form, techne or technical know-how. This refers to the skill of the artisan in following the rules necessary to produce things. In social life we have to apply the 'right' moral rules to produce social life but there are important differences too between phronesis and techne. Social or moral rules are different in that they *engage* us in a consideration of what is right or just in this particular situation, which is rather more than the *correct* application of given rules to achieve known ends that characterises technical production. With these thoughts in his mind Gadamer starts to unpick Habermas' misunderstandings.

Phronesis, praxis, and social rationality

Despite Habermas' claim that hermeneutics has not come to terms with the importance of science in the modern world, Gadamer makes clear that it has been concerned with this issue since its inception. Indeed "it cost Socrates his life demonstrating the ignorance of the artisans' specialised knowledge about that which is really worth knowing, i.e. the good".

Characteristically Gadamer does not simply argue that Habermas and Apel have misunderstood the way Aristotle distinguished different forms of knowledge, but tries to show us that there has been an ovrsimplification, by questioning the issues once more. He notes that even in the *Ethics* of Aristotle where the differences between technical and practical knowledge are worked out, it is not clear how these relate to the political wisdom of the statesman, political activity in general, or the technical knowledge of the professional. What is clear however, is that if we are concerned with practical-political decisions (and of course Habermas claims to be so), we cannot follow the technical model as this will not allow us to glimpse 'the good'. Human happiness cannot be taught directly, and those that claim it can, as Plato and Aristotle demonstrated, are deceiving people through sophistry. The indirect target in this is Habermas' Critical Theory, which Gadamer sees as daring to assume it knows ahead of everyone else what 'the good society' is (2), and moreover intends to adopt technical and scientific means of bringing it about.

However, beyond this, Gadamer declares, there is still the issue of what kind of 'theory' or 'science' is capable of recognising and teaching the distinctions between phronesis, techne, and episteme to others ? 'Practical philosophy' or 'philosophical hermeneutics' (he takes the latter to be an extension of the former), is his answer, and in a complicated series of moves he describes the similarities and differences between them and other kinds of 'theory'. Broadly speaking this involves a three way description of what philosophical hermeneutics draws from phronesis, episteme, and techne, and what it leaves behind.

Philosophical hermeneutics, he maintains, is neither a higher level of phronesis (as Habermas takes it to be), nor a theoretical enterprise (as Habermas would like Critical Theory to be). It is similar to, but also different from both. Like other forms of knowledge, he insists, it must be seen as being "determined by its 'object' which is mutable human praxis". But this should not lead us to assume its conclusions are merely "praxis based" and thus tied to particular conditions (as Habermas does) for it has theoretical elements in it too. Like (scientific) theory it does not specify what someone should do in a practical situation but :-

Rather it brings about 'general' knowledge of human behaviour and the forms of its 'political' existence (Dasein). (Gadamer in Ormiston & Schrift 1990:275)

Essentially Gadamer is clarifying how the hermeneutic conception of the relationship between the general and the particular marks it off as an enterprise from other outlooks. But he also wants to highlight how important is the link between this relationship and the hermeneutic 'object'. In doing this he is affirming the way his hermeneutic description of life is intimately tied in with a specific account of how the 'general' and 'particular' are related. If Habermas accepts this description, which he appears to do, he cannot then foist other versions of objectivity drawn from 'scientific' or 'theoretical' criteria on it without at the same time distorting it. The implication being, that while Habermas is an advocate of undistorted communication at one level, he is inadvertently imposing distortion at another.

So what does philosophical hermeneutics do ?

Gadamer maintains that the power of philosophical hermeneutics lies in its capacity to critically reflect on the automatic nature of our everyday understanding, and to expose the naivety of objectivistic ways of thinking. He notes again that Critical Theory uses hermeneutic reflection to expose the prejudices that make up ideology. Wherever a break in the apparent good order of our understanding happens, where we suspect deception, there hermeneutic reflection swings into action. He cites several examples including a philosophical one where the idea of 'nothing' as used by Hegel and Heidegger was dismissed as meaningless by positivist philosophers. Gadamer points out that the concept of 'nothingness' is only unintelligible where inappropriate standards of logic are brought to bear on it. Philosophical hermeneutics is able to show that these positivist objections do not correspond to hermeneutic experience, and that such a concept can be rendered intelligible by showing how it relates to a whole movement of thought.

Hermeneutic reflection then involves the correction of self-understanding, and I suspect that he has in mind the need to correct the 'positivist' slips in self-understanding that betray Habermas' ambitions. But ostensibly the point is a broader one. The power of hermeneutic reflection is based not on invoking a particular method, but on the possibility of reaching a common agreement through the 'universal' linguistic nature of our human life. This commonality through language is not something that one acquires through learning to use the correct method, but is available to us by virtue of our belonging to a speech community. In short, coming to a proper self-understanding, and establishing what is right or good in a particular situation is a thoroughly hermeneutic activity.

Absolutely no experience is excluded

As much of Habermas' second critique was devoted to describing what lies outside the hermeneutic realm, Gadamer takes some time and effort to reaffirm the idea that nothing is excluded:-

> Neither the specialisation and increasingly esoteric operations of the modern sciences nor material labour and its form of organisation, nor the political institutions of domination and governance which bind society together find themselves outside this universal medium of practical reason (or unreason).
> (Gadamer in Ormiston & Schrift 1990:277)

Given that Gadamer still insists that nothing, in principle, lies outside language, which is the dialogic medium of practical reason, what are we to make of Habermas' claim that some forms of knowledge are monologic ?

Gadamer's response to this is that nothing Habermas has said really shakes the specific kind of claim to 'universality' that hermeneutics makes. His response, which is tinged with a certain amazement, is threefold. First, Habermas himself recognises that monologically constructed theories still need to be rendered understandable in everyday dialogue; and hence ordinary language remains the backdrop against which scientific monologues take place. So the idea that some theories bypass ordinary language as the "last meta-language" is, in effect, denied by Habermas himself.

Secondly, despite what Habermas says, hermeneutics has never been *only* concerned with the colloquial communication. The difference between colloquial and technical speech has existed for thousands of years. Certainly, mathematics is nothing new, and the skills of the professional, the doctor, and the shaman have also traditionally defined themselves as being beyond ordinary understanding. All this is not new to hermeneutics either, perhaps the only new thing about it is that the modern professional no longer thinks it his task to communicate his expertise to everyday life.

Thirdly, Gadamer has no dispute with the idea that there are mathematical disciplines which make no reference to colloquial language. There are also the genetic discoveries of Piaget, to which Habermas drew attention, these suggest there are pre-linguistic cognitive categories. In fact Gadamer adds the names of Plessner, Polanyi. and Kunz to that of Piaget, as authors who have also analysed phenomena that exists outside the colloquial use of language. But this is beside the point. It is quite absurd for Habermas to suggest that for hermeneutics our experience consists only of the words we use to describe it. What Habermas has tried to do, and what Gadamer refuses to accept, is the narrowing down of his account of the 'linguisticality of being' to mean 'language creates reality'. This would produce the stunning naivety that if things were not in colloquial language they would not exist. Gadamer made it clear in *Truth and Method* that language is not independent of the world but has its being only in the power it has to disclose the world. Language and world always sit together and the task of hermeneutic reflection remains what it has always been

> ...to integrate into the unity of linguistic world interpretation that which is not understood, or that which is uncommon: 'understandable' only to the initiates. (Gadamer in Ormiston & Schrift 1990:278)

In other words the hermeneutic task appears so restricted only because Habermas has closed it down to allow space for his own epistemological ambitions. Gadamer insists that we recognise the full potential of language to come to terms with what is not yet known. Hermeneutic reflection constantly renews itself in bringing things to a common understanding, be they ideological deceptions, misunderstandings, or scientific insights - all are taken up into this ongoing communicative dialogue.

Psychoanalysis and the authority of tradition

Inevitably, given the attention devoted to it by Habermas, Gadamer returns to the role psychoanalysis is supposed to play as the exemplary model to be adopted by a critical sociology. It is a model that according to Habermas, embraces the virtues of both hermeneutic and scientific ways of going on. The problem, as before, is that the 'hermeneutic' and 'scientific' do not sit together in happy union. The universality that Gadamer finds in the linguistic-interpretive way we live our lives is at odds with the universality Habermas ascribes to science, and wants to see incorporated into his theory.

Gadamer notes that psychoanalysis exercises the kind of critical reflection that should emancipate neurotic patients from their 'distorted communication'. However, he also notes with a little sarcasm that when this process is transferred across to the social sphere, we have to conclude that anyone who finds themselves in agreement with the status quo, is by definition socially neurotic and in need of treatment.

His objection is as much a moral one as anything else, being based on what he sees as the manipulative potential that arises when the analyst's role is extended to embrace the social consciousness of others. He reiterates the criticism he levelled in his first response but embraces the concept of legitimacy, which had been used by Habermas to attack hermeneutics, and directs it back towards him :-

> It cannot fall within the socially legitimate function of the doctor, or the lay analyst, to move outside of the professionally therapeutic situation and 'treat' others as 'ill' by engaging in emancipatory reflection concerning their social consciousness.. Such 'treatment' is not to be described as a technique, but as a common work of reflection" (1990: 280)

Of course he acknowledges there is likely to be some overlap between professional expertise and ones normal engagement in social intercourse, but it is quite unjustified, both socially and hermeneutically, to transpose one entirely onto the other. For example, suppose one is engaged in fierce political debate to the point where the other party gets angry. Should one fall back on the assumption that because they are angry they are exhibiting neurotic symptoms, i.e. like a repressed psychoanalytic patient they are resisting the 'truth' of your case ? Clearly Gadamer finds such an idea both amusing and disturbing, for it has nothing to do with a hermeneutic partnership that could generate the ground for social solidarity.

The central issue Gadamer returns to again and again is the scope being claimed by Habermas et al for psychoanalysis, emancipatory reflection, undistorted communication, regulative ideals, and so forth. He senses that their scope is being massively, indeed potentially dangerously overrated. For example if we transpose psychoanalysis onto history are we not left with having to see it as either an "impenetrable contingency" understood only by prophets, or as something *potentially wholly rational*. Gadamer acknowledges that the discussions presented by Habermas, Geigel and Apel, are richly informative but he is fearful that they may be incorrect in being so one sided. Apel for example, seems to imply that human nature consists wholly in our being able to transcend instinctual life and bring it entirely under rational control (3).

The problem with Habermas' sketch of depth-psychology, according to Gadamer, is that it moves so unquestioningly from the individual to the social. He uses Chomsky's theory of linguistic competence to develop his own theory of communicative competence, and uses this in conjuction with psychoanalysis to justify the claim to see through distorted communication. But is this move justified ? Is it not the case that a genuine communicative consensus is based on a relationship between groups of individuals living in agreement, and that such groups break up and reform quite differently from the way neurotic individuals are split off from their speech community? The point being that the characteristics of linguistic competence a la Chomsky are quite different from the characteristics of a social consensus. If we follow Habermas and apply his psychoanalytic model to society how would we go about the *desymbolisation* of its concept of democracy ? In other words, how could Habermas justify taking a particular society's concept of democracy apart and *resymbolising* it according to the abstract principles of communicative competence ?

Clearly Gadamer is much troubled by the prospect. He knows full well that Habermas justifies his theory of communicative competence by arguing that all communication has the ideal speech situation as its *telos* or aim. He also knows that the principle of ideal speech in a sense contains 'democracy' and 'freedom' in that the essence of communication is that only the force of the better argument should hold sway. And clearly Habermas wants this used as a counterfactual principle to regulate society. But what more terrifying force could there be than the force of pure reason, how could one resist, how would one dare resist its demands? In fact Gadamer believes that Habermas has adopted and amplified the very criticism he levelled against hermeneutics. According to Habermas hermeneutics was guilty of marrying together reason and authority, yet this seems to be precisely what he wants to do when he recommends that the reasonableness of ideal speech should become the authority that regulates all our lives ! By contrast his own claims about the relationship between reason and authority were far more modest and less tied to 'ideal' conditions. For him the allegiance authority wins can never be measured in terms of an abstraction, there are no 'ideal' conditions. It has rather to be grasped through the actual, 'living' conditions that make up the tradition through which people live their lives. That is through :-

> ..all the circumstances of concrete experience in terms of which one speaks of natural authority and the following which it finds. It seems to me a dogmatic prejudice concerning what one means by human 'reason' to always speak in such cases of coercive communication: e.g. where love, the choice of ideals, submissiveness, voluntary superiority or subordination have reached a level of stability. (Gadamer in Ormiston & Schrift 1990:287)

If the relationship between reason and authority is not a straightforward one of coercion, then it is not clear how Habermas' theory of communicative competence is going to dissolve the barriers between opposing social groups. Gadamer is arguing that because reason and authority are entwined with each other, it will never really be possible to disentangle them in situations where opposing but interelated groups accuse each other of using reason manipulatively. It will never be possible to claim that reason lies all on one side, and coercive authority on the other. It has to be recognised that a political situation is not a *theoretical* situation and as such different kinds of (Aristotelean) criteria are appropriate to it. Gadamer is advocating that Critical Theory be restrained by hermeneutic understanding, and seek more modestly to bring about communication where before there was none.

In the same way that his critics have failed to see the possible validity of the connection between reason and authority, perhaps not surprisingly they have misunderstood his account of tradition. He declares that the emphasis he put on the phrase, 'connection to tradition' did not indicate any preference for those traditional customs and attitudes to which we automatically respond, as against those which challenge the status quo. His claim was only that we are immanently connected to a tradition that exceeds what our consciousness can grasp. In other words, whether we consciously affirm or deny the status quo, we extend tradition insofar as our efforts are always moulded by forces that draw us up into its movement; indeed "tradition exists only in becoming other than it is", i.e. it exists only in change. In fact, Gadamer claims that authentic critique depends upon recognising this relation to tradition and not upon forming *general* criticisms pitched at dominant groups and their ideas. Such an instrument is too blunt and undiscriminating to be effective.

Ironically, he notes that it is Habermas who takes for granted, and wants to adopt for society the unequal relationship between psychoanalyst and patient. Here, the authority of the analyst and the voluntary submission of the patient is the "supporting foundation" or consensus, which is used with some force, to uncover repression. This authority/tradition relationship illustrates well what Gadamer means by the legitimacy of true authority. In *Truth and Method* he described authority as not ultimately to do with mere obedience, but the knowing acceptance by one party that the judgement of another is superior and should hold sway. However, while the psychoanalytic relationship is exemplary in this respect within the boundaries of its own claims, it is not so beyond them. Gadamer finds it odd that Habermas, who has been so critical of him over the authority of tradition, should so blithely want to impose this 'authority' model onto social life. For in social life the supporting consensus, on Habermas' own account, involves mutual resistance between groups, not acceptance.

In fact Gadamer expresses amazement that his critics should think that he denies the significance of revolutionary consciousness and only applauds conformity. His point has been to argue that in the social world we cannot know in an automatic way whether the consciousness of the revolutionary or the consciousness of the conformist is justified. Hermeneutics cannot decide from within its own theoretical resources which is legitimate, this is something that belongs to the social-political arena, and should be agreed upon there, hopefully on the basis of dialogue.

On praxis and not always knowing best

The issue of Critical Theory claiming to know the truth ahead of others is continued in Gadamer's discussion of praxis. Habermas placed emphasis upon the importance of the concept of reflection and the role it has in promoting emancipation, indeed he even bolstered it with regulative principles such as 'the stance of the last historian' and 'the ideal speech situation'. These regulative principles are absent from hermeneutics but would be used by Critical Theory as ways of establishing a counterfactual agreement against which actual arrangements could be measured.

However, contained within this, Gadamer believes, is a dogmatic claim to foreknowledge and a contravention of the idea of praxis. Dialogue cannot be established by those who claim to know ahead of others the truth of a situation. In effect, they put the cart before the horse in claiming to have knowledge of the agreement that has yet to be established. Praxis is a process of *becoming* conscious of things and of convincing others, or being convinced by them, through ongoing concrete critique.

The ideal of undermining people's 'natural certainty' over things is incompatible with the human condition. Gadamer is, I think, referring to both the potential amorality of Critical Theory, and also to its irrationality in tacitly claiming an absolute status for its knowledge. Even the psychoanalyst knows there are limits to what can be done, and that nothing is ever completely and utterly analysed. Against Habermas' emancipatory dogmatism, therefore, Gadamer puts forward the concept of equilibrium and the "being of play" which is its natural context. This he suggests could be seen tentatively as a measure of social health - at least ontologically speaking.

Of course this measure is not to be thought in the same way as one of Habermas' regulative principles, for hermeneutics recognises that all praxis contains within it an "effective historical factor". That is to say all agreements reached are caught up in an historical process which co-determines the consensus. This does not mean that these consensuses are flimsy because they are historically relative, quite the opposite, they are potent because they are based on the deepest convictions drawn from one's tradition. Nevertheless hermeneutic experience teaches a lesson of modesty by reminding us that our generalisations are not universals, and that what we understand speaks to us from within our tradition. Indeed the richness of the hermeneutic approach lies in the fact that it discourages us from imposing abstractions while encouraging us to bring our prejudices into play. In short "the hermeneutic experience is truly woven, completely and utterly, into the general being of human *praxis*. Critical Theory will thus not enhance, but truncate and distort it.

Rhetoric returns

Towards the end Gadamer returns to the importance of rhetoric and the common ground it shares with hermeneutics. His central point is that human communication is invariably affective in that it uses emotional arguments to convince, persuade, and arrive at common agreement. However, it is not thereby irrational as Habermas implies with his efforts to establish a counterpoint of perfect communication free from coercion. He regards it as shockingly unrealistic that Habermas should seek to circumvent the supposed coerciveness that is naturally present in speech. All social praxis, especially revolutionary praxis *requires* this element to be present. By which he means that social solidarity of *any* kind will always be secured affectively, and could never be based on pure, impersonal communication. It is thus quite misleading for Habermas to talk of authentic consensus in this way.

Because Habermas sets ideal speech in opposition to colloquial speech he is necessarily ambiguous about the concept of manipulation. It is as though, for him every emotional influence represents an illegitimate manipulation of meaning. By contrast Gadamer does not believe it is possible to have communication at all without the attempt to *convince* others of something. He senses that Habermas' "ideal speech" model is geared to the exchange of information, but not to the dialogue necessary to achieve a 'living' agreement. If the ontological account of the linguisticality of being is accurate, public communication even in technologically orientated modern societies necessarily contains a dialogic element :-

> Even the technical forms of shaping opinion which our industrial society has developed always contain at some point a moment of consent, be it on the side of the consumer who can withdraw his agreement, or be it, and this is decisive, in the way our mass media are not simply extensions of a unitary political will, but rather are the showplace of political controversies, which for their part both reflect and determine political occurrences in society. (Gadamer in Ormiston & Schrift 1990:292-3)

By contrast, if Habermas sees 'ideal speech' as a principle to regulate this, then in spite of himself he will be forced into the role of the social engineer, one who acts as the gatekeeper of public information.

Let's not forget the importance of 'the good life'

Gadamer's final discussion point is perhaps the one that challenges Habermas' enterprise most thoroughly. It is concerned with the ultimate purpose of any critical social analysis, namely, how to bring the good life into being. He accepts along with Habermas that rhetoric and hermeneutics have, as it were, built into them an anticipation of appropriate ways of living. But this anticipation cannot be turned into a regulative principle without praxis becoming deformed. Praxis requires dialogue to achieve consensus and one must therefore refrain from arrogating to one's own insights an ultimate superiority. The idea of coercion-free communication must not be used coercively, for there is always the danger that empty abstractions become filled with manic ambitions. The good life will be found through dialogue, or it will not be found at all. He expresses it this way :-

> The human good is something to be encountered in human *praxis*, and is indeterminable without the concrete situation in which one thing is preferred to another. This alone, and not a counterfactual agreement, is the critical experience of the Good. It must be worked through in the concrete circumstances of the situation. Such an idea of the correct life as a universal idea is 'empty'. (Gadamer in Ormiston & Schrift 1990:293)

The important fact being that practical wisdom is not a form of knowledge where people can assume the superiority of their ideas over those of others. Of course, in everyday life people will claim to know what is best for everyone, but living together in agreement involves convincing others about it, and this cannot be achieved by a coercion-free political discussion group. Nevertheless reason can guide politics in forming an appropriate kind of political will - one where the possibility that the opposite conviction could be correct is always seriously considered. In this the concept of play reminds us of the plurality of forces that are at work in us all, in our convictions, our arguments, and our experiences, and that the fruitfulness of these are sustained in dialogue. On this basis a community that surpasses the individual and the group is formed.

Notes

1. The essay was entitled 'Replik' and appeared in 1971 as the final contribution to the book *Hermeneutik und Ideologiekritik* edited by Habermas et al, Suhrkamp Verlag Frankfurt am Main. The translation I have consulted is by George H. Leiner and is found in Ormiston and

Schrift (1990). This contains some deliberate omissions from Gadamer's original text which refer to Geigel's work, see Ormiston & Schrift (1990: 296, note 14).

2. Readers who are familiar with Habermas' work will know that this opens up onto a wider issue. His later writings identify *justice* as the key to praxis, rather than *happiness.*

3. It might be noted that this comment may contain an oblique reference to the case brought by Horkheimer and Adorno in *Dialectic of Enlightenment (1972).* In this, the development of Western reason is seen as virtually the correlate of increasing levels of repression.

13 A discussion and evaluation of the debate

Introduction

It is a remarkable tribute to both authors that their debate, which was certainly convoluted and drew on some arcane areas of German philosophy, should still be having its significance pondered in the English speaking world some twenty years later. The interim has seen it extensively covered from a variety of angles, and though I do not intend to try and discuss these in detail some comments may be useful.

In a rough and ready sense most commentary has fallen into three broad categories, the 'convergence' category, the pro-Habermas category (1), and a rather smaller pro-Gadamer category. The convergence position entails the idea that their views are not fundamentally incompatible and that their apparent differences are mainly matters of emphasis which spring from their different theoretical starting points, or a clash between the different levels of argument on which their claims are made, viz ontological versus epistemological. Ricoeur (1973 & 1981), for example argues that their respective attitudes towards such things as critique, tradition, dialogue and communication, are dialectically related and provide a mutual critical limit. Thus, any tendency toward an excess of 'emancipation' (Habermas) or an excess of 'conservation' (Gadamer), will be checked by the respective claims of the alternative position. Other authors that could be considered to fall into this category include Kisiel (1970), Bubner (1975), Mendelson (1979), Misgeld (1977a, 1977b, 1981a, 1981b, 1991) (2), Ingram (1983), Davey (1985), How (1980), Kelly (1989). Interestingly, authors in this camp are not suggesting that the two positions *should* be fused together, this idea tends to characterise the pro-Habermas camp insofar as they follow his ambition of incorporating hermeneutics into Critical Theory.

Those which tend toward the view that Habermas' criticisms are valid include, Wellmer (1972), Wolff (1975a, 1975b, & 1981), Giddens (1976a, 1976b), Bleicher (1982), Eagleton (1983), Outhwaite (1985), Brenkman (1987), Holub (1991) and Gardiner (1992), though in being broadly sympathetic to his criticisms, they are not thereby uncritical of him. Moreover, in being so general it can easily be argued these categories conceal highly diverse and often original evaluations of the debate.

Notwithstanding this, there is a third view, to which I have found myself increasingly drawn, that Gadamer's responses were more than adequate and his case stands up rather better than Habermas and those influenced by him, would suggest. Indeed, in some of the literature Habermas' criticisms have been presented as though true *because* they were critical, and very little attention given to the complexity of Gadamer's responses in terms of how they relate to his overall case. My argument is also that in trying to assimilate hermeneutics to his own project Habermas often renders it contradictory. Those who are broadly sympathetic to Gadamer include Hoy (1978), Gall (1981), How (1985), Hekman (1986), Warnke (1987), Sica (1988), Nicholson (1991).

Language, prejudice and ideology

From the outset Habermas approached Gadamer's work for the purpose of using it to reconstruct Critical Theory, and while he never claims to be doing otherwise, it subtly affects the way he describes hermeneutics. He appears to be adopting Gadamer's ideas but actually modulates them to suit a different purpose.

For example, he goes to considerable trouble to demonstrate the ways Gadamer's account of language provides the most adequate basis for social analysis. Others have recognised the constitutive role language plays in social reality, how language-games govern what is possible within particular forms of life, but it fell to Gadamer to show its endlessly reflexive 'boundary-overstepping' capacities. Gadamer's account of the linguistic horizon, Habermas argues, had the virtue of conceptualising language not only as something that determined our reality, but as something that was being constantly re-interpreted. The boundaries of a horizon are real but porous, they allow us to grasp the real in its malleability. They allow us to re-interpret the rules of our social life as well as enabling us to understand the nature of alien ways of life. This is doubly important to Habermas as he believes the linguistic approach is epistemologically superior to positivist approaches, but it also opens up the idea that our 'linguisticality' gives us a certain critical distance from those norms and values we learn in our immediate society; it is in short, the source of human freedom.

Given the comprehensive nature of Gadamer's account and the manner in which Habermas at first takes it on board, it comes as a surprise when he starts to reverse his approval. I have already indicated that Habermas slides some distinctly un-Gadamerian ideas into his description of the hermeneutic case, as if to prepare the reader for his criticisms. Certainly at first sight Gadamer's emphasis on the projective nature of understanding seems analogous to Habermas' emphasis on language's capacity to overstep boundaries. However, Habermas ignores the wider context of Gadamer's case in pressing language toward having an almost transcendental communicative function. This is alien to Gadamer as it over amplifies the appropriative side of language, placing it at odds with other aspects of his account, such as the importance of the way prejudgements always structure understanding. It also suggests that communication is one of language's functions which we as subjects utilise with varying degrees of success. This again is at odds with Gadamer's account, in that he quite specifically argues that first and foremost, language is not something we as subjects *do things with*. Rather, it does things with us. It embraces us, and places us in relation to things before we can reflect upon them.

This kind of omission on Habermas' part comes to be of crucial importance when he introduces the concept of ideology in opposition to Gadamer's account of language. He argues that the social forces of 'labour' and 'domination' exist external to language and thus impose themselves invisibly upon tradition. These forces become institutionalised, and normalise what otherwise could be seen as illegitimate relationships of social control. Ideology then is :-

> ...not so much a matter of deceptions in language as of deception with language as such. (Habermas 1988:172)

The problem with this statement is that from Gadamer's point of view there is no such thing as "language as such". One of the fundamental errors in modern thinking, he explained in *Truth and Method*, is the habit we have of seeing language as a *thing* or an object which is neutrally available to us, i.e. something that we do things with. Gadamer believes language does not exist primarily as an objective system of signs independent of us because 'linguisticality' encompasses us, is the 'world' for us, before we can abstract objects such as 'systems' from it. Hence Habermas makes no sense when he talks of "language as such" being systematically distorted, for it implies that he has removed himself from its clutches, and taken up a position to act in a sovereign way to 'de-ideologise it'. Given that what he found so worthwhile in hermeneutics was its avoidance of the objectivism still present in the Wittgensteinian approach, as well as the way it revealed language's reflexive, boundary-overstepping qualities, it is flatly contradictory to reinstate language as an object at a later stage, declaring its meaning to be trapped inside an ideological system. One cannot have language as a dialogic process *and* as a one-way medium of social control.

Gadamer, I think quite rightly opposed Habermas' efforts to close down the range of his concept of 'linguisticality' so it came to mean only "..intersubjectively intended and symbolically transmitted meaning." (Habermas 1988:173-4). Construed in this way it could necessarily only be the basis for a very limited sociology, one that explained :-

> ...social action in terms of motives that are identical with the actors own interpretations of situations, and thus identical with the linguistically oriented meaning in terms of which the actor orients himself...(this)...rules out a distinction between observed segments of behaviour and the actor's interpretations. (Habermas 1988:177)

In doing this Habermas fudges the distinction between the interpretive sociology of Anselm Strauss and Gadamer's hermeneutics. He commits both to being able only to deal with the *expressed* claims a society's members make, which are necessarily taken to be true as they are the limit of what can be known.

However, the idea that the hermeneut is unable to grasp the disjunction between the explicit claims of an actor and "observed segments of behaviour" is a parody of Gadamer's ideas. Gadamer devoted a large amount of space to describing the *projective* nature of hermeneutic understanding, and how this followed a circular, self corrective path. He quite specifically rejected the idea that understanding involved the interpreter effacing him or herself for the sake of the 'object', i.e. the actor's own self-understanding. His critique of nineteenth century hermeneutics was based on its misguided attempt to slip into the mental outlook of historical actors. In fact he has frequently pointed out that hermeneutics only really comes into its own when an effort of interpretation is required, that is, when *there is a disjunction between what one expects to find and what one actually observes* (3).

Moreover, Gadamer also specifically rejects the centrality of an actor's consciousness as the locus of truth for social analysis, and he repeatedly challenges the Enlightenment illusion that consciousness is autonomous or transcendent. Nor is this affected by Habermas' claim that hermeneutics is tied to *intersubjective* meaning (as opposed to an individual's subjective meaning), for Gadamer's argument was that meaning *always* escapes its 'author's' intentions and is determined instead by the fusion of historical horizons. Most famously in his critique of Dilthey's historicism he pointed out that to focus on subjectivity involves us in distorting things, as the subject is constantly being overtaken by history :-

> In fact history does not belong to us; we belong to it. Long before we understand ourselves through the processes of self-examination, we understand ourselves in a self-evident way in the family, society, and state in which we live. The focus of subjectivity is a distorting mirror. The self-awareness of the individual is only a flickering in the closed circuits of historical life. *That is why the prejudices of the individual, far more than his judgements, constitute the historical reality of his being"* (Gadamer 1989:276-7)

I can think of no plainer denial of the idea that hermeneutics is tied to actors' self-understanding.

If one refuses to accept Habermas' reduction of 'linguisticality' to mean a kind of closed circuit of only 'what people believe', then his claim that hermeneutics deals with cultural tradition to the exclusion labour and domination, ceases to hold water. The charge Habermas levelled against hermeneutics was that for it, labour and domination only existed insofar as they entered public language. This implied that such forces do not exist unless they come into the public domain, whereas various authors such as Marx, Freud, and Piaget, had in fact demonstrated there was a reality that went on behind the backs of public language users. However, while this criticism might stick against an interpretive sociology committed to an epistemology limited to the subject's conscious language use, it does not against an ontological argument where language is identified as the 'house of being' (3).

On this view reality and language always happen together, with the result that labour and domination are no less 'linguistical' or less 'real' than the topics that crop up on an everyday basis in ordinary language. In fact Gadamer makes the specific claim that meaning can be understood even where it is not intended. Thus, making sense of the influence of a new mode of production is hermeneutical, even though the forms of social control that go with it have become so 'normal' and 'taken for granted' that they are not overtly expressed in ordinary, or natural language. Such a critical attitude is possible by virtue of language. The point being, that for Gadamer language is not 'ordinary' in the way Habermas tries to make it. It is not a flat, direct expression of a fixed non-linguistic world, but rather that which allows us to be both a part of the world *and* apart from it. In other words, language is not an obstacle to critique, it is not mechanically tied to a society's material forces, but has the distance necessary for critique built into it. What is odd is that at times Habermas does seem to recognise this.

Even so in his second critique he still tries to manoeuvre Gadamer's account of language into the same corner. He substitutes the term 'natural language' for 'linguisticality', and in doing so restricts hermeneutics to the low key epistemological task of discussing everyday topics. This weds it to a philosophy of 'the subject' or of 'consciousness' that is quite the opposite of its actual aims.

Gadamer never suggests that our linguistic consciousness determines the material basis of life, only that labour and domination have their being in language and are therefore open to hermeneutic understanding. In fact Gadamer, I think, rightly feels that hermeneutic reflection is remarkably well suited to disclosing the complexities of meaning that make up the contemporary world. One could argue that large amounts of sociology in the last twenty years, have been devoted to a hermeneutic investigation of the subtleties of social control in all its various guises.

Yet at face value it might still be claimed that much of this work confirms Habermas' belief that meaning in the areas of, for example, gender or ethnicity, or the state's management of poverty involves 'systematic distortion', in that tacit ideological assumptions can be shown to structure the outcome of social action. Is Gadamer therefore right to assume that his account of prejudices *includes* what Habermas means by ideology ?

Clearly at one level they are not the same. Prejudices are the ground of our historical situatedness, and will change as temporal distance reveals new aspects of them, so that what is concealed from view at one point will be revealed at another. On the other hand, an ideological claim, as Warnke (1987:115) points out, involves more than the idea that it has an implicit or 'yet to be revealed' source in the social system. Rather, it presents itself in such a way that makes it difficult to disentangle what is warranted in the claim, from what is unwarranted. To be able to distinguish between the two, according to Habermas, one needs an objective "system of reference" i.e. a general theory of society that includes the hermeneutic dimension, but goes beyond it to explain how other elements are related to it.

This seems to me to be nub of the issue. Gadamer would not deny the existence of ideology in a weak sense, in that the "linguisticality of being" means that reality, including the material organisation of society, is tied in with society's self-understanding. Hence, the regular patterns of social practice which are entwined with regular patterns of ideas, will indeed make it difficult to disentangle the warranted from the unwarranted aspects of self-understanding. But just so - difficult - the task is no less hermeneutic for being that.

By contrast the existence of ideology in the strong sense, one that Habermas employs when he uses the phrase 'systematically distorted communication', is implausible. It suggests that the system is machine like in being impervious to new forms of self-understanding, and on this view it can only reproduce the ideological meanings for which it is programmed. However, apart from the doubtfulness of seeing language as a mere conduit for ideology, this also runs counter to another feature of Gadamer's case to which Habermas nominally adhered. The rules which orientate social practices, he noted (1988:165), were not to be seen as technical rules in that their application did not follow mechanically from an "abstract universal". They involved application in the Gadamerian sense of a reciprocal interpretation between the general and particular. This necessarily involves an ongoing process of re-interpretation, not a reduplication of the rules of a static status quo.

To make sense of ideology in terms of Habermas' first critique it would be necessary to establish a theory that was beyond the language tradition that is its interpretive starting point. Gadamer rightly denies this possibility. Moreover, as there can be no Archimedean point beyond language, it becomes a morally dubious illusion to suppose one can possess an 'objective' theory of society from which warranted or unwarranted claims can straightforwardly be distinguished. In reality, distinguishing between the two always presupposes an embedded understanding of what is at stake. It is not theory, but the fore-structure of our understanding, i.e. our prejudices that always provide us with a sense of what is better or worse, right or wrong, more or less justified.

Psychoanalysis and hermeneutics

In his second critique Habermas seems to acknowledge the impossibility of moving entirely outside language, but still hankers after theories which he hopes will somehow "cheat" or "bypass" natural language. He is still concerned that in some circumstances even the most strenuous hermeneutic efforts will not reveal the truth of a situation.

He uses psychoanalysis as an exemplar of a theory that is appropriate where the very tools of public communication are distorted so much that they run up against a wall of incomprehension. He cites both dreams and neuroses as examples of behaviours that meet the criteria of being specifically unintelligible, in that they break the rules of public communication. They involve condensations, displacements, and reversals of meaning, which can only be rendered intelligible by an *explanation* using Freud's theory.

There were three specific ways in which he claimed hermeneutics was "bypassed" by psychoanalysis.

(1) In psychoanalysis the ontological version of understanding has to be temporarily suspended and replaced by a 'genetic' or 'functional' method of explanation. This means that the behaviour of the patient has to be 'understood' in terms of a *theory* of personality, and read as a symptom of a traumatic scene from childhood.

(2) In psychoanalysis the doctor-patient relationship cannot simply be one of dialogue. The doctor has to control the process of "scenic transference" in a quasi-experimental way, in order that undistorted dialogue can start.

(3) In psychoanalysis the doctor selects as significant, particular expressions from the gamut of a patient's actual expressions. This involves a deliberate 'seeing' of what is relevant on the basis of theory, and not allowing what is relevant to emerge dialogically.

Even if we allow for Habermas' reduction of linguisticality, in what sense do these arguments bypass ordinary language as the ultimate meta-language? In what sense do they count against Gadamer ? It seems to me that in either case they don't.

Habermas' initial point was that unintelligible or neurotic behaviour could be defined in terms of the fact that it *broke* with normal language and the forms of behaviour that accompany it. But, in effect this indicates that the psychoanalyst in using theory does not break with, but *presupposes* an interpretive understanding of normal everyday life. To understand how condensations, displacements or reversals of meaning break with normality, one must already know what normality is.

With regard to the specific points (1)-(3) above, their effectiveness as criticisms depends on the spurious limitations Habermas has placed on hermeneutics in redescribing it. Habermas claims that hermeneutic dialogue is suspended in the psychoanalytic situation, because the relationship between doctor and patient has to be asymmetrical, so as to overcome systematic mental distortions in communication. The doctor is in the dominant role, in that he or she can see through to what is relevant, and control the patient's "scenic transference". But nowhere does Gadamer suggest that his model of dialogue is one of perfect symmetry between human subjects. As I have already indicated Gadamer's work is clearly not centred on the human subject, and the model that anticipates perfect symmetry is Habermas' own, imposed from the outside, and based on his notion of "the ideal speech situation". Habermas' complaint that hermeneutics wrongly *assumes* perfect symmetrical dialogue already exists, looks rather like an invention designed to make hermeneutics seem naive.

For Gadamer, dialogue between human subjects is but one variation on the ontological dialogue through which we have a 'world'. It is not primarily a relationship between subject and object, and certainly not one that could be purified of constraint. An important feature of Gadamer's account is that dialogue can certainly exist in situations where there is a distinct lack of symmetry. For example, in the first section of *Truth and Method* he made clear that the understanding of art was a dialogic process, but he also emphasised that art takes hold of us, it grips us in an unmistakable way that exceeds our deliberate control. It does not rely on the norms of equality and perfect partnership. When poetry 'speaks' to us it does not ask our opinion, but commands our attention, it uses all the linguistic and imaginative power available to present something convincingly.

Hence the fact that the psychoanalytic relationship is asymmetrical in no way counts against it being hermeneutical. Moreover, from Gadamer's point of view even the idea of 'systematic distortion' as a description of an *individuals'* communicative behaviour is not without credibility. It only becomes incredible if we follow Habermas and try to apply it to whole social systems. Psychoanalysis depends on assumptions about normality that are specific to Western societies at a particular time in their history. Describing certain kinds of communicative behaviour as deviating in a systematic way from specific cultural norms is therefore legitimate, because it does not claim that these norms or prejudices are universal, it does not try situate itself beyond its own historical tradition (4).

There is a problem attendant on this, which is that Freud saw his own work as being more than culturally local in origin and application. Nevertheless Gadamer's claim would be the same, viz that regardless of what Freud thought, psychoanalysis is legitimate (only) to the extent that it is an interpretation based on the norms of a living consensus, and not a spuriously universal norm such as perfect communication (ideal speech).

As can be seen it is not the existence of method in psychoanalysis that Gadamer objects to, but the application of method based on norms that are falsely claimed to be universal. It is only when Habermas tries to extend the methodic practices of psychoanalysis in this way, that Gadamer suspects a kind of emancipatory coercion is at work.

In the psychoanalytic situation there is an active seeking of help by the patient, both doctor and patient relate to each other in a mutually understood, if asymmetrical way. The doctor has the authority, but the legitimacy of both roles is sustained by common understanding, and is limited to their very specific professional relationship. However if this is extended to a general critique of ideology one is drawn into the incongruous situation of imagining that the Critical Theorist has the right to diagnose others as socially ill.

Gadamer was surely right to claim that differences in self understanding between groups is not necessarily the result of faulty communication or ideology, but of differences in the concrete circumstances that constitute their lives. There is thus no apriori way that one group can legitimately charge another with 'ideology'. Gadamer wisely warns against the habit of thought that claims to know 'everything beforehand'; a critique of ideology that claims to know the truth before it has understood anything, eliminates differences and from the outset nullifies authentic hermeneutic experience (5).

The authority of tradition and unconstrained dialogue

Gadamer's reply on the issue of language/ideology echoes his response to the criticism that his work is conservative because it encourages an uncritical submission to tradition, and is comparably adequate.

Holub (1991:68), for example, argues along with Habermas that hermeneutics has no way of distinguishing between freely accepted authority, and authority that is imposed through domination. Gadamer's account of our 'linguistic tradition', according to Holub, presents us with a view that only permits an acceptance of it. The priority Gadamer gives to prejudices and the process of tradition, makes the idea of critique a slender affair.

Gadamer's response to this line of criticism was to point to the peculiar way Habermas had reduced his account of language, and that he had fallen for the Enlightenment illusion that made polar opposites of reason and the authority of tradition. This produced in Habermas' account a naive belief that tradition was invariably wrong and those who accepted it, deluded.

Holub suggests that Gadamer over-read Habermas' criticism, and that what he actually meant, was that reason gives us the power to reflect on those things which have been dogmatically imposed, so that we can *decide* whether to accept them or not. That is, it is the specifically *dogmatic* elements in our tradition that Habermas wishes to challenge, not all aspects of tradition (1988:170). There is something in this view but it still misses the fullness of Gadamer's case.

It must be remembered that it was Habermas who argued that Gadamer had removed any distinction between reason and the authority of tradition, and he therefore saw it as his task to find some ground that was independent of tradition on which to place his theory. This does suggest that he was looking for something that could stand in *opposition* to tradition, something which could challenge its authority in an autonomous, principled way. On this basis I regard Gadamer's rejection of Habermas' 'polar-opposite' view of reason and authority as quite justified.

Gadamer, I think is right to refuse the sort of blackmail which demands that one *must* be 'for' or 'against' Enlightenment reason, such that if you are not for it, you are bound to be wholly against it. His insistence on an attitude of ambivalence towards authority, rather than one of automatic acceptance or rejection, offers a far more adequate way of dealing with the fact that all our judgements are embedded in and complicit with the tradition that we are, and thus reason can claim no final autonomy from it (6).

Although we cannot break absolutely with tradition this does not mean that we are unable to challenge or disagree with it, only that in opposing it we necessarily justify ourselves in relation to it. It is this process of justification which Habermas wants to extricate from tradition, but in so doing unwittingly ties himself to a version of pure reason; something to which he is formally opposed. There is something hollow in the concept of reflection that Habermas recommends as an antidote to tradition, for it suggests that an act of pure cognition is possible. It suggests that consciousness is autonomous at some point, in that it is able to escape the prejudices that constitute it and reflect back upon their legitimacy. Yet it was the ability of Gadamer's hermeneutics to surpass these limitations, characteristic of (Schutz's) phenomenological sociology, that recommended it to Habermas.

It is the wisdom of Gadamer to have shown that 'seeing through' prejudices is itself a prejudiced act, not a transcendental one. This is not to deny that the insight which ensues is real, only that the process of clarification should not be thought of as one of cumulative enlightenment. The temporal and finite nature of our existence requires of us a certain modesty. It asks us to recognise that in bringing to light aspects of our lives that were obscured, we necessarily throw others into the shade.

Notes

1. In using the term 'convergence' I am following Hekman (1986:138)

2. Misgeld's position is complicated as in both his 1981 articles he is somewhat critical of Habermas' theoreticism, and uses hermeneutics to challenge it, whereas in his 1991 essay he shifts to a more affirmative view of Critical Theory.

3. Hekman (1986:137-8) makes a similar point, but makes the distinction instead between Wittgenstein's linguistic epistemological case and Gadamer's ontological argument.

4. I owe something here to Georgia Warnke's incisive account of this issue (1987:127-8).

5. Habermas responded to this kind of criticism in *Theory and Practice* (1971), arguing that he had in mind to increase self-understanding in general, rather than providing ammunition for one group to convict another, adversarial group, of ideology. If the adversarial group did not accept the 'ideology critique' of themselves, he admits that one would have to remain satisfied with the scientific adequacy of the explanation alone. As Warnke (1987:128-29) points out, this does not address the deeper Gadamerian point that Critical Theory itself is only "parochially grounded", i.e. a particular, historically situated interpretation of things.

6. Holub (1988:68) claims that when Gadamer puts inverted commas round the word - freely - to describe the way authority is (dogmatically) accepted, he shows the precariousness of his argument. It seems to me the reverse is true. Gadamer puts - freely - in inverted commas because he knows full well that our freedom to accept or reject authority is always an ambiguous one. There is no pure freedom from authority, and an ambivalent attitude is preferable in that it expresses both our sense of belonging to a tradition, as well as our ability to challenge it. The translation in Mueller-Vollmer includes these inverted commas, the one in Linge does not.

14 Concluding remarks and some possibilities

It will apparent that my own view of the debate finds Gadamer's hermeneutics well equipped to stand up to the criticisms levelled against it. However, in the long run it matters less who won the debate than in working out the implications it has for different areas of academic endeavour. The myriad insights that both authors produced provide a wealth of opportunity for those wishing to undertake this task. It would however, be unhermeneutical of me to pre-empt it by declaring this or that principle should be adhered to, by those working in this or that area. And of course Gadamer has frequently reiterated, he never sought to improve the methods used in the social sciences, that task belongs to practitioners. Nevertheless some broad theoretical implications do follow from the debate.

Perhaps the most obvious implication springs from the way it challenged the objectivist assumptions that still underpin much thinking in the human sciences. To be sure most of these disciplines have undertaken a critique of positivism in their recent history, but this has often been based on the relative inadequacy of the way such methods fail to live up to expectations. By contrast Gadamer's work has shown in a comprehensive way the thoroughly temporal and hermeneutic nature of existence. If this is our condition, then explanations which deny or otherwise forget it, are at best inadequate, at worst downright dangerous.

Though there were important differences between them over the nature of objectivity, both authors opposed its traditional status. They accepted that there is no neutral point outside historical tradition, and thus those who would 'diagnose the times' should soften their claims, and acknowledge the situatedness of their aspirations.

Hermeneutics and history writing

Clearly if human existence is deeply 'historical' then Gadamer's work has implications for history writing. His work here, as elsewhere, has opened up a reflection on the limits of the knowledge we produce through methodic practice, while not denying the importance of methodic practice as such. This reflection should not be done in a negative fashion to simply disparage traditional notions of objectivity, but in a way that enhances our self-understanding through recognising how much we, and our knowledge, belong to tradition.

For example in the Afterword to *Truth and Method* he points out that the methods used by the historian are in no way undermined by his account of the way the historian's own historical standpoint feeds into the writing of history :-

> If every historian's own standpoint is always discernible in his findings and valuations, then this discovery implies no criticism of his claim to be scientific. It says nothing about whether the historian has erred by being bound to a standpoint and has misunderstood or misprized tradition, or whether, thanks to the advantage of his standpoint he succeeded in putting something hitherto unobserved in its proper light because of its similarity to something observable in immediate contemporary experience.

The point being that while the historian is in no way exempt from using the most adequate methods available, the truth of his account will become apparent via another source, viz, the resonance with which something in the past speaks to us in the present. Moreover, this is something we cannot prescribe, or know ahead of time, but can only become apparent in the way an interpretation unfolds.

While Gadamer recognises the importance of reflexivity to the historian, he does not follow Habermas in wanting to turn it into a methodological precept. Our self awareness enables us to ask questions of our tradition, it does not enable us to take up the 'stance of the last historian' somewhere beyond history.

The fundamental implication of hermeneutics for the historian can be put in the form a question. 'How can the historian best write history historically' ? There is no formal answer to this, for it can only be addressed within the framework of particular historical issues as they speak to historians in a particular historical tradition. Nevertheless, if we accept the ontological basis of Gadamer's work, such a background question should guide the practice of history writing.

Sociology and the reality of appearances

With regard to sociology, Gadamer has shown that many of the criticisms levelled by Marxists against interpretive sociology would not hold good against a a sociology informed by his hermeneutics. In fact one of the supposed weaknesses of interpretive sociology, its failure to get beyond the level of appearances, can be reversed and shown to be its strength.

One of the failings I identified in Habermas's critique of Gadamer, was the way he gradually reduced the idea of 'linguisticality' to meaning no more than what is overtly expressed in ordinary language. Though Habermas claimed that Gadamer's approach exceeded those available in interpretive sociology, he still fell back on the orthodox Marxist criticism that it fell prey to ideology. Like interpretive sociology generally, he claimed, hermeneutics was naively tied to the actors self-understanding, and as such denied the role that structural factors play in providing the context for self-understanding. In ignoring these structural factors, Habermas tried to commit hermeneutics to being able only to deal with *appearances*. In contrast, he argued, Critical Theory would be able to deal with the *reality* that lies behind appearances as well.

Now, as I have already pointed out, this criticism may apply to interpretive sociology, but it does not affect Gadamer's hermeneutics. In fact, I believe that one of the implications of hermeneutics is that the complexities of the relationship between appearance and reality is far better dealt with by it, than Critical Theory.

An adequate account of a sociological situation would certainly have to go beyond what we could, following Ricoeur, call a hermeneutics of faith, i.e. an interpretation based entirely on the validity of expressed meaning. However, Habermas seems to side prematurely with its opposite, a hermeneutics of suspicion that treats expressed meaning as an illusion, a mere consequence of more *'real'*, structural factors, working behind the scenes. Indeed most contemporary sociology takes the distinction between appearance and reality for granted, identifying the locus of truth in social situations with the latter.

Gadamer's hermeneutics reminds us is that neither appearance nor reality are static entities, but are elements inter-related through language and tradition. The reality of a situation at one point will fade and seem to be a mere appearance, as the reality of something new reshapes our understanding. Alternatively, what seems at one point to be no more than a surface appearance, may then be shown to be of decisive importance in describing the meaning of a situation.

William Connolly (1982) has spelt out some of the implications of challenging the appearance-reality dualism. Like Gadamer he is suspicious when too sharp a distinction is made between the two, and of theories that claim to be have pierced appearances and grasped the fixed structural reality lying behind them. He accepts that an interpreter may well find a discrepancy between what appears to be the case from the actors point of view, and the underlying reality that is its context, but rather than rushing to the conclusion that they are suffering from 'ideology', he suggests we examine more closely *the reality of appearances*. In doing this he focuses attention on the idea that appearances have an important role in determining the nature of reality, indeed that changes at the level of appearances will actually alter the way we understand the underlying reality of things.

To illustrate the point, he uses the example of American blue-collar workers who have adopted "the ideology of sacrifice". They submit to rigid and authoritarian work practices, which denies them dignity and self-respect. Yet in submitting to these regimes the worker does not just try to maximise his family's short term affluence, he also finds dignity and self-respect in the sacrifice he makes. The temptation is to simply conclude that he is deluding himself, because he fails to see how his life and his illiberal views are the product of his material circumstances. However, Connolly rejects in this outlook the sudden diminishment of concern for the dignity that has been found in sacrifice, and how central this is to the very identity of the worker.

Of course Connolly, no more than Gadamer, is suggesting that the limits of an interpretation are provided by the worker's self-understanding. In fact he fully accepts that the worker's self-understanding, does in part 'misrepresent' the situation. But self-understanding, 'accurate' or otherwise is not a static phenomenon. Like understanding generally it modifies itself, and in so doing necessarily alters the way material constraints have to be understood.

If this is the case then the standard criticism that hermeneutics has conservative implications is wide of the mark. If one relaxes 'the fit' between ideas and material circumstances, and allows the validity of implicit meanings to speak more clearly, then the interpretive possibilities of our tradition are widened, not closed down.

Notes
1. Apart from Connolly's book, I owe a debt to Michael Gibbons' 'Introduction' to *Interpreting Politics*, Gibbons (1987)

Bibliography

Abel. T. (1948) 'The Operation Called Verstehen', *American Journal of Sociology* 54, pp211-218.

Adorno. T. & Horkheimer.M. [(1947) 1972] *Dialectic of Enlightenment*, Herder & Herder.

Adorno. T. (1973) *The Jargon of Authenticity*, Translated by K.Tarnoski & F.Will, Rourledge & Kegan Paul.

Adorno. T. [(1951) 1974] *Minima Moralia: Reflections From A Damaged Life,* translated by E. F. N. Jephcott, New Left Books.

Adorno. T. et al. (1976) *The Positivist Dispute in German Sociology* translated by G. Adey. & D. Frisby, Heinemann Educational Books.

Adorno. T. (1991) *The Culture Industry: Selected Essays on Mass Culture* Edited with an Introduction by J. M. Bernstein, Routledge.

Alexander. J.C. (1987) 'The Centrality of The Classics' in Giddens. A. & Turner.J. eds. *Social Theory Today*, Polity Press.

Anderson.R.J. et. al. (1987) *Classic Disputes In Sociology*, Allen & Unwin

Apel. K-O. (1967) *Analytic Philosophy of Language and The Geisteswissenschaften*, Dordrecht/D. Reidel.

Apel. K. O. et. al. (1971) *Hermeneutik und Ideologiekritik*, Suhrkamp Frankfurt

Apel. K-O. (1972) 'The Apriori of Communication and the Foundation of The Humanities', in *Man and World: An International Philosophical Review*, No. 5, pp3-37.

Apel. K-O. (1980) *Towards A Transformation Of Philosophy*, translated by Glyn Adey & David Frisby, Routledge & Kegan Paul.

Arato. A. & Gebhardt. E. (1978) *The Essential Frankfurt School Reader*, Basil Blackwell.

Bauman. Z. (1978) *Hermeneutic and Social Science*, Hutchinson.

Bauman. Z. (1989) *Modernity and The Holocaust*, Polty/Basil Blackwell.

Bauman. Z. (1990) 'Effacing The Face: On The Social Management of Moral Proximity', *Theory Culture and Society* Vol 7, pp5-38.

Baynes. K. Bohman. J. & McCarthy T. eds. (1987) *Philosophy: End Or Transformation ?*, M.I.T. Press

Baynes. K. (1989-90) 'Rational Reconstruction and Social Criticism: Habermas' Model of Interpretive Social Science', *The Philosophical Forum*, Vol.XX1, Nos.1-2, pp122-145.

Benhabib. S. & Dallmayr. F. eds. (1990) *The Communicative Ethics Controversy*, M.I.T Press.

Bernstein. R. (1975) *The Restructuring Of Social And Political Theory*, Methuen & Co. Ltd.

Bernstein. R. (1983) *Beyond Objectivism and Relativism: Science Hermeneutics and Praxis*, Basil Blackwell.

Bernstein. R. ed. (1985) *Habermas and Modernity*, Polity/Basil Blackwell

Bleicher. J. (1980) *Contemporary Hermeneutics: Hermeneutics as MethodPhilosophy and Critique*, Routledge & Kegan Paul.

Bleicher. J. (1982) *The Hermeneutic Imagination: Outline of a Positive Critique of Scientism and Sociology*, Routledge & Kegan Paul.

Brenkman. J. (1987) *Culture And Domination*, Cornell University Press

Bryant. C. G. A. & Jary.D.eds. (1991) *Giddens' Theory Of Structuration*, Routledge

Bubner. R. (1975) 'Theory And Practice In The Light Of The Hermeneutic-Criticist Controversy', *Cultural Hermeneutics* 2, pp337-352.

Bubner. R. (1981) *Modern German Philosophy*, C.U.P.

Canovan. M. (1977) *The Political Thought Of Hannah Arendt*, Methuen & Company

Canovan. M. (1983) 'A Case Of Distorted Communication', *PoliticalTheory*, Vol 11, pp105-116.

Clark. J. Modgil. C.& Modgil. S. eds. (1990) *Anthony Giddens: Consensus And Controversy*, Falmer Press

Cohen. I. (1989) *Structuration Theory*, Macmillan

Connerton. P. ed. (1976) *Critical Sociology*, Penguin.

Connolly. W. E. (1982) *Appearance And Reality In Politics*, Cambridge University Press

Craib. I. (1992) *Anthony Giddens*, Routledge.

Danto. A. C. (1968) *The Analytic Philosophy Of History*, Cambridge University Press.

de Man. P. (1971) *Blindness And Insight:Essays On The Rhetoric Of Contemporary Criticism*, Oxford University Press.

Dews. P. ed. (1986) *Habermas: Autonomy And Solidarity: Interviews With Jurgen Habermas*, Verso.

Dilthey. W. (1989) *Introduction to the Human Sciences: An Attempt toLay a Foundation for the Study of Society and History,* Harvester/Wheatsheaf.

Douglas. J. et.al. (1977) *The Nude Beach*, Sage Publications.

Duckhorn. K.(1980) 'Hans-Georg Gadamer's Truth And Method', *Philosophy And Rhetoric* Vol 13, No.3, pp160-80.

Eagleton. T. (1983) *Literary Theory: An Introduction*, Basil Blackwell

Eldridge. J. E. T. (1971) *Max Weber: The Interpretation Of Social Reality*, Michael Joseph Ltd.

Ermarth. M. (1981) 'Transformation of Hermeneutics: 19th Century Ancients and 20th Century Moderns.' *Monist* 64, pp175-94.

Fay. B. (1975) *Social Theory And Political Practice*, Allen And Unwin.

Feenberg. A. (1986) *Lukacs, Marx And The Sources Of Critical Theory*, Oxford University Press.

Feenberg. A. (1988) 'The Bias of Technology' in Pippin, Feenberg, & Webel, (1988)

Frank. M. (1989) *What is Neostructuralism?*, University of Minesota Press.

Frisby. D. (1972) 'The Popper-Adorno Controversy: The Methodological Dispute in German Sociology', *Philosophy Of The Social Sciences* Vol1, No.2, pp105-119.

Frisby. D. (1974) 'The Frankfurt School: Critical Theory and Positivism' in Rex. J. *Approaches to Sociology*, Routledge and Kegan Paul.

Gadamer. H. G. (1989) *Truth and Method*, second edition, translation revised by Joel Weinsheimer and Donald G. Marshall, with afterword by H.G. Gadamer, London/Sheed & Ward. First English version translated and edited by Garrett Barden and John Cumming, London Sheed & Ward 1975. German original *Wahrheit und Methode*, J. C. B. Mohr (Paul Siebeck) Tubingen (1960).

Gadamer. H. G. (1970) 'The Power Of Reason', translated by H. W.Johnstone, *Man And World* Vol 3, pp5-15.

Gadamer. H-G. (1975) 'Hermeneutics And Social Science: "Summation", "Response", *Cultural Hermeneutics* 2, pp307-316,329-30, 357.

Gadamer. H. G. (1976) *Philosophical Hermeneutics*, Translated and Edited by David. E. Linge, University of California Press.

Gadamer. H. G. (1979) 'The Problem of Historical Consciousness', in Rabinow. P. & Sullivan. M. (1979). Original English version in *The Graduate Faculty Philosophical Journal*, Vol.5 No.1, Fall 1975, pp2-52.

Gadamer. H. G. (1981) *Reason In The Age Of Science*, Translated by Frederick G. Lawrence, The MIT. Press.

Gadamer. H. G. (1984) 'The Hermeneutics of Suspicion' in Shapiro. G. & Sica. A. (1984)

Gadamer. H. G. (1986a) *The Relevance Of The Beautiful And Other Essays*,edited and introduced by B. Bernasconi and translated by N. Walker, Cambridge University Press

Gadamer. H.G. (1986b) 'Rhetoric, Hermeneutics, And The Critique Of Ideology: Metacritical Comments On Truth And Method' in Mueller-Vollmer (1986)

Gall. R. S. (1981) 'Between Tradition And Critique: The Gadamer-Habermas Debate', *Auslegung*, Vol. 8, No.1, pp5-18.

Gardiner. M. (1992) *The Dialogics Of Critique: M. M. Bakhtin And TheTheory Of Ideology*, Routledge.

Garfinkel. H. ([1967] 1984) *Studies In Ethnomethodology*, Polity Press.

Gibbons. M. T. (1987) 'Introduction : The Politics Of Interpretation', in Gibbons. M. T. ed. *Interpreting Politics*, Basil Blackwell.

Giddens. A. (1976) *New Rules Of Sociological Method*, Hutchinson

Giddens. A. (1979a) *Central Problems In Social Theory: Action Structure And Contradiction In Social Analysis*, Macmillan.

Giddens. A. (1979b) *Studies in Social And Political Theory*, Macmillan

Giddens. A. (1984a) *The Constitution Of Society*, Polity Press.

Giddens. A. (1984b) 'Hermeneutics And Social Theory' in Shapiro G. & Sica A. (1984)

Gouldner. A. (1971) *The Coming Crisis In Western Sociology*, Heinemann Educational Books.

Guerin. D. (1977) *Class Struggle in The First French Republic:Bourgeois and Bras Nus 1793-1795*, translated by I. Patterson, Pluto Press.

Haan. N. & Bellah. R. et al. (1983) *Social Science as Moral Inquiry*, Columbia University Press.

Habermas. J. (1966) 'Knowledge and Interest', *Inquiry*, 1X.

Habermas. J. (1971) *Knowledge And Human Interests*, Beacon Press.

Habermas. J. (1972) *Towards A Rational Society*, Heinemann.

Habermas. J. (1973) *Theory And Practice*, translated by John Viertel, Beacon Press

Habermas. J. (1977a) 'Martin Heidegger: On The Publication of Lectures From The Year 1935', *Graduate Faculty Philosophy Journal* Vol.6, No.2.pp155-180.

Habermas. J. (1977b) 'Hannah Arendt's Communications Concept Of Power', *Social Research* 44, pp3-24.

Habermas. J. (1979) *Communication and the Evolution of Society*, Heinemann Educational Books.

Habermas. J. (1983) 'Interpretive Social Science vs. Hermeneuticism', in Haan. N. & Bellah. R. et. al. (1983)

Habermas. J. (1984) *The Theory Of Communicative Action: Vol 1: Reason And The Rationalization Of Society*, Heinemann.

Habermas. J. (1986) 'On Hermeneutics' Claim To Universality' in Mueller-Vollmer (1986), another translation can be found in Bleicher (1980), the German original can be found in Apel (1971).

Habermas. J. (1987) *The Philosophical Discourse of Modernity*, with an introduction by T. McCarthy, Polity/ Basil Blackwell

Habermas. J. (1988 [1967]) *On The Logic Of The Social Sciences* Polity/Basil Blackwell

Habermas. J. (1990) *Moral Conscoiusness And Communicative Action*, translated by Christian Lenhardt & Shierry Weber Nicholson, introduced by Thomas McCarthy, Polity Press

Hans. J. S. (1978) 'Hans-Georg Gadamer And Hermeneutic Phenomenology', *Philosophy Today* Vol 22, pp3-19.

Heaton. J. (1993) 'Language Games, Expression and Desire in the Work of Deleuze', *Journal Of The British Society For Phenomenology*, Vol 24,Number 1, pp 77-87

Heidegger. M. (1927) *Sein und Zeit*, English Translation, *Being and Time*, translators Macquarrie. J. & Robinson. E, Harper Row (1962).

Heidegger. M (1978) *Basic Writings*, Routledge & Kegan Paul.

Hekman. S. (1983) 'Beyond Humanism: Gadamer, Althusser, And The Methodology Of The Social Sciences', *Western Political Quarterly* Vol 36, pp98-115.

Hekman. S. (1986) *Hermeneutics and the Sociology Of Knowledge*, Polity Press.

Held. D. (1980) *Introduction To Critical Theory: Horkheimer To Habermas*, Hutchinson.

Held. D. & Thompson. J. B. eds. (1989) Social Theory Of Modern Societies: Anthony Giddens And His Critics, Cambridge University Press

Hirsch. E. D. (1967) *Validity in Interpretation*, Yale University Press.

Hirsch. E. D. (1976) *The Aims Of Interpretation*, Universtity of Chicago Press.

Holub. R. C. (1991) *Jurgen Habermas: Critic In The Public Sphere*, Routledge.

Hollis. M. & Lukes. S. eds. (1982) *Rationality And Relativism*, Basil Blackwell/Oxford.

Honneth. A, McCarthy. T, Offe.C, & Wellmer. A. eds (1992) *Philosophical Interventions in the Unfinished Project of Enlightenment*, translated by William Rehg, MIT Press.

Horkheimer. M. [1937 (1972)] 'Traditional and Critical Theory' in Horkheimer. M. *Critical Theory: Selected Essays*, Herder and Herder.

How. A. R. (1980a) 'Debate Language and Incommensurability: The Popper-Adorno Controversy', *Journal of the British Society for Phenomenology*, Vol.11, Number 1, pp3-15.

How. A. R. (1980b) 'Dialogue as Productive Limitation in Social Theory:The Habermas-Gadamer Debate', *Journal of The British Society For Phenomenology*, Vol. 11, No. 2, pp131-143.

How. A. R. (1985) 'A Case of Creative Misreading: Habermas's Evaluation of Gadamer's Hermeneutics', *Journal of the British Society for Phenomenology*. Vol 16, No. 2. pp132-144.

Hoy. D. C. (1978) *The Critical Circle: Literature, History, and Philosophical Hermeneutics*, University of California.

Hoy. D. C. & McCarthy. T. (1994) *Critical Theory*, Basil Blackwell

Ingram. D. (1983) 'The Historical Genesis Of The Gadamer-Habermas Debate', *Auslegung*, Vol10, Nos1-2, pp86-151.

Ingram. D. (1987) *Habermas and the Dialectic of Reason*, Yale University Press

Jay. M. (1973) *The Dialectical Imagination*, Heinemann Educational Books.

Jay. M. (1984) *Marxism and Totality: The Adventures of A Concept From Lukacs to Habermas,* Universty of California/Polity with Basil Blackwell

Kellner. D. (1989) *Critical Theory, Marxism and Modernity*, Polity.

Kelly. M. (1987) 'Hermeneutics And Science: Why Hermeneutics Is Not Anti-Science', *The Southern Journal Of Philosophy* VolXXV. No.4. pp481-500

Kelly. M (1988) 'Gadamer and Philosophical Ethics', *Man and World*, Vol 21, p327-346.

Kelly. M. (1989) 'The Gadamer-Habermas Debate Revisited: The Question of Ethics', *Philosophy and Social Criticism*,Vol 14, Nos.3-4, PP369-389. Reprinted in Rasmussen. D. (1990b)

Kelly. M. (1989-90) guest editor of, 'Hermeneutics In Ethics And Social Theory', Special Double Issue of *The Philosophical Forum: AQuarterly*, Vol. XX1, Nos 1-2.

Kisiel. T. (1969) 'The Happening Of Tradition: The Hermeneutics Of Gadamer and Heidegger', Man and World 2, pp358-85

Kisiel. T. (1970) 'Ideology Critique And Phenomenology', Philosophy Today No. 14, Fall, pp151-60.

Kisiel. T. (1978) 'Habermas' Purge Of Pure Theory: Critical Theory Without Ontology', Human Studies 1. pp167-83.

Larmore. C. (1986) 'Tradition, Objectivity, and Hermeneutics', in Wachterhauser (1986)

Laska. P. (1974) 'Habermas and the Labour Theory of Value', *New German Critique*, Number 3.

Lefebvre. H. (1975) 'What is The Historical Past', *New Left Review* 90. pp27-43

Lowith. K. (1988) 'The Political Implications of Heidegger's Existentialism', *New German Critique* 45, pp117-134.

Lukacs. G. [(1922) 1971] *History and Class Consciousness*, Merlin Press

Marcuse. H. [1928 (1969)] 'Contributions To a Phenomenology of Historical Materialism', *Telos* 4, pp3-34.

Marcuse. H. [1936 (1968)] 'The Concept of Essence', in *Negations*, Allen Lane/Penguin Press

Marcuse. H. (1972) *Studies In Critical Philosophy*, translated by Joris De Bres, New Left Books.

Marcuse. H. (1974). 'On Science and Phenomenology', in *Positivism and Sociology*, ed. A. Giddens, Heinemann Educational Books.

Marcuse. H. (1977) 'Heidegger's Politics: An Interview with Herbert Marcuse' conducted by F. Olafson, *Graduate Faculty Philosophy Journal*, Vol 6, No. 1, pp28-40. Reprinted in Pippin, Feenberg & Webel (1988).

Marcuse. H. (1980) 'Theory and Politics: a discussion with H. Marcuse, J. Habermas, H. Lubasz, and T. Spengler, *Telos* 38.

Marcuse. H. (1986) *One Dimensional Man: Studies in The Ideologies of Advanced Industrial Societies*. Routledge/ARK.

Marshall. G. (1980) *Presbyteries And Profits: Calvinism And TheDevelopment of Capitalism in Scotland 1560-1707*, Clarendon/Oxford

Mattick. P. Jr. (1986) *Social Knowledge: An Essay On The Nature And Limits Of Social Science*, M.E. Sharpe Inc.

McCarthy. T. (1973) 'On Misunderstanding 'Understanding', *Theory and Decision* 3, pp351-370.

McCarthy. T. (1978) *The Critical Theory Of Jurgen Habermas*, Heinemann.

Mendelson. J. (1979) 'The Habermas-Gadamer Debate', *New German Critique*, 18, pp44-73.

Merleau-Ponty. M. (1973) *Adventures of The Dialectic*, Evanston /Northwestern University Press.

Michelfelder. D. & Palmer. R. eds. (1989) *Dialogue And Deconstruction: The Gadamer-Derrida Encounter*, State University Of New York Press.

Misgeld. D. (1977a) 'Critical Theory And Hermeneutics' in O'Neill (1977)

Misgeld. D (1977b) 'Discourse And Conversation: The Theory Of Communicative Competence And Hermeneutics In Light Of The DebateBetween Habermas And Gadamer', *Cultural Hermeneutics* 4.

Misgeld. D. (1979) 'On Gadamer's Hermeneutics', *Philosophy of Social Science* 9, pp221-239.

Misgeld. D. (1981a) 'Science, Hermeneutics, And The Utopian Content Of The Liberal-Democratic Tradition: On Habermas's Recent Work: A Reply To Mendelson', *New German Critique*, No. 22, pp123-144.

Misgeld. D. (1981b) 'Habermas's Retreat From Hermeneutics: Systems Integration, Social Integration, and the Crisis of Legitimatiom', *Canadian Journal of Political and Social Theory*, Vol.5, Nos. 1-2, p8-44.

Misgeld. D. (1985) 'Critical Hermeneutics Versus Neo-Parsonsianism', *New German Critique*, Spring/Summer, p55-82.

Misgeld. D. (1991) 'Modernity And Hermeneutics: A Critical-Theoretical Rejoinder' in Silverman ed. (1991)

Mueller-Vollmer. K. (ed) (1986) *The Hermeneutics Reader*, Basil Blackwell.

Norris. C. (1992) *Uncritical Theory: Postmodernism, Intellectuals And The Gulf War*, Lawrence & Wishart.

Nicholson. G. (1991) 'Answers To Critical Theory' in Silverman ed. (1991)

Ormiston. G. L. & Schrift. A. D. eds. (1990) The Hermeneutic Tradition: From Ast To Ricoeur

O'Neill. J. ed. (1977) *On Critical Theory*, Heinemann Educational Books.

O'Neill. J. (1988) 'Marcuse, Husserl, and the Crisis of the Sciences', *Philosophy of the Social Sciences*, Vol. 18, pp327-42.

Outhwaite. W. (1975) *Understanding Social Life: The Method Called Verstehen*, London/Allen & Unwin.

Outhwaite. W. (1985) 'Hans-Georg Gadamer' in Skinner (1985)

Outhwaite. W. (1987) *New Philosophies of Social Science: Realism, Hermeneutics and Critical Theory*, Macmillan.

Palmer. R. (1969) *Hermeneutics: Interpretation Theory in Schleiermacher, Dilthey, Heidegger, and Gadamer*, Evanston, Northwestern Unoversity Press.

Pannenburg. W. et al. (1967) *History and Hermeneutic*, Harper Row.

Parkin. F. (1982) *Max Weber*, Ellis Horwood.

Parsons. T. (1968) *The Structure of Social Action,* Two Vols.The Free Press.

Piccone. P. (1975) 'From Trajedy to Farce: The Return of Critical Theory', *New German Critique*7, pp91-104.

Piccone. P & Delfini. A. (1970) 'Herbert Marcuse's Heideggarian Marxism', *Telos* 6, pp36-46.

Pippin. R. Feenberg. A. Webel. C. eds. (1988) *Marcuse: Critical Theory and the Promise of Utopia*, Macmillan.

Plummer. K. (1975) *Sexual Stigma: An Interactive Account*, Routledge & Kegan Paul.

Rabinow. P & Sullivan. W. M. (eds) (1979) *Interpretive Social Science: A Reader*, University of California Press.

Rasmussen. D. (1990a) *Reading Habermas,* Basil Blackwell.

Rasmussen. D. (ed) (1990b) *Universalism vs Communitarianism: Contemporary Debates in Ethics*, MIT Press.

Ray. L. J. (1979) 'Critical Theory And Positivism: Popper And The Frankfurt School', *Philosophy Of The Social Sciences* 9, pp149-73.

Ricoeur. P. (1970) *Freud and Philosophy: An Essay on Interpretation*, translator Savage. D., Yale University Press.

Ricoeur. P. (1973a) 'The Task of Hermeneutics', *Philosophy Today*, No.17, pp112-28. (also in Ricoeur 1981.)

Ricoeur. P. (1973b) 'Ethics and Culture: Habermas and Gadamer in Dialogue' *Philosophy Today*, Summer, pp153-65.

Ricoeur. P. (1974) *The Conflict of Interpretations: Essays in Hermeneutic*, ed. Idhe. D., Northwestern University Press/Evanston.

Ricoeur. P. (1976) *Interpretation Theory: Discourse and The Surplus of Meaning*, The Texas Christian University Press.

Ricoeur. P. (1977) 'Schleiermacher's Hermeneutics', *Monist* 60, pp181-91.

Ricoeur. P. (1981) *Hermeneutics and The Human Sciences*, edited and translated by J. B. Thompson, Cambridge University Press.

Robinson. J. M. & Cobb. J. B. Jnr. eds. (1964) *The New Hermeneutic*, Harper & Row.

Rockmore. T. (1989) *Habermas on Historical Materialism*, Indiana University Press

Roderick. R. (1986) *Habermas and the Foundations of Critical Theory*, Macmillan.

Rovatti. P-A. (1973) 'Critical Theory and Phenomenology', *Telos* 15, pp24-40

Sahay. A. ed. (1971) *Max Weber and Modern Sociology*, Routledge and Kegan Paul

Sensat. Jnr. J. (1979) *Habermas and Marxism: An Appraisal*, Sage.

Sensat. Jnr. J. (1986) 'Recasting Marxism: Habermas' Proposals' in :Buczkowski. P. & Klawiter. A. *Theories of Ideology and Ideology of Theories*, Amsterdam/Rodopi.

Schleiermacher. F. D. E. (1977) *Hermeneutics: The Handwritten Manuscripts*, ed. Kimmerle. H., Translators: Duke. J. & Forstman. J, Missoula, MT: Scholars Press.

Schmidt. A. [1968 (1988)] 'Existential Ontology and Historical Materialism in the Work of Herbert Marcuse', in Pippin Feenberg & Webel (1988).

Shapiro. G. & Sica. A. eds. (1984) *Hermeneutics: Questions and Prospects*, University of Massachusetts Press.

Sica. A. (1988). *Weber, Irrationality, and Social Order,* University of California Press

Silverman. H. J. ed. (1991) *Gadamer And Hermeneutics*, Routledge.

Skinner. Q. (1975) 'Hermeneutics and The Role of History', *New Literary History* 7, pp209-232.

Skinner. Q. ed. (1985) *The Return Of Grand Theory In The Social Sciences*, Cambridge University Press.

Skjervheim. H. (1974) 'Objectivism And The Study Of Man', *Inquiry* 17, Part 1 pp 213-39, Part 2 pp265-302.

Smith. C. (1979) 'Gadamer's Hermeneutics and Ordinary Language Philosophy', *The Thomist* Vol 43, pp296-321.

Soboul. A. (1964) *The Parisian Sans-Culotte and The French Revolution*, Oxford University Press.

Spender. D. (1980) *Man Made Language*, Routledge & Kegan Paul.

Stauth. G & Turner. B. (1992) 'Ludwig Klages (1872-1956) and the Origins of Critical Theory', Theory, *Culture & Society,* Vol.9, No.3, pp45-63.

Tawney. R. H. (1978) *Religion And The Rise Of Capitalism*, Penguin.

Taylor. C. (1985) *Philosophical Papers Volume One: Human Agency And Language; Philosophical Papers Volume Two: Philosophy And The Human Sciences*, Cambridge University Press.

Therborn. G. (1971) 'Jurgen Habermas: A New Eclecticism', *New Left Review,* Number 67.

Thomas. P. (1979) 'The Language of Real Life: Jurgen Habermas and the Distortion of Karl Marx, *Discourse* Vol.1, Part 1.

Trevor-Roper. H. (1967) *Religion, The Reformation And Social Change*, Macmillan.

Turner. S. P. (1980) *Sociological Explanation As Translation*, Cambridge University Press.

Vattimo. G. (1988) *The End Of Modernity: Nihilism and Hermeneutics in Post-modern Culture*, Translation and Introduction by J. R. Snyder, Polity Press.

Wachterhauser. B.R. (ed) (1986) *Hermeneutics and Modern Philosophy* State University of New York Press/Albany.

Warnke. G. (1987) *Gadamer: Hermeneutics, Tradition and Reason*, Polity Press with Basil Blackwell

Weinsheimer. J. (1985) *Gadamer's Hermeneutics: A Reading of Truth and Method*, Yale University Press.

Wellmer. A. (1972) *Critical Theory Of Society*, Seabury Press.

Wiggershaus. R. (1994) *The Frankfurt School: Its History, Theories and Political Significance,* translated by Michael Robertson, Polity Press

Wilson. B. ed. (1974) *Rationality*, Basil Blackwell.

Wilson. H. T. (1977) 'Science Critique And Criticism' in O'Neill. J. (1977)

Winch. P. (1958) *The Idea Of A Social Science And Its Relation To Philosophy*, Routledge & Kegan Paul.

Winch. P. (1964) 'Understanding A Primitive Society', *American Philosophical Quarterly* XLVIII, pp307-324.

Wittgenstein. L. (1968) *Philosophical Investigations*, Basil Blackwell.

Wolff. J. (1975a) *Hermeneutic Philosophy And The Sociology Of Art*, Routledge and Kegan Paul

Wolff. J. (1975b) 'Hermeneutics and The Critique of Ideology', *Sociological Review*, pp811-829

Wolff. J. (1981) *The Social Production of Art*, Macmillan Education Ltd.

Wolin. R. (1991) 'Introduction To Herbert Marcuse and Martin Heidegger: An Exchange of Letters', *New German Critique* No.53, pp19-32.

Index

Abel T, 21
Adorno T, 2, 3, 6, 10, 12, 14, 15, 21, 57, 102, 103, 104, 105, 106, 107, 108, 109, 110, 111, 113, 114, 118, 158, 176, 179, 212
aesthetic consciousness, 25, 26, 27, 31, 33, 106, 107
Alexander J.C, 51
Anderson R.J, 58
anticipation of completeness, 106, 107
Apel K.O, 12, 14, 21, 62, 63, 137, 138, 195, 199, 200, 201, 202, 206
application, 11, 51, 54, 57, 59-62, 62-7, 70, 71, 72, 74, 75, 76, 77, 79, 80, 92, 104, 113, 119, 120, 132, 137, 144, 174, 179, 183, 188, 190, 193, 201, 219, 221
Arato A & Gebhardt E, 10
Arendt H, 137, 178
Aristotle's Ethics, 62, 76, 77-80, 159
art, 1 2, 3, 24-6, 27, 28, 29-34, 156, 161, 162, 182, 193, 221
authenticity, 2, 3
authority, 28, 139-144, 171-3, 178, 196, 197, 205-8, 221, 222-3, 224
Ayer A.J, 149, 150
Azande, 62, 67, 68, 69, 70, 71, 75, 76, 119

Baudrillard J, 100
Bauman Z, 7, 14, 15
Baynes K, 17, 114, 138
belonging, 61, 130, 203, 224
belongingness, 126, 127
Benhabib S.& Dallmayr F, 77, 138
Bernstein R, 14, 30, 34, 63
Betti E, 16, 60
Bhaskar R, 3

Bleicher J, 7, 21, 101, 194, 197, 214
Brenkman J, 214
Bronner S. & Kellner D, 10
Bryant C. G. A. & Jary D, 63
Bubner R, 138, 163, 200, 214

Canovan M, 137
Cassirer E 89
causality, 117, 148-150, 185, 191
causes, 5, 117, 148-153, 178
Chomsky N, 121, 180, 181, 187, 206, 207
Christian prayer, 71, 75
Cicourel A, 5, 118
Clark J, Modgil C. & Modgil S, 63
class, 5, 124, 137, 145, 152, 170, 178, 191
classic texts, 50-7
Cohen I, 63
colonisation of the life-world, 18
communication, 15, 16, 17, 18, 20, 22, 42, 88, 94, 113, 115, 118, 119, 122, 123, 127, 134, 137, 144, 145, 146, 156, 158, 185, 186, 187, 188, 189, 190, 191, 192, 193, 194, 195, 196, 197, 198, 199, 203, 204, 205, 206, 207, 208, 210, 211, 213, 215, 219, 220, 221, 222
communicative action, 16, 102, 134, 135, 154
communicative competence, 182, 184, 185, 193, 194, 198, 206, 207
Connerton P, 7, 10, 198
Connolly W, 228
consciousness, 18, 25, 26, 27, 31, 33, 36-8, 39, 55, 95, 102, 112, 118, 127, 147, 150, 156, 161, 167, 174, 175, 184, 185, 187, 194, 195, 196, 197, 206, 207, 208, 209, 210, 211, 217, 218, 223
consensus, 15, 16, 17, 18, 20, 35, 40, 94, 113, 123, 125, 134, 135,

136, 154, 180, 183, 185, 187,194, 195, 196, 197, 206, 207, 208, 209, 210 211
conversation, 18, 19, 20, 28, 40, 41, 42, 56, 64, 87, 115
Cooley, 148
Craib I., 63
Critical Theory, 5, 6, 12, 13, 14, 18, 21, 80, 81, 89, 102, 103, 105, 112, 116, 117, 127, 131, 132, 133, 134-7, 155, 161, 163, 174-7, 195, 196, 197, 198, 199, 202, 203, 208, 209, 214, 223, 224, 227
critique, 6, 12, 13, 14, 16, 17, 18, 20, 21, 22, 24, 25, 28, 31, 100, 104, 105, 109, 110, 112, 113, 116-138, 139-154, 155, 158, 171, 172, 177, 178, 180, 181, 185, 187, 188, 193, 196-7, 204, 208, 209, 213, 216, 217, 218, 219, 222, 224, 225, 227

Danto A.C, 128-131
Dasein, 9, 70, 203
Davey N, 179, 214
death, 3, 68, 72, 73, 74, 75, 76, 89
depth hermeneutics, 189-190, 198
Dews. P. ed, 140
dialogue, 15, 16, 19, 22, 23, 35, 90, 118, 119, 123, 134, 135, 139, 143, 144, 145, 175, 181, 183, 185, 186, 194, 195, 197, 198, 204, 205, 208, 209, 210, 211, 213, 220, 221, 222
Dilthey W, 8, 37, 38, 39, 43, 62, 67, 119, 217
domination, 10, 12, 28, 77, 104, 139, 141, 145, 160, 167-173, 195, 196, 204, 215, 217, 218, 222
Douglas J, 19, 20, 50
Droysen, 50, 178
Duckhorn, 162
Durkheim E, 54

Eagleton T, 214
effective-historical consciousness, 55
Eldridge J.E.T, 58
empirical, 3, 8, 9, 11, 16, 31, 45, 50, 54, 57, 58, 69, 70, 86, 93, 97, 98, 105, 111, 112, 113, 118, 129, 140, 141, 145, 147, 153, 162, 181, 192
Ermarth M, 7
ethnography, 19
ethnomethodology, 40, 100, 115, 118
Evans-Pritchard, 62, 67, 68, 71, 75, 119
existentialism, 2, 5, 21
experience and the structure of openness, 81-3
experience of art, 1-3, 24-6, 27, 28, 29, 31, 34, 36, 156, 161

falsifiability, 105
Fay B, 137
Feenberg A, 10, 12
finitude, 81, 82, 165
flight from dualism, 168-171
form of life, 24, 64, 66
Foucault M, 54, 57
Frank M, 57
Frankfurt School, 1, 2, 3, 5, 6, 9, 10-6, 103, 105, 108, 109, 111, 121, 133, 159, 161
French Revolution, 52, 53, 111, 178
Freud, 18, 117, 147, 149, 150, 151, 152, 175, 188, 189, 190, 192, 193, 217, 220, 221
Frisby D, 21, 104
fusion of horizons, the, 38, 41, 56, 92, 124, 126-8, 135, 168, 179, 217

Gall R.S, 214
Gardiner M, 214
Garfinkel H, 5, 115, 118

geisteswissenschaften, 8, 37, 105, 127
Gibbons M.T, 63, 85, 228
Giddens A, 63, 85, 214
good life, the, 20, 79, 211
Gouldner A, 124, 137
Guerin D, 58

Haan N. et al, 102
Hamlet, 33
Hans J, 91
Heaton J, 137
Heidegger M, 2, 3, 4, 5, 7, 8, 9, 12, 14, 20, 21, 30, 34, 42, 45, 46, 57, 100, 140, 153, 160, 163, 177
Hekman S, 66, 84, 85, 120, 124, 214, 223
Held & Thompson, 63
Held D, 10
hermeneutic circle, 44, 45, 46, 113, 119, 126
hermeneutic tradition the, 7-10, 11, 36, 125
hermeneutics of faith, 16-20, 227
hermeneutics of suspicion, 16-20, 227
Hermes, 7, 82
Hirsch E.D, 22, 41, 57
historical consciousness, 36-8, 102, 165, 174
historical materialism, 3, 4, 5, 12, 154
historical tradition, 2, 10, 24, 28, 30, 34, 38, 43, 55, 81, 83, 85, 106, 107, 108, 123, 125, 126, 135, 165, 166, 221, 226, 227
historically effected consciousness, 55, 81, 164-7
historicity, 4, 5, 37, 48, 53, 81
history, 4, 6, 8, 12-3, 20, 33, 34, 37, 48, 53, 81, 103, 110, 111, 114, 117, 156, 164, 165, 166, 178, 206, 217, 221, 226
Hollis M & Lukes S eds, 63
Honneth A et al, 199
Horkheimer M, 3, 6, 12, 13, 14, 15, 158, 212
How A, 21, 104, 110, 214
Hoy D.C & McCarthy T, 137
Hoy D.C, 7, 35, 55, 136, 137, 138, 214
Humboldt, 91, 92, 100

ideal speech situation, the, 134, 137, 138, 181, 185, 198, 199, 207, 209, 221
idealism, 66, 147, 148, 167, 170, 172
idealist illusions, 144-7
ideology, 11, 120, 146, 154, 158, 161, 163, 167, 171, 174, 175, 177, 181, 188, 197, 203, 214-9, 222, 224, 227, 228
ideology-critique, 101, 153, 161, 172, 175, 180
immanent critique, 13
Ingarden R, 59
Ingram D, 22, 214
Institute for Social Research, 10
instrumental reason, 13, 14, 109, 120, 121, 199
interpretation, 8, 9, 17, 18, 20, 21, 29, 33, 34, 41, 44, 45, 46, 47, 50, 53, 55, 56, 57, 59, 60, 63, 66, 71, 72, 74, 75, 77, 79, 113, 117, 118, 120, 123, 126, 127, 128, 132, 133, 135, 146, 148, 149, 150, 151, 152, 153, 154, 181, 186, 187, 190, 194, 195, 197, 205, 216, 219, 221, 224, 226, 227, 228
interpretive sociology, 66, 95, 123, 124, 137, 147, 148, 170, 216, 217, 227, 228

Jacobins, 52, 53
Jay M., 10, 22
Joyce, 32

Kant, 10, 25
Kellner D, 10
Kelly M, 77, 114, 177, 214
Kisiel T, 199, 214
Kohlberg L, 78, 102, 140, 151
Kuhn T, 34, 114
Kunz, 204

Language as world-disclosure, 91-2
language-games, 86, 87, 90, 118, 119, 120, 123, 138, 140, 146, 165, 190, 214
language-world relation, 95-9, 156, 217
Larmore C, 41, 57
Laska P, 22
Lefebvre H, 52, 53
Levi-Strauss C, 88
Liebnecht K, 4
Linge. D, 224
linguisticality, 156, 157, 159, 160, 164-7, 178, 215, 216, 217, 218, 220, 227
linguisticality of being, 22, 205, 210, 218
Lorenzer A, 181, 188, 189, 192, 198
Lowith K, 3, 21
Lukacs G, 5, 10
Luxembourg R, 4
Lyotard, 179

MacIntyre A, 74, 150, 151
Marcuse H, 2, 3, 4, 5, 6, 10, 11, 12, 20, 21, 54, 109, 154, 158, 163
Marx, 3, 4, 10, 11, 18, 54, 103, 104, 109, 147, 154, 163, 217
Marxism, 4, 5, 6, 12, 17, 20

Marxist, 4, 5, 6, 11, 12, 14, 18, 22, 42, 52-4, 57, 58, 103, 107, 146, 180, 227
Mattick P.Jr, 63, 71
McCarthy T, 85, 114, 137, 138, 154, 198
Mead G.H, 148, 196
Mendelson J, 214
Merleau-Ponty M, 21, 58
method, 1, 2, 3, 5, 6, 8, 9, 15, 17, 23, 24, 26, 28, 30, 32, 34, 36, 37, 38, 39, 40, 41, 43, 47, 50, 52, 53, 55, 57, 62, 64, 75, 76, 81, 104, 105, 106, 107, 108, 109, 118, 124, 140, 147, 152, 156, 159, 161, 162, 166, 174, 177, 179, 180-1, 184, 187, 188, 193, 198, 203, 205, 220, 221, 225, 226
Michelfelder D. & Palmer R, 107, 108
Misgeld D, 214, 223
modes of production, 146
Mommsen, 50
moral knowledge, 78-80
Mueller-Vollmer K, 7, 37, 57, 101, 155, 162, 163, 168, 169, 170, 172, 175, 177, 182, 184, 185, 186, 190, 192, 197, 224
Munz P, 178

Nicholson G., 214
Nietzsche, 3, 18
not always knowing best, 209

O'Neill J, 20
objectivism, 126, 127, 134, 165, 166, 167, 169, 216, 225
objectivity, 7, 9, 15, 16, 17, 36, 38, 40, 43, 61, 96, 104, 105, 127, 156, 165, 178, 186, 195, 203, 226
observation, 11, 36, 38, 41, 127, 129, 149, 186

observational attitude, 26, 119, 127, 173
Odysseus, 58
Oedipus myth, 88
Offe C, 12, 14
openness, 47, 48, 81-3, 84, 103, 137
Ormiston G.L. & Schrift A.D, 101, 197, 203, 204, 205, 207, 210, 211, 212
Outhwaite W, 21, 84, 85, 214

Palmer R, 7, 107, 108, 162, 163, 177
Pannenburg W, 7
Parkin F, 58
Parsons T, 21, 110, 140, 141, 142, 153
pessimism, 12, 13
phenomenology, 2, 4, 5, 7, 18, 20, 149, 223
Piaget, 140, 180, 181, 185, 186, 204, 217
Piccone P, 21
Plato, 87, 89, 90, 100, 156, 160, 163, 177, 202
plausibility, 157, 183
play, 26-29, 32, 33, 34, 49, 52, 55, 56, 63, 75, 86, 87, 90, 142, 146, 209, 211
Plessner, 204
Plummer K, 154
Pocock J.G.A., 85
Polanyi, 204
Popper P, 17, 21, 34, 103-113, 117, 118, 120
Popper-Adorno controversy, the, 103-114
positivist, 3, 13, 21, 102, 103, 104, 117, 132, 133, 134, 135, 140, 148, 149, 150, 156, 159, 161, 179, 203, 215
positivistic assumptions, 37, 116

postmodernism, 144
praxis, 4, 78, 112, 137, 142, 156, 159-160, 171, 184, 201, 202-3, 209, 210, 211, 212
prejudgements, 46, 47, 50, 76, 131, 137, 142, 151, 215
prejudices, 39, 44-50, 51, 52, 55, 66, 128, 130, 131, 139-144, 154, 171, 183, 195, 197, 203, 209, 214-9, 221, 222, 223
presuppositions, 104, 113, 119, 220
Proust, 32
psychoanalysis, 147, 150, 151, 152, 153, 174, 175, 177, 180, 188-9, 190, 192, 193, 194, 205, 206, 219, 220, 221
psychological understanding, 38-43
purposive-rational action, 15, 146, 187

Rabinow P. & Sullivan W. M, 102
Ranke, 178
Rasmussen D, 22, 77
rational reconstruction, 184-8
rationalisation, 11, 16
Ray L.J, 104
realist philosophy, 114
reality of appearances, 227-8
reflection, 55, 81, 90, 142-4, 152, 157, 162, 166, 167, 169-73, 174, 176, 184, 185, 186, 189, 197, 200, 201, 203, 205, 206, 209, 218, 223, 226
Rhetoric, 87, 155, 156-162, 163, 167, 182, 183, 187, 210
Ricoeur P, 7, 8, 17, 18, 19, 20, 22, 61, 88, 153, 213, 227
Robinson J.M. & Cobb J.B, 7
Rockmore T, 22
Roderick R, 22
Rovatti P.A, 20
rule, 28, 63, 64, 65, 66, 67, 113,

118, 119, 123, 124, 125, 133, 144, 149, 150, 184, 189, 219

Sahay A, 21
Sans-Culottes, 52, 53
Saussure, 89, 90, 100
scenic understanding, 188, 189-193
Schleiermacher F.D.E, 8, 37, 38, 39, 40, 45, 57
Schmidt A, 4, 21
Schutz, 5, 223
science, 1, 5, 6, 7, 8, 9, 10, 11, 12, 13, 14, 17, 21, 24, 34, 36, 37, 38, 39, 40, 43, 44, 47, 50, 52, 54, 55, 57, 88, 96, 99, 102, 103, 104, 105, 106, 108, 109, 110, 111, 112, 113, 114, 116-8, 120, 125,126, 127, 129, 130, 133, 134, 135, 139-142, 143, 144, 145, 146, 147, 149, 150, 151, 153, 154, 157, 158, 159, 161, 162, 163, 173, 174, 177, 179, 180, 181, 182, 183, 186, 187, 195, 198, 199, 200, 201, 202, 205, 225
scientific, 3, 6, 10, 11, 12, 16, 17, 24, 26, 30, 34, 60, 63, 66, 67, 68, 69, 70, 77, 80, 81, 82, 97, 102, 103, 104, 105, 106, 108, 109, 110, 111, 112, 113, 114, 118, 120, 121, 124, 129, 130, 132, 133, 140, 151, 152, 156, 157, 158, 159, 160, 161, 162, 163, 166, 174, 175, 176, 177, 179, 181, 185, 186, 187, 192, 198, 201, 202, 203, 204, 205, 224, 226
scientization, 3,11
Sensat J. Jnr, 22
Shakespeare W, 26, 33
Shapiro G, 7, 21
Sica A, 7, 22, 114, 120, 214
Skinner Q, 57, 84, 85
Skjervheim H, 21
Smith C, 66, 87, 100
Soboul A, 52, 53, 57

speculative structure of language, 98, 122, 169
stance of the last historian, 128-131, 136, 137, 209, 226
Strauss A, 148, 216
subject-object, 47, 57, 61, 83, 127, 173, 185, 221
symbolic interactionism, 19, 40, 84, 148
systematic distortion, 145, 188, 189, 190, 218, 220, 221
systematically distorted communication, 16, 188, 192, 194, 195, 197, 198, 216, 219
systems theory, 17, 111, 116, 117, 141, 142, 201

Taylor C, 99
technology, 11, 12, 14, 133, 140, 146, 147, 154
theory, 5, 6, 12, 13, 14, 17, 18, 20, 21, 35, 48, 51, 63, 70, 77, 78, 80, 81, 89, 90, 110, 111, 112, 117, 134, 136, 146, 147, 149, 151, 152, 153, 159, 163, 167, 171, 176, 178, 180, 185, 187, 188, 193, 194, 196, 202, 206, 207, 208, 218, 219, 220, 222
Therborn G, 22
Thirty Years War, 128, 129
Thomas P, 22, 148
totality, 12, 103, 106, 107, 108, 109, 110, 112, 120, 130, 131, 141, 167, 176, 179
tradition, 2, 3, 5, 6, 7-16, 23, 24, 25, 26, 28, 29, 30, 32, 34, 36, 37, 38, 40, 42, 43, 44, 46, 47, 48, 49, 50, 87, 92, 95, 98, 102, 105, 106, 107, 108, 120, 123, 124, 125, 126, 127, 128, 129, 131, 135, 136, 137, 139-144, 145, 147, 148, 149, 152, 153, 156, 157, 158, 159, 160, 161, 162, 163, 165, 166, 167, 168, 171,

172, 173, 174, 177, 178, 181, 183, 193, 194, 195, 196, 197, 198, 205-8, 213, 215, 217, 219, 221, 222-3, 224, 226, 227, 228
traditional theories, 6, 13, 226
tragedy, 26, 82
Trevor-Roper H, 58
truth, 2, 5, 7, 24, 25, 29-34, 35, 36, 40, 41, 43, 45, 47, 48, 49, 54, 55, 89, 90, 95, 99, 136, 137, 140, 145, 152, 157-9, 160, 162, 168, 175, 179, 181, 194, 195, 196, 197, 206, 209, 217, 219, 222, 227
Truth and Method, 5, 9, 23-35, 36-58, 86-100, 101, 102, 114, 120, 122, 140, 156, 160, 162, 163, 164, 166, 168, 175, 179, 205, 208, 215, 221, 226
Turner S.P, 3, 63

unconcealment, (aletheia), 30
unconstrained dialogue, 163, 195-6, 222
understanding, 2, 4, 5, 6, 8, 9, 10, 15, 17, 21, 24, 25, 26, 28, 32, 34, 36-58, 59-85, 86, 92, 93, 94, 97, 99, 102, 106, 107, 109, 111, 112, 113, 116, 119, 120, 122, 123, 125, 126, 127, 128, 130, 131, 132, 137, 139, 140, 141, 142, 146, 147, 153, 155, 157, 159, 160, 162, 165, 166, 168, 174, 176, 177, 180, 182-4, 186, 187, 188, 194, 203, 204, 205, 215, 216, 217, 218, 219, 220, 221, 228

Van Gogh. 31
Vattimo G, 34

Wachterhauser L, 30
Warnke G, 7, 33, 34, 40, 41, 57, 107, 214, 218, 224
Weber M, 3, 9, 11, 14, 21, 54, 58, 66
Weinsheimer J, 23, 24, 43, 55, 80
Wellmer A, 14, 195, 214
Wiggershaus L, 10
Wilson B. ed, 63, 68
Wilson H.T, 104
Winch P, 5, 21, 57, 62-7, 68, 69, 70, 71, 72, 73, 74, 75, 76, 77, 84, 85, 86, 87, 118, 119, 124, 148, 164
Wittgenstein L, 5, 64, 66, 85, 86, 87, 118, 119, 120, 123, 124, 164, 184, 216, 223
Wolin R., 21
Wolff J., 1, 214
World-disclosure as language, 92-5